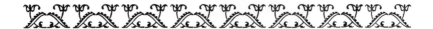

Companionship Therapy

Studies in Structured Intimacy

Gerald Goodman

COMPANIONSHIP
THERAPY

Jossey-Bass Inc., Publishers
San Francisco · Washington · London · 1972

Cop. 1

COMPANIONSHIP THERAPY
Studies in Structured Intimacy
by Gerald Goodman

JACKET DESIGN BY WILLI BAUM

FIRST EDITION

Code 7232

The Jossey-Bass
Behavioral Science Series

General Editors

WILLIAM E. HENRY
University of Chicago

NEVITT SANFORD
Wright Institute, Berkeley

Preface

Companionship Therapy describes an experiment with nonprofessional therapists in a community setting. The experiment was designed to provide findings relevant to the structure, process, and effects of therapies using nonprofessional or paraprofessional agents. Some of this work is directed at the specialist in therapy and interpersonal process research, but most of the book was written for a mixed audience of students and professionals in community mental health, clinical psychology, public health, social welfare, education, and psychiatry.

The mental health field is going through an unprecedented period of innovation. Much of the activity centers around new therapy formats and new designs for utilizing a nontraditional work force. These events, along with convincing predictions of an increasing gap between social needs and professional manpower, point to a future where nonprofessionals will be a major adjunct in the delivery of mental health service. Early signs of preparation for this new prospect in mental health work can be seen in the professional literature. There has been a burst of publication describing pilot programs and theoretical models for the application of service and calling for studies on nonprofessional effectiveness. We now have an impressive stockpile of innovation awaiting empirical assessment. We can expect that nonprofessional therapy will shift into an advanced phase where the proliferation of untested inventions and the rationales for legitimization are diminished in favor of systematic research on effectiveness. The shift will require special research models and a body of findings large enough to attract substantial numbers of investigators. These convictions influenced the design of the project described in *Companionship Therapy*. Efforts were geared toward making contributions to a generic model of program research in community settings and toward yielding findings applicable to a variety of nonprofessional therapies.

Much of the book is organized as a manual for establishing and studying nonprofessional therapy projects. Most of the methods, problems, and findings are relevant to other program designs. I have attempted to include guiding material for students, project administrators, and professional investigators. The chapters are organized to approximate the chronology of events. Chapter One reviews changes in the mental health field, then outlines the scope and logic of nonprofessional therapy. A capsule history of companion programs from 1935 to the present highlights key events. Examples of successes and failures of the project in community intervention are given. Chapter Two details a format for recruiting and selecting troubled children in a school setting. Their problems are listed and rank ordered according to frequency; comparison profiles of moderately troubled and typical classroom children are displayed. Chapter Three is primarily a detailed presentation of the Group Assessment of Interpersonal Traits (GAIT). This device shows promise as an inexpensive and reliable method for selecting individuals with therapeutic talent. A detailed set of administrative and scoring procedures is offered along with reliability and validity findings gathered in this project and by other investigators. The chapter also includes findings on the major motives that impel students to participate in the nonprofessional therapist role. Chapter Four deals with the effects of program structure on relationship processes. A plan is presented for building economical portable programs that simultaneously serve research and therapeutic goals. Chapter Five offers several methods for tracing process dimensions of companionships and other forms of two-person helping relationships. The associations among activity patterns, conversation topics, and the onset of intimacy are described in Chapter Six. The findings suggest clues for the early detection of deteriorating relationships. Procedures for structuring initial contact and reducing trauma during the termination of companionships are discussed with findings. Chapter Seven focuses on change in the boys who participated in the program. The findings were drawn from responses by parents, counselors, teachers, classmates, and participating boys. Systematic observations were made at the start of the program, at termination, and about one year after termination. Several measurement issues are raised and solutions suggested. Chapter Eight presents a strategy for identifying characteristics of the most successful companionships. Outcome is related to specific boy, student, and relationship variables. A detailed profile of the effective companion therapist is outlined. Chapter Nine reviews changes in the student counselors' interest patterns, career goals, and interpersonal styles. Chapter Ten summarizes all findings, offers conclusions, recommends a set of procedures for nonprofessional therapy projects, and speculates on new directions in the field.

Because *Companionship Therapy* describes a community experiment, it required the help of an especially large number of people and agencies. I must acknowledge a small, durable companionship program that began forty years ago in Berkeley, California. It attained a reputation with enough strength to aid the entry of our unusual project into the community. Inspectors Albert Riedel and Victor Vieira, of the Berkeley Police Department, and many others kept that big brother program alive over the decades. Impetus for converting the big brother program into a large research project came from the Berkeley Council of Social Welfare, the Mayors' Committee on Children, and the Berkeley Council of Social Planning. William J. Davis, general director of Stiles Hall (the Berkeley University YMCA), pursued a lengthy campaign to gather talent, community cooperation, and funds for launching the experiment. He enlisted the active collaboration of a multidisciplinary group of professors at the University of California: Milton Chernin (social welfare), John Clausen (sociology), Hubert Coffey (clinical psychology), William Schutz (educational psychology), Clyde Sullivan (law), Staten Webster (education), and Robert Westfall (psychiatry). Mr. Davis also fostered the support of the Berkeley schools through Alan Foord, Herbert Wenneberg, and Neil Sullivan; the support of the health department through Carl Wells; and the support of the California Department of Mental Hygiene through Eli Bower. The Stiles Hall Advisory Board encouraged Mr. Davis to develop a proposal for funds with the counsel of Professors Coffey, Schutz, Sullivan, and Webster. These men gave much time and care in preparing an initial proposal, which was eventually supported by a three-year grant from the Applied Research Branch, National Institute of Mental Health (No. 00992).

I came to Berkeley after the groundwork was prepared. Bernice Neugarten at the University of Chicago pointed my way; and Professor Clausen welcomed the project into the Berkeley Institute of Human Development, which served as a research wing to Stiles Hall. The close collaboration between a very academic university department and a social-action-oriented YMCA enhanced the amalgamation of research and application within the project. The authors of the initial proposal were flexible and cooperative when the study component was redesigned. In fact, Stiles Hall and all the collaborating agencies respected our autonomy in making the many changes required during the pilot phase.

The immediate project staff was a closely knit group that remained intact over three years. Warren Robinson and Betty Smelser were there at the beginning and worked with genuine commitment in a variety of roles in getting the program launched. Mr. Robinson focused on counselor selection and supervision. Evelyn Scheffer Talbert specialized in the collection and analysis of process data. Barbara Short ran our sociometric studies and organized the mass of data and computer work. Roberta Black gave scrupulous care to the details of office management. Earl Brennen, the associate director of the project, brought his considerable social work skills into managing the program, designing research, interviewing subjects, relating to agencies, interpreting data, and preparing sections of *Companionship Therapy*. But the division of labor was not distinct. Everybody helped with everything.

Encouragement to write *Companionship Therapy* came from Donald Fiske, Henry Maas, Scott Moss, John Shlien, William Smelser, and Brewster Smith. Donald Fiske helped me believe that the design was worthwhile, although I know its execution falls short of his elegant standards. He has never stopped being my teacher and concerned friend. Jean Dames Murphy gave me her love and enthusiasm as I started the book. Further encouragement came from Emory Cowen, Bernard Guerney, Stuart Golann, James Kelly, and Carl Rogers after reviewing a partial manuscript.

William Henry never returned the TAT assignments I did for his course twelve years ago, but he recently rescued this book. His superb editorial sense guided me throughout.

Most of this book was written at UCLA with support and appraisal from my colleagues—especially James Coleman, Kent Dallett, Seymour Feshbach, Gilbert Frietag, Michael Goldstein, Barbara Henker, Ivar Lovaas, Charles Nakamura, and Eliot Rodnick. Jennifer Carter brought care and quiet competence to the organization and typing of the manuscript. She also provided compassion at my fretful moments. Katherine Hord and Helen Brown helped with the typing and tedious proofing and offered few complaints. Mary Madison also helped and never complained. Some final detailing was done with a little help from my friends and students: Barbara Witlin, Joe Fabricatore, Ada Molinoff, David Dooley, Naomi McCormick, Diana Solar, and Dieter Bruhl.

A grant from the Institute of Human Development (University of California, Berkeley) paid for some last-minute data analysis. UCLA granted me a summer salary for writing, and the department of psychology financed the preparation of the manuscript.

I was away when a canyon fire threatened my Topanga home and the manuscript for this study. My neighbors Gerard Haigh, Harold McBride, and Bob Hill rescued the manuscript. I hope they feel this book warrants their risk.

Obviously, the project is indebted to the hundreds of students who served as companion therapists and their schoolboy clients, and to the parents and teachers who gave thousands of hours responding to our research instruments. I hope they have satisfying recollections about the risks they took with us.

My own companion therapist is Cathy Chase, who attended my book-writing pathologies with a consummate interpersonal talent that can come only from a combination of friendship and love.

Los Angeles   GERALD GOODMAN
August 1972

Contents

Preface   ix

1. Context of Companionship Therapy   1

2. Troubled Boys   15

3. Assessing Psychotherapeutic Talent   26

4. Structuring Companionships   51

5. Initial Meeting, and Companionship Activities   73

6. Conversation, Feelings, and Termination   96

7. Change in Boys   125

8. Predictors of Change   173

9.   Impact on Counselors   200

10. Summary, Speculation, Suggestions   224

A   Problem List for Elementary School Boys   268

B   Classmate Descriptions   271

C   Group Description Scale   272

D   Counselor-Boy Relationship Index   274

E   Retrospective Questionnaire   275

F   Follow-Up Interview with Parents   278

G   Boys' Story of Companionship   281

     References   285

     Index   293

Companionship Therapy

Studies in Structured Intimacy

I

Context of Companionship Therapy

The project described in this book was built to study an experimental form of psychotherapy. College students were the therapeutic agents; their "patients" were troubled school children; their "office" was the community at large; the "treatment" was companionship. More specifically, because of stipulations in the YMCA proposal funded by the National Institute for Mental Health, the companionships were restricted to boys; and we further restricted our subjects to fifth- and sixth-grade boys in the Berkeley, California, public schools.

Our research questions focused on the effectiveness of companionship as a therapeutic format. We also studied the differential

1

impact of various companionship structures and processes and developed a promising method for selecting therapeutically talented nonprofessionals. When the preliminary research design was complete, we faced the task of introducing the entire unorthodox project to a wary community. The initial challenge was to earn trust and obtain acceptance.

The acceptance task was eased by two factors: (1) the small but long-established and generally respected Berkeley Big Brother Program developed by the Police Department and Stiles Hall–University YMCA; (2) promises of cooperation and support gathered from major agencies by William Davis, who was the prime catalyst for bringing the project idea into reality. In contrast to the Big Brother Program, our plan called for some rather heavy intrusions into the personal lives of participants, and our approach was frankly therapeutic. We were viewed as a new program with new methods aimed at new populations of participants. Public acceptance would vary through our good works and bad mistakes. A careless procedural mistake or two, showing cause for mistrust and generating serious community complaint, could close down the project. We therefore sought to reduce risks by establishing some global operating principles that would simultaneously protect our participants and our research goals.

Eventually, the principles took the form of a general approach, or a "clinical attitude" toward the community, consistent with the client-centered theory of effective therapist-client relationships. That is, we would try to empathize with any complaints about us, accept community apprehension and protective activities, and disclose our own needs and plans—including the global intervention strategy (see Chapter Four for details). Sometimes we also disclosed the motives for our disclosures (metadisclosure). Implementing this approach took extra time initially, but it brought trust and proved efficient in the long run.

Much of our first year was spent developing assessment procedures, negotiating with the schools, exploring recruitment and selection procedures for students and children, and establishing ties with the community. Teacher descriptions of the six hundred boys in Berkeley's fifth-grade classrooms were obtained with a bipolar rating scale of behavior characteristics. Teachers were also asked to nominate boys with emotional problems. We then used the behavior profiles and referrals to select one hundred boys with the highest frequency of rated problems. Their parents were sent detailed project descriptions and applications. Seventy parents applied—a surprising number. We selected forty for participation and asked the remainder to serve as controls. This procedure went through several modifications and eventually involved a more systematic multiobserver format utilizing descriptions from parents, teachers, and classmates (see Chapter Two). Using a multiple-interview selection procedure, we then recruited students from the University of California campus and randomly paired them with the boys. Again, the selection procedure went through many revisions and eventuated in a very promising group-assessment method, described in Chapter Three. A trial run of these forty companionships lasted ten weeks and allowed us to spot some problems and generate research ideas. The companions met two or three times a week according to convenience and inclination, and contacts lasted from one to five hours. Counselors (designated "Activities Counselors") were paid a substandard hourly wage because previous experience had shown that unpaid volunteers are less reliable and frequently leave their post when paying jobs become available (Davis, 1957). Some rudimentary research was aimed at instrument and design development.

The final project format described throughout this book began to take shape during our second year—in spite of some trouble that began as we started the second-year recruitment. We decided to focus on preadolescent fifth- and sixth-grade boys and could handle fifty participants and fifty controls. To aid our selection, we sent short questionnaires to all 1,250 parents of boys in our target population. Although we did mention that response to the questionnaire was optional, we did not emphasize that fact. As a result, complaints were made to the school board. The board in turn complained that some parents would feel coerced to respond. The issue received prominent mention in the local press, and the number of returned questionnaires dropped sharply. The final return was about 40 per cent, but the adverse publicity lowered our morale and cost considerable staff energy. We were more than ever determined to maintain very honest communications with the community.

Of those who returned the questionnaires ($N = 506$), nearly two thirds ($N = 317$) asked for a project application. The figure would have been higher without the adverse publicity and the prior drain of some sixth-grade boys who, as fifth graders, had participated in our pilot program the preceding year. The evidence clearly indicates that many parents are willing to let their children participate in a companionship therapy program. We eventually learned that boys were eager to join the program and almost never regarded their participation as a stigma.

Shortly after the incident over parent questionnaires had settled down, a new complaint emerged concerning our plans for obtaining children's views of each other's behavior in the classroom (see Chapter Two). A few school board members, along with some parents, regarded the procedure as an invasion of privacy and a source of trauma. Once again, the issue received publicity in the local newspaper. This time, we were intent on using our intervention principles of empathizing with community concerns, displaying our understanding, and disclosing our needs. The matter was scheduled for review at a hearing of the school board. We prepared an open letter to the board. In it we listed the potential dangers in the planned sociometric screening and the potential benefits for the community; we also explained our strategy for avoiding harm to children and disclosed our research needs. Apparently, some were surprised by the open letter because we listed potential dangers that were not imagined by the critics. The hearing resulted in an approval of the sociometric screening plan, along with official encouragement for its eventual use as a school-wide program for detecting emotionally troubled children.

During the second and third year of the study, we secured data that helped in establishing the final versions of our parent, teacher, counselor, and boy rating instruments (Chapter Seven); our control-group format and dyad matching method (Chapter Two); and our study design for measuring the companionship process (Chapters Five and Six). We also settled on the criteria for structuring the companionships (Chapter Four) and selecting counselors (Chapter Three). A stratified random sample of two hundred "normal" boys was selected and assessed over time for future comparisons. Crude findings on the truncated companionships produced a mixed outcome picture, with hints of greater gains for specific subgroups. That is, the early clues suggested that particular classes of boys, counselors, dyad types, and even companionship-process patterns might be associated with therapeutic improvement. In other words, it became apparent that the total sample of companionships should really be divided into many subgroups—a difficult procedure with only fifty companionships.

We therefore decided to extend the project into a fourth year, with an additional program that strictly replicated the third year. The expansion would create a sample of one hundred companionships for study and would prohibit program changes between years (since such changes might prevent the blending of the separate programs into one large research sample). The National Institute of Mental Health agreed with the plan and granted funds. Enlarging the final study sample turned out to be a critical move. It enabled us to learn that the effectiveness of companionships is associated with such variables as counselor characteristics, boy and dyad types, and the properties of ongoing companionship process.

Scope and Logic of Nonprofessional Therapy

The rationale for exploring companionship as a therapeutic device becomes clear when viewed in the context of current mental health planning. The literature of community psychology, social work, community psychiatry, and applied social psychology is filled with calls for radical changes in the delivery of mental health services: a shift from private to public models, the utilization of new manpower resources, the proliferation of alternate theories and therapeutic inventions, and a concentration on prevention procedures—especially for children (Adelson and Kalis, 1970; Albee, 1968; Arnhoff, Rubinstein, and Speisman, 1969; Cowen, Gardner, and Zax, 1967; Grosser, Henry, and Kelly, 1971; Guerney, 1969). Most observers believe that the changes have been fostered by the hopelessly widening gap between professional resources and community need, but few regard manpower deficit as the only instigator.

Some point to the eroding confidence in the medical-practitioner or illness model for mental health applications (and urge abandonment of the orthodox fifty-minute hour). Psychotherapists are trading individual therapy for groups, consultation, program administration, teaching, and research. Also cited as causes for the new movement are the rise of humanistic psychology, the increased acceptance of second-generation-therapy theories, the therapeutic-community model in mental hospitals, congressional investigations of the mental health enterprise, the civil rights struggle, and the war on poverty. We can predict, then, that the next decade of development in mental health strategies will be dominated by the nonprofessional therapeutic agent.

With some hindsight, we can view the coming of the nonprofessional as a logical phase in the developmental history of mental health economics. Almost every significant structural change in the therapy enterprise over the past fifty years has been influenced by the social demand for greater output or less expense (upgrading effectiveness has been a secondary issue). An increased output of therapy hours came with the advent of the "functional alternatives": clinical and counseling psychologists, social workers, pastoral and marriage counselors, and the like. Cost per hour took a dip, but then advanced to earlier highs. Briefer forms of therapy also became popular and reduced expense, but demand still exceeded supply. With the invention of group therapy, supply was expanded and costs cut; again, however, there was not enough to go around. After that, a great number of therapeutically intended or change-producing programs rapidly emerged: encounter groups, behavior-modification, growth centers, grass-roots programs (Alcoholics Anonymous, Synanon, half-way houses, Big Brothers), and other comparatively inexpensive procedures with potential for wide distribution. Nonprofessional manpower has been involved in all these developments. Thus, the change-seeking or psychologically distressed individual now has many affordable options.

The professional also has new options, which sharply increase the number of clients he can work with. Not long ago, the therapist was limited to orthodox individual therapy (long term: one therapist to one patient format). He worked with about one hundred patients during his entire career. With the popularization of the interpersonal, existential, experiential, and behavior-modification therapies (short term: one therapist to one patient), his range was expanded. The legitimization of group therapy provided another option with economic advantages (long term: one therapist to several patients). Now the numerous possibilities range from crisis intervention (brief term: one to one) to encounter groups (brief term: one to several) to supervising nonprofessionals (variable term: one to several nonprofessionals to several clients = one professional to many patients). By supervising nonprofessionals, a single professional could conceivably oversee the therapy of a hundred clients in a year instead of a lifetime. Unfortunately, little is known about which option does what for whom, because systematic investigation of effectiveness was a neglected factor in the rush of events. That is, we have succeeded in developing a wide variety of accessible new procedures that may not provide therapy. They exist mostly on faith, excitement, good intentions—and economic need.

It is difficult to estimate the scope of nonprofessional therapy because many programs are not described in print. On occasion, programs are mentioned in newspapers or on television, but the clearest indicator of the movement's magnitude comes from edited collections in the professional literature (Cook, 1970; Cowen, Gardner and Zax, 1967; Ewalt, 1967; Grosser, Henry, and Kelly, 1971; Gruver, 1971; Guerney, 1969; Hart and Tomlinson, 1970; Iscoe and Spielberger, 1970; Simon, 1971; Sobey, 1970). The National Association for Mental Health has been actively promoting nonprofessionals through its eight hundred state and local chapters, but an accounting of all programs has not yet been prepared (see Matarazzo, 1971). The burst of activity in nonprofessional work is evidenced by the narrow time span encompassing these publications. Almost all of the programs described focus on homogeneous groups of therapists or clients. The most frequently used agents are college students, who are easily accessible to professional program initiators. In addition to being an easily captured group, students represent an enthusiastic, bright, idealistic, inexpensive, flexible—and very large—manpower pool. The host of other groups utilized as therapeutic agents almost form a representative social cross section: high school students, "empty-nest" housewives, indigenous neighborhood

workers, nurses, retardates, retired people, delinquents, businessmen, police, drug addicts, ex-offenders, hospital attendants, scout
leaders, military men, welfare workers, alcoholics, parents (with
their own children), and bartenders.

The homogeneous program pattern may eventually break
down with the development of systematic selection procedures for
locating personal attributes most effective for particular classes of
clients. Also, selection probably will become an active issue because,
as recent findings (for instance, Truax and Mitchell, 1971) suggest,
successful therapy as well as efficiency results when skill training is
replaced by talent selection.

Most of the published programs employed minimal in-
service supervision or brief orientations, although some attempted
to emulate professional instruction; and Rioch, Elkes, and Flint
(1965) went the distance and produced a small group of profes-
sionals-without-credentials in an intensive two-year clinical training
program. Rioch's spearhead program, along with the "new careers"
model of manpower utilization, has influenced the numerous two-
year training programs in junior, community, and state colleges—
programs aimed at producing Associate of Arts mental health technicians or "generalists." As expected, first reports indicate some
institutional resistance to these paraprofessionals, so that their entry
into the field probably will be slow and complicated by their marginality (Simon, 1971).

In any case, paraprofessionals alone will not bridge the
manpower gap; nonprofessionals, systematically selected and lightly
trained, will probably form the largest component of the manpower
pool. Their use in auxiliary or primary helping relationships should
not be complicated by marginality or career problems, and supervision can come from professionals or paraprofessional technicians.
Apparently, then, mental health work is headed for a tripartite
stratification: professionals, paraprofessionals, and nonprofessionals.

The great variation of nonprofessional personnel in therapy
roles is paralleled by the variety of their client populations. Hospitalized mental patients are probably the largest customer pool, but
other client groups are appearing more frequently: troubled schoolchildren, clinic outpatients, drug addicts, distressed college students,
alcoholics, welfare and court clientele, prisoners, retardates.

Diversity of populations and procedures has been spawned by the atmosphere of free experimentation. In general, the nonprofessional literature seems composed of strategies for action, program descriptions, historical accounts, manpower issues, and large conceptual frameworks. Research is missing (see Zax and Cowen, 1972), but there is some indication that it may soon be underway. The few early studies (for instance, Holzberg, Gewirtz, and Ebner, 1964; Poser, 1966; Zunker and Brown, 1966) have been joined by two larger systematic investigations—one, of students with chronic patients (Rappaport, Chinsky, and Cowen, 1971); the other, of housewife mental health counselors (Magoon, Golann, and Freeman, 1969). The slow but irresistible legitimization of academic community psychology within universities will increase research output. As of now, this burgeoning new field appears to be building a conceptual base, testing the administrative feasibility of diverse therapeutic agents and client populations, exploring radical procedures, and just starting the serious business of doing believable research.

Capsule History of Companionship Programs

The companionship program appears to be one of the durable elements in the evolution of nonprofessional therapy. The following programs trace a history of companionship experiments and provide a context for the project described in this book.

The Cambridge-Somerville Youth Study, begun in 1938, stands as the granddaddy of companionship programs (Powers and Witmer, 1951)'. In this study, about 650 preadolescent boys were matched into pairs and split into participating and control groups. Most of the counselors were men, and many had had training in social work. Visit frequency and length were very inconsistent and poorly regulated, with some pairs meeting once a month or less. The average relationship lasted about five years. "Maturity" and "good will" were seen as the potential inducers of change. Case histories, delinquency records, and adjustment ratings provided outcome data. The findings were negative: Controls and participants showed similar gains. Gordon Allport's foreword to the Powers-Witmer book was essentially a plea for not abandoning the companionship idea. He pointed to the lack of specificity in the main hypothesis, the lack of refined subgroups, the crude measurement, and the need for follow-up studies. He even located one counselor with a high success rate and urged readers not to disregard the implication: that nonauthoritarian, nonprofessional warmth may be more therapeutic than a professional approach. The McCords (1959) heeded Allport's appeal and reanalyzed the data on twenty-four matched pairs. They found that improvement was significantly associated with frequency of contact, age of the boys, and the boys' willingness to disclose personal matters. According to these investigators, "the program might have been more successful had a greater number of boys been seen at least once a week, and had treatment started during the first decade of the boys' lives" (p. 47). The Cambridge-Somerville study falls short of modern research standards, but it remains as a classic pioneer of community psychology and a model of scrupulous reporting.

The Berkeley Big Brother Project, the precursor of the program described in this book, got underway in the early 1930s. At that time, the Berkeley Police Department began pairing delinquent boys with older "high-caliber" volunteer college men on the assumption that the friendship would provide a medium for guidance and constructive modeling behavior (Davis, 1957). The effort was joined by Stiles Hall, the University YMCA, which initially served as a recruitment agency but soon became a full partner. When the volunteer arrangement proved impractical, students were paid with funds donated at first by the Junior Chamber of Commerce and later by fraternities on the University of California campus. About fifteen to twenty companionships were maintained, and administrative costs were born by Stiles Hall and the Police Department. This successful joint venture attracted the attention of other communities throughout the country and provided a model for program initiation.

Around 1960, William Davis, the General Secretary of Stiles Hall, began a methodical campaign to systematize and study the program with widespread community involvement. He was able to gather commitments from the Public Health Department, the Public Schools, the Recreation and Parks Department, the Council on Social Planning, and an interdisciplinary group of faculty from the University of California. Several proposals were collaboratively prepared and rejected by funding agencies. Eventually, the National Institute of Mental Health awarded a large grant for the establishment and study of a four year companionship program that would involve fifty pairs of college men and emotionally troubled boys each year. That grant supported the central studies reported in this book.

Another large and successful companionship program is the Big Brothers of America, a national institution of scattered agencies pairing fatherless boys with adult males—frequently businessmen. Their emphasis is on prevention, and their approach has taken much from social casework. Relationships are quite unstructured, with some concern for allowing the boy a successful reliving of the earlier trauma created by his loss of a father. The leaders of the Big Brother organization have shown interest in testing their assumption that the relationships are beneficial (Jahn, 1962). The Big Brother Program of the Jewish Board of Guardians has recently heightened its emphasis on systematic pairing and selection (Lichtenberg, in Guerney, 1969).

In 1952, a small group of volunteer Harvard students began work at Boston Psychopathic Hospital under the direction of Donald Schneiderman. It was the earliest college student companion program with hospitalized mental patients. In 1954, a group of enthusiastic students started the Harvard-Radcliffe program at Boston's Metropolitan State Hospital, and over two thousand students became involved during the next decade (Umbarger, Dalsimer, Morrison, and Breggin, 1962). That figure has probably more than doubled by now. Volunteers worked in one-to-one companionships with adults and children, and with case aides, and assisted in a variety of group projects. In 1957, the idea of the Harvard program was incorporated into the abnormal psychology course at Wesleyan University. The course grew into the Connecticut Valley State Hospital Companion Program (Holzberg, Knapp, and Turner, 1967), which, in turn, has expanded to seven additional colleges. Students and patients visit both in and out of the hospital. Studies of the program have focused on changes in students.

The wave of student companionship activity with adult and

juvenile mental patients has spread to hundreds of colleges and clinical settings. An accurate survey does not exist, but an estimate of six hundred programs feels conservative. We also know little about the effectiveness of these thousands of therapeutically intended companionships. Research on selection, process, and patient change has been lacking; but the situation may be improving, as evidenced by the systematic work of Rappaport, Chinsky, and Cowen (1971). Their monograph on student-led groups of chronic patients is an example of program evaluation that should provide a model and stimulate more investigation.

Apparently, the scattered student-child companionship programs existed and terminated without much knowledge of each other. Programs in South Dakota, Chicago, New York, Boston, California, and Vermont were in progress around 1960, but did not mention the existence of kindred efforts. The Vermont project —Student Volunteers and Troubled Children—used students from Goddard, Montpelier, and Vermont colleges (Mitchell, 1963). Some of the four- to fifteen-year-old children participated up to three and four years. The project was without outcome research, but the director's experience led to a theoretical paper in defense of volunteers over paid workers (Mitchell, 1966a).

The first sophisticated process and outcome study of a companionship program for college students and troubled children was conducted at the University of Rochester (Cowen, Zax, and Laird, 1966; Cowen, 1971). Pilot work for their small study began earlier (Cowen, Izzo, Miles, Telschow, Trost, and Zax, 1963) and paralleled the start of our own pilot investigation in 1962. Similarities between the Rochester study and our work are not limited to timing. Both projects were designed to ask questions about selection, training, and change in students—along with change in children and the association between process and outcome. Unfortunately, the two projects were independently initiated and provide another example of the communication gap between companionship programs. Cowen and his colleagues saw their work as a first step in evolving a model for integration in long-range programs aimed at early detection and prevention of emotional disorders in the school setting. They selected seventeen students via interviews, briefly oriented them, and provided a one-hour group consultation twice a week—after each contact with the children. The primary-grade children were selected with the aid of a teacher's rating scale (for problems), an adjective check list, and a written description of the child's problem. Contacts involved a range of after-school activities and lasted about seventy minutes. The companionships lasted for about fourteen meetings. The investigators realized that a larger, longer program and even more design refinement were needed for a rigorous assessment of outcome, but reasoned that a modest study could serve as an impetus for further work. Participating children were compared with a non-participating control group on pre-post outcome measures. No significant differences were found—probably for the following reasons: (1) The limited sample size made it difficult to partition for more successful subgroups. (2) The brief companionship duration worked against high levels of disclosure and intimacy. (3) The visits were too short. (4) There was no selection procedure for obtaining students with high levels of openness, empathy, and other qualities that we found associated with greater improvement. (See Chapters Eight and Nine for findings related to these four points.) The seventeen male and female students showed some pre-post change in attitudes: "a diminution of the idealized image of institutional concepts" and more accepting attitudes toward emotionally disturbed children. The investigators' attempt to relate process measures of companionship activities (taken at three points during the program) to the children's outcome scores was admittedly hampered by the small sample size, but the limited findings provide some important clues. Positive outcome was associated with higher frequencies of "talking activities" and lower frequencies of "running activities." These trends show some correspondence to our process findings (Chapters Five, Six, and Eight), and we regard this type of research as having great potential for linking interpersonal processes to therapeutic change. Further, we see companionship programs in general as providing a major vehicle for the expansion of such research (Chapter Nine). Cowen and his associates are continuing work on process analysis (McWilliams, 1971). They are also studying the problems of companion selection (Cowen, Dorr, and Pokracki, 1972) and the longer-term effects of companionships on children (Cowen, Dorr, Trost, and Izzo, 1972).

Investigators have only scratched at the tremendous research potential for studying long-standing therapy questions with non-professional programs. A few dozen programs pairing students and troubled children have appeared in collections (Gruver, 1971; Guerney, 1969; Sobey, 1970), but most just mention the research possibilities; not one includes the type of serious investigation described by Cowen and his associates. While the lack of research is disappointing, there is a good deal of imaginative exploration. The frequently cited Project RE-ED, developed by Hobbs (1966), trains students for nine months to staff a radically conceived live-in school for reeducating disturbed children. Hobbs's school may be the prototype of a future standard in mental health technology. Here are a few representative samples of other student-child programs that emerged in the past decade: Reinherz (1969) brought students to children in mental hospitals in an extension of the Harvard-Radcliffe program; Davison (1966) trained undergraduates as social reinforcers for autistic children with little measured effect; student companions in the Pattersons' (1967) program worked with adolescents from an outpatient clinic; and Linden and Stollack's (1969) students employed play therapy techniques with younger children.

Companionship programs have reached for innovation by varying large components such as relationship structure and participating populations. We are building a stockpile of inventions without knowledge of their therapeutic effects. Evaluation has been confined mostly to problems involving the *administrative* feasibility of particular formats. That is, greater confidence has been established for a wide range of initiation strategies, recruitment procedures, and program-maintenance strategies for the many new therapeutically intended relationship combinations. As we settle into the knowledge that almost anything is administratively possible in the recently liberalized mental health field, the striving for innovation should be supplemented by an increased concern for program effectiveness—and a willingness to replicate last year's invention in this year's research design. The refinement and study of *specific* program formats for *specific* populations seems the logical next step. If we locate some reproducible situations that consistently yield successful outcomes, the nonprofessional therapy revolution can become a major force in mental health work.

II

Troubled Boys

As the "patients" in our companionship study, we hoped to select moderately troubled boys who were still capable of attending public school and who were willing to make some interpersonal contact with a college student twice a week for the school year. Boys with severe behavior or organic problems would have required special care unavailable in a lightly supervised and mobile companionship program. The boys we sought, in short, could be grossly categorized as a preclinical, or a prevention, sample.

In addition, we decided to limit our recruitment to pre-adolescent or early-adolescent boys because (1) their problems are not complicated by the common physically induced crises of adolescence, (2) most are in a developmental period that makes demands upon the interpersonal skills necessary for collaboration with a single friend, and (3) they are old enough to enjoy a wide range of interesting activities with a college student. We limited our recruitment to the fifth and sixth grades (boys mostly in their tenth and eleventh years).

Public school systems usually do not have a good accounting of their emotionally troubled children, and Berkeley was no exception. The school guidance offices were understaffed and without any systematic screening procedure, so that most of the moderately troubled children remained unlocated within the school system. Our research design required almost two hundred troubled boys, and we were faced with the problem of locating them without causing much disturbance. After initial resistance, the board of education agreed to let us use a sociometric instrument to screen all 2,400 children in the fifth and sixth grades and to send project announcements to all the parents of the boys.

The two-page announcement described most facets of the program. It included details on the selection and characteristics of our activities counselors, a list of activities pursued by pairs during the pilot program, our research objectives and sponsoring agencies, the special nature of structured cross-age companionships (frequent individual contact with a nonfamily, nonprofessional adult; rare use of discipline; absence of customary adult demands). We emphasized that counselors would not attempt to intervene as professional therapists but rather would build gradual friendships, whose potential therapeutic effects were under study. The purpose of sharing these details was to engender parental trust in an experimental enterprise launched by a frequently suspect group—university researchers. The announcement also underlined our focus on boys with emotional problems (that is, boys who seemed hostile, depressed, withdrawn, or lacking in self-esteem) who were experiencing serious difficulty in performing schoolwork. To discourage possible coercion by parents, we stipulated that boys must show a clear interest in joining. We also informed parents of the research demands of the program: a lengthy set of questionnaires at the beginning and end of companionships. Those interested made formal application by returning a postcard.

Twelve hundred fifty announcements were distributed to classrooms for boys to take home to parents at the start of both program years. During the first year, about 25 per cent of the parents asked for applications. We were surprised that one of every four parents found interest in a program aimed at emotionally troubled boys. Our staff did some phone consultation with prospective applicants and discouraged about 5 per cent, who described obviously superficial problems. We assume that another 5 per cent changed their minds or were reluctant to fill out the lengthy and personal application form and questionnaires, since we eventually received 186 completed applications (nearly 16 per cent of the almost 1,200 announcements estimated to have reached parents). Completed applications for the second program year fell to 10 per cent (see Chapter One for details).

We received completed applications for about 14 per cent of the boys in the fifth and sixth grades over the two program years and eventually selected about 10 per cent to participate in companionships and serve as controls. Assuming that we received applications from at least two thirds of the troubled boys who could meet our criteria, we speculate that the boys in our final sample are fairly typical of the most troubled fifth- and sixth-grade boys in the Berkeley schools.

For each of the two program years (the third and fourth ones of our study), about one hundred boys described as most troubled by parents, teachers, and classmates were formed into fifty closely matched pairs. The remaining boys were then used as secondary matches. We managed to do some rather close matching on variables such as age, school grade, socioeconomic status, race, neighborhood, intactness of home, religious commitment, and birth order (see Table 1). We also matched boys according to the classification "quiet" (problems with isolation, depression, withdrawal) or "outgoing" (pervasive aggression, attention-seeking behavior, rebelliousness). Boys were placed in these categories by three project staff members after their review of parents', teachers', and classmates' ratings. The interjudge reliability was .93.

We assigned the two groups to companionship participation or rejection status by the flip of a coin. Over the two years, about half of the parents of rejected applicants volunteered to serve as controls by responding to future assessment. With some realignment and use of secondary matches, we obtained a large control group ($N = 90$). At the closing of the program, attrition reduced the

Table 1

GENERAL AND FAMILY CHARACTERISTICS OF BOYS

Variable	Participants ($N = 88$) Per Cent	Controls ($N = 74$) Per Cent
Fifth grade	57	69
Sixth grade	43	31
Age	11.2	11.0
White	69	70
Black	28	26
Oriental	3	4
Income below $6,000	30	29
Between $6,000 and $9,000	25	19
Between $9,000 and $12,000	16	29
Above $12,000	30	23
High socioeconomic position = 4	24	23
3	27	28
2	24	26
Low socioeconomic position = 1	25	23
Intact home	66	70
Broken home	34	30
Some religious affiliation	67	61
No affiliation	33	39
Religiously committed home	31	33
Mild commitment	35	27
Very little or no commitment	34	40
Only child	8	10
First born	28	32
Middle	41	42
Last born	23	16
Never spanked	24	27
Rarely	58	54
Monthly	13	12
Weekly	7	7

Note: None of the frequencies differed significantly among groups.

group to seventy-four, but it remained closely matched to the participant group of eighty-eight boys (Table 1). Of course, the control group was also matched with participants in their motivation to join the project—a motivation that carried them through the laborious application phase. However, they were biased by their willingness to serve as controls and their experience of rejection. Speculation on the effects of the bias are offered in Chapter Seven.

Combining the control samples for the two programs was appropriate because they were extremely similar on virtually all variables. The same was true for the two participant groups. This similarity was a result of strict replication of recruitment and selection procedures (see Chapter Seven for details).

Characteristics of Boys

As Table 1 shows, almost all the boys (92 per cent) were in their tenth and eleventh years as the program started. None was younger than nine or older than twelve, making the sample mostly preadolescent and partially early adolescent. Mean ages for the participant and control groups were similar, as were the remaining variables shown in Table 1. Both groups were about 70 per cent white, 27 per cent black, and 3 per cent Oriental. Our black sample slightly underrepresented the Berkeley black population, because, we suspect, black families were reluctant to apply to an experimental mental health program with a white staff. Family income tended to be bimodal, with 30 per cent below six thousand dollars and a substantial proportion with above-average incomes, especially control families, 50 per cent of whom earned nine thousand dollars or more. The Berkeley median family income was near seven thousand dollars. Table 1 shows a more symmetrical distribution of the sample on Hollingshead's (1957) Index of Social Position, which is based only on occupation and education. The high incidence of low incomes was generated by the many fatherless homes containing well-educated mothers working part time. The potential use of our college counselors as temporary father surrogates attracted applications from a high proportion of mothers with "fatherless" boys. Over half of the applications we rejected (because of few problems or low pathology scores from school ratings) were for such boys. About one third of the final samples were fatherless; fewer than 5 per cent were from homes with only a father. The birth order of our sample was close to that of the general population.

Parents' Initial Descriptions

All applicants were described by parents on the reliable Adjective Check List (ACL), discussed in Chapter Seven. In a study comparing parental ACL ratings with a large battery of tests, interviews, and other background information, Scarr (1966) found systematic correlations—which suggests that the ACL is valid for describing children. However, since the ACL was standardized on adult self-descriptions, the meaning of the original scale names requires some stretching for application to children. In our study, original designations are accompanied by a set of revised scale names, which seem more appropriate to our data. Revised names were determined by the correlations of each ACL scale with the Problem List for Elementary School Boys and the Peer Nominations Inventory (described later), along with a content analysis of the adjectives used by parents. Original and revised names for the twenty-four scales are shown on Figure 4 (in Chapter Seven), along with initial mean scores for participants and controls. As the figure shows, no significant differences were observed between the two groups at initial testing. In general, the findings seemed to characterize the sample boys as primarily unmanageable mischief makers who demanded attention, created disorder, felt restless, and lacked friends.

The Problem List for Elementary School Boys (Goodman, 1966) contains thirty-five typical problems of preadolescent boys with eight-step endorsement scales ranging from "never" to "always" observed (see Appendix A and Figure 5). Once again, participants and controls were rated quite similarly by their parents at the initial testing, with only two items different at the .05 level (participant boys were higher on "He is modest—doesn't like to be seen undressed" and lower on "His appetite is poor"). A total-problems score (simple summation of all ratings) was virtually identical for the two groups. Ratings for both groups ($N = 160$) were combined to produce an overall picture of problem frequency.

Table 2 uses three classes of problem severity as rated by parents: serious—problem occurs often to always, moderate-mild —slightly less than often to seldom, no problem—seldom to never. This breakdown is crude because some problems occur with greater frequency in the general preadolescent population—for example, attention-seeking and becoming very upset when scolded (both omitted from Table 2). Also, different levels of problem severity can be represented by the same level of problem occurrence. Nevertheless, Table 2 gives a fairly accurate rank order of problem severity for these boys. The level of severity was probably somewhat inflated because parents emphasized problem occurrence to enhance their chances for selection. We cannot accurately gauge the extent of this response bias. We did find many significantly positive correlations between parent ratings and school ratings (using a different instrument), which suggests that the bias is slight and that the occurrence levels are significantly above those expected from a random sample of preadolescent boys.

Fifteen problems occurred at serious frequencies (often to always) for at least one third of the sample. The most characteristic of these involved emotional and interpersonal vulnerability, or a general fragility of self-esteem: easily hurt feelings, self-dislike, feelings of being picked on, and interpersonal fears. Another set of common serious problems involved aggressive hostility: temper tantrums, edginess and irritability, and frequent teasing. Two isolation problems were frequently rated as serious: habitually concealed feelings and much solitary play. Other problems occurring frequently for over one third of the sample were overdependency, emotional lability, negativism, and worry about schoolwork. About 25 per cent of the boys, according to parents' ratings, were seriously troubled with jealousy, sleep problems, overcompetitiveness; 20 per cent were depressed much of the time; 15 per cent were phobic; and about 10 per cent had speech and eating problems. This breakdown, however, masks the severity of behavior dysfunction for the quiet and outgoing subgroups of boys. Parents of almost 80 per cent of the quiet subgroup saw them as seriously overdependent,

Table 2

FREQUENCY OF PROBLEM OCCURENCE FOR
ENTERING BOYS ($N = 160$)

Problem Rated by Parents	"Always" to "Often"	"Often" to "Seldom"	"Seldom" and "Never"
		Per Cent	
Feelings are easily hurt	66	32	2
Has "temper tantrums"—anger outbursts	53	28	19
"On edge," annoyed, irritable at small things	48	40	12
Modest—doesn't like to be seen undressed	46	29	25
Thinks poorly of himself	45	36	19
Feels everyone picks on him	44	38	18
Keeps his feelings to himself	43	46	11
Teases others	43	45	12
Plays alone	41	50	9
Depends on parents too much	40	38	12
Not sure of himself with people	39	44	17
Has mood 'swings—strong changes in feelings	38	50	12
Wants to do the opposite	34	46	20
Asks for help with schoolwork	33	53	14
Upset by new situations and activities	33	40	27
Asks for help wih schoolwork	31	55	14
Becomes very jealous	29	47	24
Does not like to share things	27	51	22
Quiet and shy	26	51	23
Gets into fights with children	25	55	20
Must win at all costs	23	56	19
Restless in sleep—has disturbing dreams	23	38	39
Has sad moods	20	56	24
Swears or curses	16	37	47
Afraid or upset by dogs, fire, dark, and so on	15	32	53
Bites his nails	15	20	65
Ruins toys or destroys belongings	13	35	52
Acts unusual—unlike other children	13	36	51
Tells fibs or lies	10	60	30
Has poor appetite	10	52	38
Has speech problems: stutters, baby talks, and so on	9	21	70
Wets his bed or soils during the day	5	15	80
Takes things not his own—steals	4	36	60

shy, and upset at new situations, while a similar proportion of the parents of outgoing boys rated them as frequently getting into fights and being extremely competitive.

Evidence for the consistency of parents' reports comes from the set of modest but significant correlations between Problem List and ACL scores. The total score on the Problem List was positively correlated in the high fifties ($p < .01$) with the ACL categories unmannerly-rude (aggression) and demanding (succorance), and negatively correlated (high fifties) with the categories well behaved (favorability), friendly-gregarious (affiliation), and good little man (adjustment). Many specific item comparisons across instruments produced significant correlations in the fifties ($p < .01$)—for example, "depends on parents too much" positively with the ACL category demanding (succorance), "tries to get attention" with the ACL category attention-seeking (exhibit), "thinks poorly of himself" with ACL weak-timid (abasement).

Teachers' and Classmates' Initial Description

Teachers and classmates rated all children in the class. Although they did not know who our applicants were, they described them as more atypical, isolated, and attention-seeking and less likeable than other boys in the classroom. We collected these ratings near the end of school years, when familiarity was greatest, and used the Peer Nominations Inventory (PNI) (Wiggins and Winder, 1961) as the sociometric instrument to gather classroom observations. The PNI organizes ratings into factors labeled isolation, hostility, likeability, and attention-seeking. We added an atypicality scale. (See Chapter Seven for details on items, scoring methods, and factors.)

A correlation of teacher and classmate scores on the five scales indicated strong agreement between the two rater groups. The five sister scales (for example, teachers' isolation with classmates' isolation scores) produced the five strongest correlations in the matrix. The average sister-scale correlation was .61 ($N = 166$), with hostility, isolation, and attention-seeking around .70 and atypicality and likeability near .50. These similarities support the validity of the measurements made in the classroom.

Participants ($N = 88$) and controls ($N = 74$) received similar scores from teachers and classmates on all PNI scales. The participants did differ significantly from a stratified random subgroup ($N = 201$) on most scales. Specifically, the participants were described as significantly more isolated and atypical by both teachers and classmates ($p < .01$). Classmates rated participants as more attention-seeking and less likeable than random boys at the $<.01$ level, while teachers did the same at the $<.05$ level. The teacher and classmate hostility scales did not significantly differentiate participants from random boys, but the trend was toward somewhat higher scores for participants. (See Table 13.) These classroom observations support the parent descriptions, indicating that the participants and their controls were a distinct group displaying moderate psychological problems at home and in school.

Summary

We decided against selecting a clinical sample with severe behavior or organic problems because the companionships were designed to be lightly supervised. Besides, a moderately troubled sample has the advantages of representing a larger segment of the general population and being more accessible from public schools. The disadvantage is that changes in moderate problems are usually more difficult to measure than are changes in severe problems. Preadolescent boys were chosen because their problems are not complicated by the physically induced crises of adolescence, they are developmentally ready for learning one-to-one collaboration, and they are old enough to enjoy a wide range of activities with a college student.

Since the Berkeley school system did not have a clear accounting of troubled boys, we screened all fifth- and sixth-grade classrooms with a sociometric device. In addition, we sent project descriptions and applications to the parents of these children. Completed applications for the two research program years represented about 14 per cent of the fifth and sixth grades. About one hundred boys were eventually selected for each program year and were considered to represent the most troubled 15 per cent in the fifth and sixth grades.

During each program year the selected boys were sorted into matched pairs. The matched pairs were then randomly split and assigned to companionship or control status. About half those designated as controls agreed to serve by responding to future assessment. Thus, the controls were tainted with a volunteer bias but were well matched on motivation for applying to the program. At project termination there were seventy-four controls and eighty-eight boys who participated in companionships.

Evidence supporting the assumption that our final applicants were moderately troubled came from a comparative study using 201 children randomly selected from the same classrooms. Compared with the random group, participants were rated significantly more isolated, atypical, attention-seeking, and less likeable by both classmates and teachers on the PNI. The two groups were not significantly different on PNI hostility.

Most boys in the samples were in their tenth and eleventh years (70 per cent white, 27 per cent black, 3 per cent Oriental). One third were from broken homes. Participants and controls were closely matched. Parent ratings allowed an overall characterization of the boys as unmanageable mischief makers who demanded attention, created disorder, felt restless, and lacked friends. An extremely wide range of problems were seen by parents. The findings suggest that the boys could be globally characterized as an emotionally and interpersonally vulnerable group who tended to be socially isolated and experienced low self-regard.

In sum, the samples appear to distinctly represent a cross section of emotionally troubled boys with problems of moderate severity. Observations from parents, teachers, and classmates are adequately reliable and concur in describing the participant and control groups as appropriately matched for study into the effects of a companionship intervention.

III

Assessing Psychotherapeutic Talent

We needed fifty counselors for each program year. A small advertisement placed in the campus newspaper promised $1.40 an hour for six to nine hours a week and a free training program. About one hundred college men applied each year, but it would have been easy to recruit many more applicants. Few students were discouraged by the substandard pay rate or by the demanding set of requirements spelled out in the project announcement. Apparently, work on mental health projects is appealing to a large and diversified segment of college students. They form a bright and eager manpower pool. Since we did not consider brightness and eagerness sufficient attributes for maintaining therapeutic relation-

26

ships, our next step was to search for better criteria and prepare selection procedures aimed at therapeutic competence.

Very little has been published about the selection of non-professionals for therapeutic roles. Programs often use the judgment of an interviewer or the information on an application form as selection criteria. The effectiveness of these criteria is rarely studied. Developing reliable selection procedures becomes especially important where training is minimal. Indeed, training may be less important than appropriate selection in programs using nonprofessionals—particularly since therapeutic competence probably is more a matter of untutored talent or interpersonal sensitivity than of skill learned during a training course.

Traditional screening procedures used in selecting students for professional clinical training were inappropriate and seemed more concerned with academic achievement than therapeutic talent. We wanted to devise an inexpensive selection method that would be open to research and adaptable to varied program needs and manpower sources. Multiple structured interviews, in which each applicant was seen and rated by a male and female staff member, were useful as a reliable pathology screen but showed a constricted view of the applicant's interpersonal style. Only after the counselors had been selected and on the job for awhile did we get a good sample of their intepersonal styles—from observing their behavior in supervision sessions and small sensitivity-training groups and from reading their accounts of the companionships.

In the midst of our dilemma over selection, we decided to experiment with small-group sessions as a context for selecting counselors. In setting up such an experiment, we faced many problems: building an assesment device, establishing rejection criteria, devising the actual group procedure, and preparing a research design to study the entire selection method. But our first major problem was to choose the variables: the interpersonal traits related to untutored therapeutic talent. This step required a clarification of our assumptions.

Criteria

Perhaps there never will be any generally accepted criteria for therapeutic talent. Each system of therapy holds its own view of effective therapist behavior and its own training methods. Clinical training programs in and out of the universities have offered little empirical or theoretical work on therapeutic talent. It appears to be thought of as either a minor variable or an impossible concept. Schools usually select their students with criteria based on academic achievement; for indication of therapeutic talent, committees at best attempt to extrapolate intuitively a few clues about personality into judgments of future success in the therapy role. Thus, therapists are usually brought into professional training on evidence that often has little to do with the critical skills they must actually use in the field.

One might begin forming a model for selection by listing the characteristics necessary for the traditional psychotherapist. But the traditional therapist usually attempts to use his expert knowledge to understand his patient better than his patient understands himself; his therapeutic techniques seldom depart from the historical conception of a professional healer. Traditional theories, therefore, cannot provide a working model for nonprofessional therapists, who do not have the expertise to formulate or prescribe.

In contrast, client-centered theory seems to provide an appropriate model for selecting nonprofessional criteria. Each of the necessary and sufficient conditions of therapeutic personality change formulated by Rogers (1957) can be seen, in less obvious fashion, in everyday behavior—in the person regarded as a good listener who understands the other person's feelings; in the person regarded as spontaneous, open, "straight," self-disclosing; or in the person described as having an accepting nature. A few unusual people possess these traits in combination. We wanted to find people with these combined traits. Some previous studies showed promising results in assessing client-centered conditions from tape recordings of interviews (Carkhuff and Truax, 1965) and questionnaires (Barrett-Lennard, 1962), but they are too elaborate for a large-scale selection program.

The project's attempt to operationalize and quantify such vague variables as openness, understanding, and acceptance is only a promising first step. We invented a structured small-group situation where students were asked to rate each other after trying to listen and disclose to a stranger (a fellow applicant). The sessions were often stressful and revealing for the students. Some major measurement issues must be clarified before the procedure can be used with confidence. For example, the constancy of interpersonal style over time and situation is still a question for study. In addition, variance in the composition of assessment groups and disparities between group and dyadic behavior will reduce predictability. Nevertheless, some early informal observations and a few findings suggest that this new technique—referred to as GAIT (Group Assessment of Interpersonal Traits)—can be superior to interviews or paper-pencil self-descriptions at quantifying interpersonal traits.

Group Assessment of Interpersonal Traits (GAIT)

Seven or eight applicants gather into structured groups, where they perform several interpersonal tasks and prepare systematic descriptions of each other. As they enter the room, each applicant receives a written set of instructions and a sociometric rating scale, along with a rationale for the entire procedure. During a warm-up period, students are invited to ask the *group* a personal question "as if" it were an individual. Anyone who wishes can answer the question briefly, and the questions and answers continue around the group until all participants have asked and answered once. Next, the applicants are asked to think of two immediate interpersonal concerns that they could share with the group and to state them briefly in writing during a coffee break. Most of these statements tell of discomfort with alienation, guilt, dependency, self-worth, and honesty; they usually involve girl friends, parents, pals, and siblings. The self-descriptive statements are used as catalysts to start dialogues between pairs of applicants: one person elaborates or explores his own statement; the other person attempts to understand feelings. Here is an outline of the procedure*:

1. The applicants sit in a circle and wear letter tags. Mr. A begins by reading one of his statements to the group. He is designated as *the discloser*.
2. Any applicant can spontaneously respond to the discloser and engage him in a five-minute dialogue. The applicant who responds

* A copy of the detailed description of procedures is available from the author.

is called *the understander*. Other group members are asked to remain silent. A kitchen timer (bell type) passed from one discloser to another can be used to time dialogues.

3. In the rare instance where no response is offered to the discloser's first statement within a minute, the discloser is asked to read his second statement.

4. Understanders are asked to avoid giving advice, making judgments, asking questions, or offering interpretations. Instead, they should reflect feelings, disclose their own relevant thoughts or immediate reactions, or simply "listen very hard" while saying nothing.

5. When the five-minute dialogue has terminated, the understander tries a brief (thirty-second) summary of the interaction.

6. The discloser then rereads his initial statement. The juxtaposition of initial statement and summary gives the group a sharper view of the understander's grasp of the situation and his success at facilitating the expansion of the problem presented.

7. Mr. B now becomes the discloser, and anyone except the person who responded to Mr. A can now respond to Mr. B. The group continues to form dyads in this manner until everyone in the circle has performed both tasks.

8. Each applicant is asked to rate the other applicant on sociometric scales describing such interpersonal traits as understanding, openness, acceptance, rigidity. The same scale is used by attending staff members to rate applicants.

9. When the scales are completed, the group is open for free discussion, with the staff answering questions. The entire procedure takes about an hour and a half.

We realized that this task would ask much of applicants, and we told them so. Some would be dissatisfied with their performance, and we also told them that. But a sustained relationship with a troubled boy might ask more of them and cause frequent feelings of self-dissatisfaction. For us, the central product of GAIT is the direct assessment of each applicant's solution to two difficult problems: (1) how to go about disclosing an important part of one's self in conditions far from ideal; (2) how to enter another person's frame of reference and understand his feelings with few questions and no judgments or interpretations or advice.

Applicants who feel excessive anxiety about performing the tasks are left with avenues of escape. They can simply leave the group after reading the instructions or during the coffee break; or they can remain but avoid disclosing themselves by reading an abstract or less personal statement to the group. Similarly, they can avoid the listening task by interjecting small lectures on unrelated matters or by responding to the discloser's statement with unrealistic "quickie" solutions. Those few who seemed to need escape were usually rejected through the poor ratings given by other applicants and staff.

The sociometric instrument contains seven statements descriptive of interpersonal style (Appendix C). It also contains space for rank-ordering the applicants on judged potential as successful counselors. The statements (see Table 3) are lined with six-step scales ranging from "very much like him" to "very much not like him." Terms in parentheses are variable names; asterisks denote selection criteria thought to reflect attributes suggested by client-centered theory.

Table 3

GROUP DESCRIPTION SCALE

Sociometric Item	Variable Name
1. I feel he understands what others really mean.	*(Understanding)
2. He seems sad, blue, discontented.	(Depressed)
3. He appears honest, frank, emotionally open.	*(Open)
4. I see him as a mild, reserved, quiet person.	(Quiet)
5. He seems warm, patient, and accepting.	*(Accepting-Warm)
6. He appears set in his ways.	(Rigid)
7. I see him as a relaxed, easygoing person.	(Relaxed)
8. A composite of items 1, 3, and 5.	*(Therapeutic Talent)

Scoring Method and Score Patterns. Scoring procedure will be described in detail here for those who wish to experiment with the GAIT procedure. Two methods for scoring an individual's performance were studied. The first utilizes the mean rating given an applicant on each item by all observers. This score has a potential range of 1 to 6, corresponding to the six-statement GAIT scale: "very much not like him" to "very much like him." The second method uses the percentage of observers that rate an individual on the positive half of the six-statement GAIT scale. It is a simple index of positive endorsement. A "yes" score is given any rating from "probably like him, or more like him than not" to "very much like him." The endorsement method of scoring collapses the six-step scale into a two-step dichotomous scale. The potential range is 0 to 100 per cent. Both types of scores were completed for about 180 applicants on each of the scale items. A comparison of the two methods yielded correlations around .90, with a range of .83 (open) to .93 (quiet).

The strong correlations between the two sets of scores allowed us to discard one scoring method. Several slight advantages favored the percentage-of-endorsement method. First, raters appeared to be using the scale in a dichotomous fashion, with the majority of responses falling around the point of transition from positive to negative endorsement; therefore, the percentage-of-endorsement procedure, which collapsed the scale into a "yes" or "no" vote, seemed a better approximation of the actual rating behavior of the observers. Second, percentage scores (for example, "81 per cent described him as open") are easier to discuss because they do not require external scale referents (as in "His score on open was 5.3") for meaning. All scores used in this chapter are indices of positive endorsement.

Table 4 shows the mean percentage-of-endorsement scores (in rank order) for third- and fourth-year applicants combined. Analyses for the separate program years produced very similar results. Similarity of scores for the two program years suggests a stability of observer response and group performance. The rank pattern of scores yields a rough picture of the average applicant's performance.

The trait seen as most characteristic of the average applicant was openness. This rating was probably based on the way an applicant disclosed a personal concern to a peer in front of the group—and possibly on his response to a question during the warm-up period and his stance while trying to understand a fellow applicant. The project staff was impressed by the applicants' willingness

Table 4

GROUP-ASSESSMENT SCORES FOR MALE COLLEGE
STUDENT APPLICANTS $(N = 179)$

Trait	Mean Endorsement	Standard Deviation
	Per Cent	
Open ("honest, frank, emotionally open")	81.3	15.9
Accepting-Warm ("warm, patient, and accepting")	74.0	20.8
Understanding ("understands what others really mean")	72.5	19.0
Quiet ("a mild, reserved, quiet person")	57.7	26.9
Relaxed ("a relaxed, easygoing person")	51.9	21.1
Rigid ("set in his ways")	48.7	22.3
Blue ("sad, blue, discontented")	35.7	22.9

to share meaningful concerns with the group. We had expected more guarded behavior. However, the most frequently mentioned motive for applying (to enhance interpersonal sensitivity) appears consistent with taking the chance of disclosing in a strange environment. The average applicant also was described by most of the raters as accepting, warm, and understanding. Impressions for these ratings were probably drawn from the applicant's behavior while he was trying to empathize with a fellow applicant. Table 4 shows that raters were also willing to make socially undesirable descriptions. The average applicant was described as rigid ("set in his ways") by half the raters. Similar patterns of scores were found in a separate analysis of staff ratings, which further weakened the case for an overall positive-response set.

The group ratings often showed strong agreement in describing an individual as quiet. The mean score (nearly 58 per cent) suggests a balanced group of applicants, with a few more quiet types—or perhaps a few more made quiet by the structured nature of the groups. Some degree of tension or excitement or intense concentration was attributed to half the applicants. These nonrelaxed descriptions are assumed to be products of a special risk-taking and problem-solving situation.

The last item on the GAIT form uses a rank-order format in place of the six-step scales. All observers are asked to "Indicate in order of preference (1, 2, 3, 4) the four applicants you feel would make the best counselors." An individual's score is based on the frequency of endorsement by others, stated in percentages; for instance, an individual included in half of the listings receives a score of 50 per cent. On occasions where only seven applicants are present, the first three choices are used in the scoring.

Measurement Issues. In our project each applicant was usually described on all the interpersonal items by nine male observers: six student applicants and three staff members. Applicants did not describe themselves. Differences between students and staff seemed capable of producing two independent sets of ratings. Staff members had more sophisticated and inbred ideas about empathy and self-disclosure and were prone to be more demanding than applicant observers. In addition, staff members were about fifteen years older and did not have to perform the GAIT tasks or to experience the apprehension of being rated. Also, since they had witnessed many GAIT groups, they had a wider basis for judgment. In spite of these apparently sharp differences, however, the ratings of the two groups were somewhat similar. Correlations of student and staff ratings on 179 applicants ranged from .23 to .52, which were modest but significant at the .01 level (an r of .19 or higher = $p < .01$ for N of 179). The highest correlations were generated by the categories quiet (.52), blue (.44), accepting-warm (.43), and therapeutic talent (.38). Lower correlations occurred for best counselor (.33), open (.29), relaxed (.29), and understanding (.23). Mean student ratings fell in the more socially desirable direction on every item, whereas staff ratings were always less positive than the student ratings were. Nonetheless these two subgroups did display some measure of agreement in making abstract judgments from brief samples of very complex behavior.

Interjudge reliability for the three staff raters was computed on all GAIT items and produced a mean coefficient of .51 (Spearman-Brown correction). The mean reliability for staff raters on the three therapeutic talent items was about the same, at .54. Similar reliabilities for therapeutic talent ratings from three observers of mixed-sex GAIT groups were subsequently found by Chinsky and Rappaport (1971)—a mean coefficient of .52 ($N = 48$); D'Augelli, Chinsky, and Getter (1971) also found a mean coefficient of .52 ($N = 66$). Both studies used advanced clinical psychology graduate students as observer-raters. The consistency of reliabilities over all three studies (.54, .52, and .52) indicates that the GAIT therapeutic talent items are modestly reliable when used by sophisticated observers for same- and mixed-sex groups.

We decided to move directly toward studying the reliability of *combined* student-staff ratings, since a single set of combined GAIT scores would simplify comparison with other instruments and would provide broader-based measures due to the amalgam of vantage points (combining internal-external, experienced-inexperienced, conceptually homogeneous and heterogeneous subgroups of raters). We performed a split-half reliability study by randomly dividing each set of student raters into subgroups of three or four. Staff raters were randomly split into two and one and randomly assigned to the student subgroups. This procedure typically split the combined pool of student-staff raters into subgroups of four and five. Reliabilities were found to range from .44 to .79 (Table 5).

Table 5

SPLIT-HALF RELIABILITIES OF COMBINED
STUDENT-STAFF GAIT RATINGS[a]

Item	Reliability[b]
Quiet	.79
Understanding	.64
Accepting-Warm	.63
Rigid	.62
Blue	.59
Open	.54
Relaxed	.44

[a] For 174 project applicants.
[b] Using Spearman-Brown correction.

Here are the split-half reliabilities for the therapeutic talent items, followed by the findings of Chinsky and Rappaport (in parentheses): understanding, .64 (.70); accepting-warm, .63 (.41); open, .54 (.56). As mentioned earlier, the Chinsky-Rappaport reliabilities were for mixed-sex participant raters only. Mean reliability for the three items in our study is .60, compared to .56 for the Chinsky-Rappaport study. The only sign of disagreement occurs for the accepting-warm item. Taken together, these findings indicate modest to moderate reliability for the principal component of GAIT. As expected, the high-visibility quiet item was the most reliable.

A test-retest study of GAIT using forty-one male and female UCLA undergraduates provides further reliability findings (Dooley, 1972). Eight groups of seven to nine students took GAIT on two occasions approximately three weeks apart. The study was confined to ratings made by students; no external judges were used. Coefficients ranged from .66 to .86, with a mean of .80. The three therapeutic talent items produced a mean of .73 (understanding, .78; open, .71; accepting-warm, .69).

Interrelation of GAIT Items. Evidence for the internal coherence of the GAIT measures comes from their intercorrelations (Table 6). Correlation patterns make sense; they create designs that fit our intuitive expectations based on item definitions. For example, best potential (based on upper-half rankings as best counselor by all raters) is well correlated with understanding, accepting-warm, open, and relaxed; it is negatively correlated with rigid and blue, and shows no patterned relation to quiet. That is, raters tend to see good counseling potential as requiring understanding, acceptance, and openness, along with minimal or no tension, rigidity, and depression. Furthermore, good potential is seen in both quiet and outgoing students.

As expected, the therapeutic talent composite formed spurious and strong correlations with its three components (accepting, open, understanding). As Table 6 shows, this construct takes on additional meaning in the minds of our observers: Someone high on therapeutic talent is also someone who is relaxed, somewhat quiet (reserved-mild), and tends not to be rigid or blue or discontented. Observers predict that such a person will become a good counselor.

Table 6

CORRELATIONS AMONG GAIT VARIABLES

	Accept-ing-Warm	Quiet	Open	Under-stand-ing	Relaxed	Blue	Rigid	Best Poten-tial
Therapeutic Talent	.84	.24	.77	.84	.45	−.14	−.61	.69
Accepting-Warm		.35	.48	.54	.49	−.22	−.50	.55
Quiet			.12	.09	−.06	.34	−.32	−.03
Open				.52	.22	.02	−.48	.48
Under-standing					.38	−.13	−.54	.65
Relaxed						−.43	−.13	.48
Blue							−.12	−.26
Rigid								−.44
Best Potential								X

Note: For $N = 179$, an r of .12 $= p$ of .10; r of .15 $= p$ of .05; r of 20 $= p$ of .01.

None of the correlations among traits jarred our expectations. On the other hand, some of the intercorrelations approach the limit set by their reliabilities, so that the measures are not always sharply distinguished from each other. In general, however, most of the findings on GAIT suggest a coherent internal order among the GAIT items.

Relation of GAIT to Other Project Indices

The initial design of our project had no provision for the study of GAIT. It was a late arrival, and most of our research on its measurement properties has a patchwork quality. Ideally, study of such complex traits would include various assessment methods with variables that parallel those used in GAIT. A comparison of traits between different methods could reveal patterns of convergence and discrimination yielding powerful evidence for validity questions (Campbell and Fiske, 1959). Falling quite short of this ideal, we decided to look for data at hand that could be considered reasonable parallels of GAIT items. Some tentative findings on the validity of GAIT variables come from a few ostensibly parallel indices, from the applicants' self-descriptions, and from applicants' scores received during later group-training sessions. Even weak associations will be presented as clues for further study.

The application form asked students to choose the term that came closest to describing them: quiet or reserved versus outgoing. These self-descriptions were strongly related to the GAIT quiet score—in the appropriate direction. There was also a positive relation between GAIT quiet and low participation in extracurricular high school activities ($p < .05$). The Adjective Check List (Gough and Heilbrun, 1965) was also given to all applicants, and its twenty-five scales were correlated with the GAIT items (see Figure 4 for the specific ACL items). The ACL exhibit scale (adjectives such as "outspoken") showed the strongest correlation with GAIT quiet: $-.28$ ($p < .01$).

Two other ACL scales appeared relevant to GAIT items. ACL unfavorably (unfavorable self-description) correlated with GAIT blue at .20 ($p < .01$); and GAIT therapeutic talent showed its strongest negative ACL correlation with defensive at $-.20$ ($p < .01$). It seems that applicants seen as sad and discontented on GAIT tend to describe themselves in unfavorable terms. Applicants described as high on GAIT therapeutic talent prepare nondefensive self-descriptions.

Further study of GAIT's ability to predict external variables was hampered because we did not collect additional data on rejected applicants. Rejection was determined by low scores on a specific set of GAIT items. Therefore, since our analyses were generally limited to medium and high GAIT scores, the probability of our locating external correlates was obviously reduced. The accepted candidates' data became more accessible to study through the formation of subgroups whose scores fell into the upper and lower thirds on each GAIT item. Thus, we could compare medium and high scores on relevant external variables to see whether the differences suggested any construct validity of GAIT variables.

A group of students receiving very high scores on accepting-warm ($\bar{x} = 96$ per cent) chose significantly ($p < .01$) more person-oriented (Rosenberg, 1957) vocational goals than a group with medium scores ($\bar{x} = 70$ per cent). The high-scoring students also described themselves as significantly less dominant, exhibiting, and self-confident ($p < .01$) and more deferent on the ACL ($p < .05$). They also scored slightly lower on ACL defensive ($p < .10$). Roughly five months after the GAIT session, the high accepting-warm students were described as tending to let others be themselves during sensitivity-training sessions. They made fewer attempts to influence others and were rated as less assertive and determined (.05). Thus, GAIT accepting-warm seems to predict persistent related behavior in future group settings, along with mild, unforceful self-descriptions.

The quiet group ($\bar{x} = 88$ per cent) had significantly fewer person-oriented academic majors and less experience working with children than the outgoing group ($\bar{x}$ quiet score $= 30$ per cent). Quiets were less involved in extracurricular activities in high school and college ($p < .10$). According to the Self-Disclosure Questionnaire (Jourard, 1962), the quiets were less ready than the outgoings to tell others about their attitudes (.10). Their ACL scores were lower on exhibit and labile and higher on succorant (all at .05). On the initial application form, the quiets, much more frequently than the outgoings, rated themselves as quiet and mild (.01). Five months later, during the sensitivity-training sessions, their fellow counselors saw them as less assertive and less disclosing (both at $<.05$).

Students with high scores on understanding others' feelings ($\bar{x} = 94$ per cent) produced somewhat higher scores ($p < .10$) than medium understanders ($\bar{x} = 67$ per cent) on the Social Insight Test (Chapin, 1942). High understanders also described people as more complex (.05) on the Philosophies of Human Nature Questionnaire (Wrightsman, 1964).

The group scoring higher on rigid ($\bar{x} = 63$ per cent) came from families with stronger religious commitment ($p < .05$) than the low rigid group ($\bar{x} = 16$ per cent). High rigids were somewhat less disclosing to their friends (.10) and saw human nature as less complex and less changeable (.05). They also tended to be described as less open during the later training sessions (.10). (Many of the extremely high rigid scores belonged to rejected applicants and were therefore lost to this analysis.)

Applicants judged as having superior potential for the counselor role ($\bar{x} = 84$ per cent) were slightly older than those rated as having moderate potential. The high potential group had higher grade-point averages ($p < .05$) and participated in a few more extracurricular activities (.10). The high group was more self-supporting (.05) and more frequently described human nature as altruistic and complex (both at .05).

Few relevant differences were found between the subgroups based on the relaxed and blue scales. Actually, few external variables seemed pertinent to these dimensions. Moderately high blues, however, described themselves with a few more unfavorable adjectives (.10). We could not form distinct subgroups on the therapeutic talent variable because all accepted applicants naturally had high scores on this variable.

Our study of GAIT's relation to other indices offers some encouragement about the validity of GAIT. The reliability findings, the meaningful intercorrelation matrix, the consistency of the small test-retest sample, the significant correlations between staff and student ratings have also provided clues to GAIT's promise as a worthwhile new assessment technique. It seems capable of generating indices on a wider range of interpersonal traits than have been used here. Administrative expense may be reduced by eliminating some or all of the professional observers. Eliminating or reducing professional biases in screening nonprofessionals may also reduce the emphasis on selecting applicants who resemble professionals in verbal skills and attitudues (see Linton, 1967). GAIT is also relatively quick, inexpensive, and easy to score. It is less cumbersome than the individual interview and appears more reliable and bias-free than interviews. (Other studies of the reliability and validity of the GAIT therapeutic talent measure are discussed later in this chapter.)

Arbitrary Standards for Hiring

Essentially, we wanted students who were described as open, accepting, and understanding by a *majority* of observers. The following acceptance criteria were established on the basis of in-

tuition, practicality, and theoretical biases: (1) a minimum score
of 60 per cent on therapeutic talent; (2) a minimum score of 50
per cent on each of the three criterion traits: understanding, open,
and accepting-warm; (3) a score of at least 30 per cent on "the
best potential" item.

The final acceptance criterion was based only on the observations of attending staff. The three staff members were instructed
to note any applicants who caused them clear doubt or appeared
emotionally unprepared for the job. These concerns were amplified
into staff vetoes. A single staff veto would cause an applicant to be
rejected. This apparently harsh criterion was used to bring the
clinical skills of the staff into focus as a pathology screen. The
incidence of psychopathology in the applicant group seemed similar
to that of a typical student population. This unsystematic observation is supported by Holzberg, Whiting, and Lowy (1964), who
found no difference in psychopathology between students wanting
to work in mental hospitals and a group of controls. It turned out
that 82 per cent of the vetoed applicants in our study were independently rejected by the first three GAIT criteria, aimed at interpersonal style rather than psychological dysfunction. Thus, the
standard scales (missing only 18 per cent of the rejections based on
vetoes by experienced clinicians) seem to produce a fairly effective
pathology screen.

Of the 179 applicants who submitted to GAIT during the
two final program years, 56 failed to meet the standards (a 31 per
cent rejection rate).

The selection criteria we chose predetermined that the
group of accepted applicants had significantly higher scores on
open, accepting-warm, and understanding than those rejected.
Rejected applicants were also rated as significantly more rigid
($p < .01$). Comparison of the two groups on personal-background
characteristics and scores on other instruments revealed the following differences significant at the .05 level or better: Accepted applicants had had more volunteer or paid work experiences in the
social service area—especially with children. More frequently than
rejected applicants, they described themselves as quiet or reserved
and not religiously committed; they were more self-supporting; and
their mothers had had more formal education and their fathers less

religious commitment than those of rejected applicants. Those accepted by GAIT more frequently sought careers in the clinical or social-helping professions. A few were receiving counseling or psychotherapy, compared to none in the rejected group. Self-descriptions (ACL) of the rejected group were higher on exhibit, self-confidence, dominance, and number checked. Accepted applicants were higher on deference and counseling readiness.

Of course, the characteristics of the accepted and rejected applicant groups would have changed if different selection criteria were chosen. Programs using different populations, or different goals, or varying therapy procedures may require criteria that differ from those presented here. Several variations are possible—by selecting new combinations of scales, modifying the cut-off points, relying solely on staff observer ratings or solely on applicant observations. Criteria could also be established on the basis of a predetermined rejection rate.

Staff Judgment

During the final year, we conducted an additional small experiment on professional judgment. In addition to the staff veto discussed above, a staff-choice vote was studied. The varying group of attending staff members and consultants (usually clinicians) were asked to note those applicants who impressed them as very good prospects for the counselor position. There was high interstaff agreement on this judgment. When at least two of the three staff members voted for an applicant, the designation *staff choice* was applied. About one third of the final year's applicants $(N = 103)$ received staff-choice labels. Using data from the application form, the ACL, and GAIT, we compared the staff-choice applicants with all the remaining applicants $(N = 67)$. A similar comparison was made for the staff-veto applicants $(N = 25)$ versus all other applicants $(N = 78)$. T-tests were used.

As expected, the staff-choice applicants also were described as significantly more open, understanding, and accepting-warm $(p < .01)$. The most dramatic differences appeared for the scores on therapeutic talent and best potential. We also found that the staff had more confidence in quiet applicants. The weakest difference in a GAIT item (.05) was produced by relaxed. Blue was not significantly related to staff choice. That is, a fine counselor prospect also could be blue or sad according to the professional judges.

A similar picture of the staff-choice group appeared when viewed through the separate ratings of student observers. Once again, the blue item was not differentiating. Students rated the staff-choice group as more accepting-warm, open, and understanding and less rigid (all at .01); also more quiet and relaxed and with best potential (all at .05). Staff-choice applicants were chosen somewhat more frequently as learning partners by their peers (.10).

Other instruments also showed significant differences between students classified as staff choice and the remaining group of accepted applicants. The staff-choice students saw human nature as much more complex ($p < .01$), more changeable (.05), and slightly more altruistic (.10) on Wrightsman's questionnaire (1964). Their ACL self-descriptions were higher on deferent ($p < .05$) and somewhat lower on exhibit, dominance, and self-confidence (all at .10). They described themselves as self-disclosing more to their girl friends (.05) while being somewhat less concealing about money matters and their bodies (both at .10). Compared with other applicants, they were less religiously committed and more of them were in psychotherapy (both at .05). They were less close to their mothers during high school years (.10) and had slightly more work experience with young boys (.10).

When the staff-veto applicants were compared with all other applicants, the significant differences were almost exactly opposite those found for the staff-choice group. Once again, student-rater patterns were very close to those of staff raters. When a staff member secretly vetoes an applicant, student observers tend to describe that applicant as emotionally closed, misunderstanding, nonaccepting, tense, and rigid; he is also not chosen as someone with best potential or as a learning partner. He could be either quiet or outgoing and either blue or not.

Findings on these two special subgroups strengthen previous observations on staff-student similarity in rating behavior. For some programs, the applicants themselves may effectively replace

professional observers (or vice versa) in the assessment of interpersonal traits.

Prediction of Performance with GAIT

Is there any association between change in emotionally
troubled boys and the truncated GAIT scores of their college
student companions? Four representative change items for boys
were arbitrarily selected: (1) two retrospective change scores on
self-esteem (positive change in "the way he feels about himself")
from the observations of teachers and parents; (2) a pre-post
discrepancy measure on the adjustment scale of the Adjective
Check List (Gough and Heilbrun, 1965) filled out by parents
before and after the companionships; (3) a composite school-
aggression score built from classmate and teacher response, pre to
post, on the Peer Nominations Inventory (Wiggins and Winder,
1961). Correlations of these change indices with the GAIT variables are shown in Table 7.

In general, the correlations in Table 7 fall in a systematic
pattern and lend some support to GAIT as a predictor of the
therapeutic talent in a field situation. Of the thirty-six correlations
shown, 32 fall in directions suggesting an association between counselors' GAIT scores and boy improvement. However, these correlations do not indicate that the predictors are powerful.

Some further support for the predictive capacity of GAIT
therapeutic talent items comes from a number of studies (Barnett,
1972; Chinsky, 1968; Chinsky and Rappaport, 1971; D'Augelli,
Chinsky, and Getter, 1971; Rappaport, Chinsky, and Cowen,
1971). Chinsky and Rappaport used several assessment procedures
as potential predictors of therapeutic ability in student volunteers.
Before the college students were assigned to their tasks as therapy
group leaders for chronic hospitalized schizophrenic patients, they
were assessed on the following scales: Whitehorn-Betz A-B Scale,
Internal-External Locus of Control Scale, Personality Research
Form, Philosophies of Human Nature Questionnaire, Self-Disclosure Questionnaire, Social Insight Test, Adjective Check List,
Semantic Differential Adaptation, and GAIT. The thirty students
led patient groups for five to six months. Patient improvement

Table 7

Correlation of GAIT Criteria Variables with Selected Change Scores for Emotionally Troubled Boys

| | GAIT Variables | | | | | |
| | Accepting-Warm | | | Open | | |
Change Items	Applicant Raters	Staff Raters	All Raters	Applicant Raters	Staff Raters	All Raters
Teachers						
Positive change in "the way he feels about himself"	.01	.14	.11	−.15	.08	−.07
Parents						
Positive change in "the way he feels about himself"	−.03	.08	.02	.14	.13	.19
ACL adjustment scale	.10	.17	.18	.10	.26[b]	.19
Classmates-Teachers						
Composite school-aggression score	−.04	−.09	−.10	−.10	−.31[b]	−.24[a]

| | Understanding | | | Therapeutic Talent | | |
Change Items	Applicant Raters	Staff Raters	All Raters	Applicant Raters	Staff Raters	All Raters
Teachers						
Positive change in "the way he feels about himself"	.08	.03	.07	−.02	.10	.08
Parents						
Positive change in "the way he feels about himself"	.11	.18	.20[a]	.09	.17	.20[a]
ACL adjustment scale	.06	.20[a]	.17	.11	.26[b]	.24[a]
Classmates-Teachers						
Composite school-aggression score	−.06	−.07	−.10	−.09	−.19	−.20[a]

[a] p of .05 for r of .195.   [b] p of .01 for r of .254. $N = 99$.

was assessed by sixteen criterion measures administered before and after the program. The measures tapped verbal fluency; thought processes; psychomotor, perceptual, and motor functioning; and ward behavior. Effectiveness was studied by correlating all criterion measures with all predictor variables. Only two of the eighty-five variables from nine instruments produced significant correlations with any outcome measures. Observer-rated GAIT accepting-warm was significantly associated with factored ward measures rated by hospital staff on the Ellsworth Behavioral Adjustment Scale: improved mood (.39, $p < .05$), cooperation (.41, $p < .05$), and total adjustment (.46, $p < .01$). GAIT understanding correlated with improved mood at .48. None of the student-rated GAIT scales were significantly related to patient outcome. This study offers evidence that observer-rated GAIT scores for accepting-warm and understanding can be effective in selecting nonprofessionals who may generate some improvement in chronic mental hospital patients.

In another study (D'Augelli et al., 1971), observer-rated GAIT therapeutic talent was related to style of participation in free-discussion groups. As part of a larger design, individuals were assigned to groups on the basis of their high, medium, or low therapeutic talent scores (HTT, MTT, LTT). Style of group participation was assessed on four levels of personal to impersonal behavior on the Group Interaction Profile (Getter, Korn, and Anchor, 1970). The investigators found that HTT groups used significantly more personal discussion than MTT groups ($p < .01$) and that MTT groups used more personal discussion than LTT groups ($p < .001$). Stated in percentages of personal discussion units, LTT = 3 per cent; MTT = 26 per cent; HTT = 32 per cent.

These findings suggest that groups composed of individuals with higher GAIT ratings on open, accepting-warm, and understanding develop environments where personal concerns are more frequently discussed. Such group environments are probably more therapeutic; but the findings, as presented, do not allow us to discard the hypothesis that the higher GAIT open scores produced most of the results. On the other hand, it seems unlikely that a group composed of participants high on open and low on accepting-warm or understanding would produce much personal discussion. In sum, these findings suggest that observer-rated GAIT therapeutic talent can predict a more therapeutic style of group participation—if one assumes that higher frequencies of personal disclosure are therapeutic.

Motives

Working with troubled children has strong appeal for students. Current programs have no difficulty with recruitment. Why do students apply in such large numbers? Are the motives too varied and complex for orderly characterization? Kantor's (1962) impressionistic study of thirty-five students who volunteered for mental hospital work offers some clues. Even though Kantor's students were not paid and their clients were severely disturbed adults, the program was similar to ours in demanding the risk of getting close to someone in trouble.

Kantor did not report quantitative results but, instead, displayed a range of motives drawn from questionnaires and inferred from interview behavior. The various motives were classified in three categories: (1) *verbalized and known motives* (the testing of conceptions about mental illness—or perhaps "morbid curiosity," career testing, relief from academic work, a chance to gain self-knowledge through contact with someone troubled, hope of relieving someone's suffering, or a chance to make more contact with students and professionals); (2) *withheld motives* (a search for differences between self and mental patient, the acquisition of prestige from peers, an opportunity to influence another's life or to receive respect from the patient, or an expression of rebellion by entering the atypical mental hospital culture); (3) *unaware motives* (a counterphobic motive based on the fear of mental illness, an "oedipal motive" for using patients as parent surrogates to work out problems such as control and independence, an impulse-release motive for identification with patient spontaneity and vicarious release of control, or a "free psychotherapy" motive for getting help with personal problems).

Kantor's observations suggest a wide range of motives for students working with troubled people, but his work gives us no clue about the relative frequency of motives. We wanted to know whether certain motives are common to many applicants. Attempt-

ing to make sense of the multiple hidden and unknown motives
seemed too large and unfruitful a task for us; so we decided upon a
simple study of expressed motives. Data from nearly two hundred
applicants were obtained from the following question inserted in
the application form: "Please think about your motives for joining
the project and describe them. What's in it for you? Is salary
important? Be frank."

The eight categories generated by our content analysis were
not mutually exclusive, nor did they have sharp boundaries. Many
students offered several motives. What seemed most prevalent was
a mixture—an idealistic social-service attitude coupled with the
need for self-improvement and earning money. The following breakdown is in order of frequency.

Forty-one per cent of the applicants hoped that the program
would help them develop better interpersonal skills: "Without trying to sound pretentious, I want to develop my own ability to com-
municate (which means more than articulateness to me). I also
see the work as an exercise in understanding."

Thirty-seven per cent mentioned the need to be nurturant,
to reach out in a responsible and sometimes fatherly manner: "I
always wanted to be something like a big brother to somebody."
"I just like the feeling of worth I get from helping someone smaller
than me—like a child."

Twenty-four per cent of the applicants thought the project
experience might clarify career goals: "I feel that kids have a
better chance to get 'straightened out' than adults. Maybe I'll
study to be a psychotherapist. This job may help me make up my
mind."

Since the project announcement called for students "who
wish to join for money only, for experience only, and for both,"
applicants probably felt free to list money as a major reason for
joining us. However, salary seemed to be the primary motivation
for only 10 per cent. Fifty-six per cent of the applicants specifically
stated that the project's major appeal was not salary, even though
they could use the money.

Nine per cent of the applicants described a kindred feeling
for boys experiencing emotional discomfort: "Not so long ago I
was in their shoes." "I still remember what it's like to feel little and
lonely and scared and wondering why parents can't make it go

away all the time. Maybe I could just be there and show that I remember."

Relief from academic work was mentioned by 7 per cent: "My scientific studies have drawn me away from people and into things. I look upon the project as an opportunity to express my need for interpersonal relations." "I want to become active in other things besides academics and sports."

Four per cent saw project work as a step toward independence: "Although I don't need the money, I don't want 100 per cent support from my parents either."

Another 4 per cent clearly expressed a yearning for putting their ideals into action: "I haven't picketed, joined CORE or anything—though I generally agree with them. I feel guilty and want to do something." We suspect that this type of motive is more prominent than our count of 4 per cent; it often seemed vaguely implied within other expressed motives.

These eight nonexclusive categories of motives were generated by responses from all applicants. In a later analysis, we divided the applicants into three subgroups: (a) those who withdrew shortly after applying, (b) those rejected, and (c) those accepted. Only a few differences were found. The group of applicants who withdrew had twice the proportion of students stating money as a primary motive (20 per cent versus 9 per cent). Perhaps some decided against our substandard hourly wage or could not afford the month's waiting period between acceptance and the start of work. Accepted applicants (compared with those rejected) reported more "academic relief" motives (10 per cent versus 5 per cent) and fewer "empathic" motives (7 per cent versus 16 per cent).

In general, our project seemed to be used by students as a vehicle for the practice of giving to others and as a testing ground for interpersonal skills. That is, many students were seeking a safe opportunity for trying out new ways of being with others. They were searching for adventure.

Summary

Faced with the need for systematically selecting counselors and the lack of research in the area, we started experimenting with group-assessment procedures. Eventually, we settled on a structured group method that utilized successive sets of dyadic interaction as performance samples for rating (GAIT: Group Assessment of Interpersonal Traits). Client-centered theory was a major influence. Participants rated each other and were also rated by three staff observers. The primary scales were understanding, open, and accepting-warm, which formed a therapeutic talent composite. Remaining scales were labeled depressed, quiet, rigid, and relaxed. Split-half reliabilities for the combined student-staff ratings ranged from .44 to .79. Mean reliability for the primary scales was .60. Intercorrelation of all scales suggests internal coherence.

GAIT's relation to external indices in our study and in other investigations offers encouragement about its validity. Selection criteria were established that rejected about one third of the "self-selected" applicants. Staff ratings were better predictors than student ratings. Work from other investigators also was described.

Finally, we studied the applicants' expressed motives for wanting to join the project and formed eight nonexclusive categories: (1) development of interpersonal skills, (2) the need to be nurturant, (3) clarifying career goals, (4) salary, (5) empathy with troubled boys, (6) academic relief, (7) need for independence, (8) putting ideas into action. The first three were most frequently mentioned, and we found elements of the eighth motive in most descriptions.

IV

Structuring Companionships

The companionship process was shaped by a structure that involved (a) matching boys and counselors into specific pairings; (b) imposing a set of visiting limits and obligations on counselors, boys, and parents; (c) sharing our goals and assumptions with all participants; (d) demanding visit reports for each contact by all counselors; and (e) providing an experimental orientation and weekly training groups for counselors. The following sections describe the rationale and administration of these program structures.

Matching Boys and Counselors

Counselors were rank-ordered on a quiet-outgoing dimension. The dimension was actually a composite derived from GAIT quiet, ACL exhibit, and a direct "quiet" or "outgoing" self-description item on the application questionnaire. These three variables intercorrelated at .37 ($N = 179$). The rank order of the final composite was divided at midpoint to form contrasting groups: quiet and outgoing counselors. These two groups were divided again by assigning half to group training and half to a self-directed status. The manipulations gave us four subgroups of counselors: quiet-trained, quiet–self-directed, outgoing-trained, and outgoing–self-directed.

Boys were also ranked on a quiet-outgoing dimension, but for them the dimension represented the quality of their interpersonal problems. All of the boy applicants were sorted into pairs that were closely matched on five variables: quiet or outgoing behavior problem, severity of presenting problem, race, father in home, and socioeconomic status. Some other important characteristics were "prematched" through our restricting applications to fifth- and sixth-grade boys attending the Berkeley public schools who were referred as emotionally troubled by their parents. One boy from each matched pair was then randomly chosen as a participant and the other assigned to the nonparticipating control group. The participant boys were next divided into four groups, each containing an equal number of black and white boys, quiet boys, fatherless boys, and so on. These four equal groups of boys were then matched with the four groups of counselors. That is, four dyad types were produced: quiet counselors with quiet boys, quiet counselors with outgoing boys, outgoing counselors with outgoing boys, and outgoing counselors with quiet boys. These four dyad types also were matched on counselor training, severity of boy's problem, socioeconomic status (70 per cent were matched into identical classes of Hollingshead's Index of Social Position, and the remainder were matched within two index positions), race, and father in home.

Other procedures have been used to pair nonprofessionals and extraprofessionals (professionals not trained as therapists) into relationships with their clients. Holzberg, Whiting, and Lowy (1964) first let their college students choose the patient each wanted to work with by arranging a social hour in which the students and mental patients mixed. Students complained of guilt feelings in having to choose and thus reject others. Eventually patients were assigned by the project staff. Mitchell (1966b) paired college students with troubled children under the assumption that no generalizations can be made about matching. He considered each pairing as a unique event and a complex task requiring a professional with special ability to interpret a cluster of variables. Mitchell's student variables were age, physical appearance, sex, personality structure, intelligence, socioeconomic class, religion, race, dress, prejudices, recreational interests, and expectations from the companionships. Variables he considered for the children were family situation, neighborhood type, and distance from campus. Intuitive pairings of this type may be most practical for many programs. However, we believed that useful generalizations about effective pairing are possible, and our findings on dyad types and boy outcome support the contention (see Chapter Eight). The complex matching procedure used by Palmer (1965) is geared to do some predicting of outcome. He matched juvenile offenders and parole officers into dyads that were later assessed on a dimension of "satisfaction-effectiveness," which shows signs of predicting recidivism. Roughly, Palmer classified three types of "treators": (1) oriented toward self-expression and building a relationship, (2) oriented toward the juvenile's self-control and providing limits, and (3) a blend of the two previous types. Eight types of juvenile offenders were classified by case history and clinical analysis: communicative-alert, passive-uncertain, hostile-defensive, impulsive-anxious, dependent-anxious, independent-assertive, defiant-indifferent, and wants to be helped and liked. It is difficult to see these types as independent. We believe that further work will shrink the typology. While Palmer has not yet discussed his methods in detail, he does offer some preliminary results. The self-expression, relationship-building "treators" were most effective with communicative-alert, impulsive-anxious, and hostile-defensive types. Treators who emphasized self-control and limits were best with wards who wanted help and liking. Treators who represented a blend of the two previous types produced better results with dependent-anxious wards, and had difficulty with the hostile-defensive and defiant-indifferent types.

The dyad types in our project were also formed to facilitate research. We wanted to avoid a common pitfall in psychotherapy research: conceiving a heterogeneous group of patients or therapists as homogeneous; that is, studying variations in patients and considering the therapists (or therapy) as a rather homogeneous constant—or vice versa. Our preference was to establish and study a few dyad types based on easily assessed or clearly dichotomous variables. Major research targets were dyads formed on the quiet-outgoing dimensions and the presence or absence of counselor training, but other promising dyad types emerged from our work.

Table 8

CHARACTERISTICS OF BOYS ASSIGNED TO FOUR COUNSELOR TYPES

Boy Characteristics	Counselor Types			
	Quiet– Trained	Outgoing– Trained	Quiet– Self- Directed	Outgoing– Self- Directed
	Per Cent			
Problem Type				
Quiet	27	26	21	26
Outgoing	27	24	22	27
Problem Severity				
High	23	28	23	26
Moderate	60	10	10	20
Low	23	26	23	28
Race				
Negro	28	20	16	36
Caucasian	27	27	24	22
Family Status				
Fatherless	22	30	26	22
Father in Home	30	23	20	27
Social Class				
High	29	24	27	20
Low	26	26	16	32

They are discussed in Chapters Eight and Ten. Table 8 displays the distribution of boy characteristics over four counselor types.

Orienting Counselors

After the pairs had been created on paper, we began to make arrangements for the orientation and initial meeting (see Chapter Five for findings on the initial meetings). All the counselors attended an orientation meeting, which comprised the bulk of "training" for many counselors. Our instructions were few and simple enough to fit on one sheet of paper. We wanted to be very open with the students—sharing our concerns, assumptions, research design, and administrative structure whenever possible or relevant. The following quotes from an information sheet should characterize the orientation:

> Counselors and boys will be paired on the basis of specific research criteria. When you have completed three teaching-machine sessions, we will send you general information about the boy assigned to you, including his age, interests, and hobbies. It will be your task to call the parents immediately and arrange a meeting with them and their boy. They will be expecting your call. We want to know when this meeting occurs and if it has proven satisfactory for everyone. Parents will call our office if they do not feel that you and the boy will get along well.
>
> You should call our office the afternoon following the initial meeting. If you and the parents and the boy feel good about starting, we will consider the relationship in progress. Arrangements for future meetings are now the responsibility of you, the boy, and his parents. . . . In sum, your obligations are: (1) Call parents upon receiving our letter. (2) Visit the boy's home. (3) Call us the next afternoon. (4) If things go well, make further arrangements to see the boy.
>
> We have prepared a brief, convenient form (Visit Report) for you to use as an aid in describing each contact. If these forms are not properly filled out by counselors, our ability to make some sense out of the relationship will be severely hampered, because your observations are a crucial aspect of the program.
>
> The form asks what you did, how long it took, and what and whom you talked about. The entire task should take ten to fifteen minutes and should be done within a few hours after you leave the boy.

Since it is our intention to establish one-to-one relationships, it would be best to avoid including a third person unless there are special circumstances. Should a third person join you during an activity, please note it on your visit report. We would like you and your boy to have much opportunity for two-person conversations, which will allow the boy greater opportunity to experience trust and a feeling of closeness. Frequent spectator activities, such as movies, or inclusion of other people may reduce your chance of establishing a meaningful relationship.

Do not promise more than you can deliver. Try not to promise the boy some activity unless you are fairly certain that it will occur. You can create an atmosphere conducive to trust by not disappointing the boy—keep your goals modest—try hard to anticipate correctly. If a visit has to be brief, let the boy know at the start. If there is some possibility that you will be late or cannot make it next time, let the boy know. In short, try to share all the things you know that touch on the relationship between you and your boy. This sharing may be difficult for you at first, but it will make you a more comfortable person to be with.

Don't use "strategy." Don't try to "treat" the boy or offer explanations for his emotional aches and growing pains. Remember that you are not a professional. Just be as honest with yourself and the boy as possible. Counselors who are genuine with their boys usually create the best relationships. We selected you carefully from a large number of applicants and feel that your best resource is your personality. Take it easy with personal advice. Let the boy know that you are getting paid (at the same time, you can let him know that you are interested in working with kids). It is absolutely necessary that during the early visits you let the boy know that the relationship will end in June. If you neglect this point, the boy may not be prepared for the separation and he may feel badly let down.

Please see the boy two or three times every week—no less, no more. Try not to visit less than one hour or more than four hours. Also, try not to see the boy less than four hours every week or more than eight hours every week. In sum:

	Minimum	Maximum
Visits per week	2	3
Hours per visit	1	4
Hours per week	4	8

We feel that this procedure will give the boy a sense of continuity, allow for a degree of consistency between relationships, and help us keep within our budget. You may break these limits on occasion if you feel it necessary, but let us know the reason.

Please remember that we want these relationships to be comfortable and want you to call us any time if you run into any difficulty, feel troubled, or are just curious. We may not have the answer, but we will work with you toward a solution. The chances are that you will find it easy to get along with your boy. Most ten and eleven year olds enjoy the exclusive attention of adults— they usually relax when adults relax.

(A copy of this information sheet will be sent to parents.)

In essence, during the orientation session we attempted to prescribe the counselor's limits and duties within the relationship. We were defining a social role without traditional precedent. We were also urging an approach to interpersonal relations that aimed at authenticity. Since only half the counselors were scheduled to attend weekly interpersonal-training groups, the orientation was an important element in shaping the counselors' attitudes.

The teaching-machine sessions mentioned in the orientation sheet refer to a programmed-instruction course on interpersonal relations (Berlin and Wyckoff, 1964). It is a ten-lesson program designed for collaborative and simultaneous use by two persons. The course moves step by step through various role-playing tasks and other forms of structured interaction designed to provide practice in empathy and openness. Selected counselors were not paired with boys until they had completed the first three lessons. Combining these lessons (which took three or four hours) with the four-hour orientation meeting provided seven to eight hours of total orientation time for half the counselors. Add an hour or two of random consultation time throughout the year, and the total professional contact with each of the self-directed counselors was about eight to ten hours. Thus, half of our counselors received very little training during their stay in the project.

The Berlin-Wyckoff teaching machine was built to replace professional manpower in human-relations training, but we had little information on its effectiveness. We therefore made a rough evaluation of the teaching machine by asking counselors for their impressions. Adequate research would have required a control group, but the project design was already complicated and could not support further subgrouping. The first evaluation came from counselor responses to an item on the Final Observations Questionnaire: "What did you think of the programmed instruction (teaching machine)?" Two judges reliably rated the responses as favorable, neutral, or negative ($r = .79$ for Kendall's Tau). About one third of the responses fell into each category. Most of the negative comments were complaints about the oversimple and frequently condescending content of the lessons: "They were fun, but seemed written for high school kids." "My partner and I learned a little about expressing our feelings, but we didn't need ten lessons—too damned long—it got boring." The positive responses often praised the program's simplicity but suggested that fewer lessons were needed: "Excellent! Covered stuff easy to learn but hard to adopt." ". . . lessons are still with me . . . put complex things into simple words that I wish I could have known sooner." ". . . reminded me of things I knew but did not know *actively.* . . . actually learned all I could after three lessons."

Counselor reaction caused us to shorten the mandatory lessons to six for the following year. We also tried to lower the counselors' expectations by emphasizing, during the orientation meeting, the limited goals of the teaching machine. Once again, counselors were questioned at the project's termination: "Did they [the programmed lessons] provide any help in your relationship with the boy?" and "Were they useful to you personally?" Both questions received the same proportion of "yes" responses: 58 per cent. Apparently, fewer lessons and lowered expectations generated more favorable reaction. We recommend the Berlin-Wyckoff program as an adjunct training device. It is inexpensive, somewhat simple, and redundant for college students, but it did seem useful to many counselors—especially those who did not receive additional group training. Perhaps the first two and the last two lessons could serve the orientation needs of nonprofessionals about to enter a one-to-one helping relationship.

After the matching, the orientation session, and the teaching-machine requirements were completed, each counselor was given brief information about his boy. The boy's "presenting problem" and his ratings by classmates and teachers were never shown to counselors.

Orienting Parents

Contact with almost all parents was by letter and phone. The project announcement letter (sent to all parents of fifth- and sixth-grade boys in the Berkeley public schools) contained information about our research, program goals, counselor selection, past programs, companionship rationale, financial support, and criteria for selecting boys with problems. The acceptance letter sent to participating parents was a major orientation vehicle. Most of it is reproduced below:

(1) We are now completing the selection of students (activities counselors). Selection is based on a detailed application covering the student's background, a personality test, a new group-assessment procedure, and a review of each student's university records to make sure he is in "good standing." This procedure has given us a fine group of young men with a rich variety of backgrounds, interests, and fields of study. Fifty students have been selected from about one hundred applicants. They will be paid $1.40 an hour.

(2) Activities counselors will be paired with boys tentatively on the basis of our research requirements and pending the approval of parents and boys.

(3) Each counselor will be given the name, phone number, and address of his assigned boy. He will be told the boy's age, interests, and hobbies. He will be asked to phone the parents for a convenient time to meet them and the boy.

(4) When a counselor calls you, please make arrangements for him to meet you and your son. Please remember that our counselors are not professionals. Some of them may be rather shy being interviewed in an unfamiliar situation. We hope you will make the counselor comfortable and tell him something about yourselves too. We are asking parents and counselors to notify us *immediately* if either feels that another counselor should be tried. If we do not hear from you, we will assume that everything is satisfactory.

(5) Counselors will contact our office one day after meeting you and your boy. If all has gone well, we will assign the counselor to your boy for the remainder of the school year. After

that, responsibility for visit times will be in the hands of parents, counselors, and boys (see attached orientation sheet for counselors).

(6) Our budget, research plan, and experience call for boys and counselors to get together two to three times each week. We would also prefer that the visits last no longer than four hours unless there is an occasional special event (a zoo trip or a sports event) that requires more time. Last year most visits lasted between two and three hours. Finally, it is strongly suggested that these relationships be primarily one-to-one, without brothers, sisters, or friends tagging along. An *occasional* third person would do no harm, but we do want these visits to be mostly between boy and counselor.

(7) We want parents to tell us how they see boys and counselors getting along. Please send us a brief note in about one month (just a few lines will do). This is our only way of knowing that the relationships are going well from your point of view.

If this outline has missed some point you are curious about, please phone us any weekday afternoon. In addition to the above general plan there are other aspects of the program that may interest you.

We will ask boys and counselors to visit our office so that we may observe how they are getting along and obtain further information about them as a pair. We will want to know what kinds of things they will be doing and would like to do. We will also suggest current community events and exhibits. At times free tickets to sports events or exhibits will be offered.

There are a few suggestions that involve the parents:

(1) Try not to give your son or his counselor money for their activities. The project allows the pair $5.00 a month for spending money (transportation, refreshments, etc.). However, *occasional* small expenditures by parents for things like model kits or paints are in line with project policy.

(2) We are asking counselors and parents not to talk about the boy when he is not present. Please do not say anything to the counselor that is a secret from your boy. We hope parents and counselors will have no reason to talk about the boy after the first meeting. It is our opinion that these relationships will grow best if boys and counselors find out about each other without the aid of parents or the project staff. Of course, certain types of information regarding diet or prohibited activities may be necessary. But please do not put the counselor in the position of knowing secrets about your boy.

(3) Please be sure to write or phone us with any com-

ments or questions as soon as they occur to you. We are depending upon parent reactions and observations to improve the program.

(4) Counselors and parents should be *sure that boys know the relationships will end in June.* Many boys will not want them to end, just as boys often feel sad about leaving a summer camp. We do not want the ending to be a surprise. In some cases the relationships may "unofficially" continue through the summer (as some did last year). However, most of the counselors will leave Berkeley during summer vacation, or may not be able to continue for other reasons.

A student will phone you soon. Let us know if he does not reach you by the end of next week. I hope you will feel free to write or phone us with questions or observations at any time during the year.

A copy of the parents' acceptance letter was given to all counselors, just as the counselors' orientation sheet was given to parents. This procedure was successful in reducing questions and seemed to engender the trust of participants in the project's attempt to keep things open. Parents were surprisingly conscientious about following suggestions. They seldom interfered with the dyads, they were extremely hospitable to counselors, they refrained from telling the counselors secrets about the boys. However, only a few sent us the note we requested on the orientation schedule; and phone calls or letters requesting information or announcing problems were rare. Even when, about two months after the companionships began, we sent parents a note asking what they thought about the program so far and whether they saw the need for some changes, we received few suggestions for change (although about three quarters of the parents responded). A few calls came in about counselors' beards or political affiliations or religious attitudes, but only one reassignment had to be made. (A boy was withdrawn because his mother demanded a primarily tutorial relationship.) We were careful to avoid coercing any participant into something he did not want. In almost all cases, the project office did not hear from participants, and the companionships were officially assumed underway.

Supervision and Training of Counselors

Systematic and repeated consultation or supervision can serve the same function as in-service training. We combined the two approaches in our weekly small-group sessions; these sessions were aimed at interpersonal-relations education but also served as devices for looking after and watching over the progress of companionships. Counselors also were supervised and consulted through other project structures: The Visit Report form prepared by counselors after each contact, individual interviews with the project staff, and letters from parents.

The Visit Report forms used various scales and checklists to collect details on each visit (see Chapter Five for a complete description). Counselors were asked to turn in Visit Reports within a week of the visit. If two weeks passed without a report, the counselor was contacted for an explanation. In a few cases overdue Visit Reports signaled a problem that required lengthy staff consultation. Every staff member carefully followed about ten companionships by reading each Visit Report for signs of trouble in the running descriptions or sudden changes in the check-list ratings. Almost 80 per cent of the counselors received one or two notes from staff during the year. Most of the notes were about tardy Visit Reports; a few had to do with various staff worries about the companionships. Approximately 20 per cent of the counselors received three or more notes from staff. About 15 per cent of the problems mentioned in notes eventually led to individual interviews. The Visit Report, then, served simultaneously as a supervision device, a source of process data, an avenue for counselor self-expression, and a source of payroll data (hours worked).

Individual contact with project staff was a supplementary source of consultation and supervision. Over half of the counselors had at least one interview during the program year. One-third of these interviews were initiated by staff and usually concerned some irregularity in visit patterns; two-thirds were initiated by counselors, who came to talk of their doubts—about themselves and the companionships. Early in the program, counselors frequently fretted over the lack of "deep" problem-oriented discussions with their boys. They seemed to doubt whether any benefit could come from simply being a friend; some of them said that they felt like "glorified babysitters." We responded to their concern with our belief that the companionship itself might be helpful through offering the boy an opportunity to try out new ways of being with people. And after the first few months, looking for problems to correct seemed a minor concern for counselors. As the companionships strengthened, they found challenge and self-worth in trying to be genuine and understanding and accepting of the way their boys needed them.

A few counselors were disenchanted because their boys were "uncooperative," "indifferent," or "ungrateful." They seemed to be saying, "My boy should reach out to me more often; what's wrong with him?" But with more experience or with consultation, some counselors changed their tune to something like "I'm afraid my boy doesn't like me very much, and I want him to; what's wrong with me?" When these problems came to us, our consultation usually took the form of listening with few questions and scarce advice. In many ways we approached our counselors as we wished them to approach their boys. Our favorite question, or piece of advice, was "Would you be able to tell your boy what you just told me?" In other words, we assumed that self-disclosure and emotional risk-taking usually facilitate relationships.

It was easy for counselors to get personal consultation. The project office was an informal and receptive place. We thought that the self-directed counselors (those not in training groups) would seek out consultation more frequently than trained counselors; but that did not happen. Both groups came in with equal frequency. However, the outgoing counselors sought help and were invited in for consultation more than quiet counselors (at a 4:3 ratio). Less frequently, counselors phoned a staff member at home for consultation. These calls were usually the result of the counselor's frustration at wrestling with a companionship problem.

Parents can also serve as an information source for consultation. Since our project parents were asked not to intrude into the companionships, they had to miss many details. Nevertheless, they would probably see the ramifications of trouble. Three fourths of the parents responded to our inquiry two months after the program's start. Critical remarks about counselors were rare. Occasionally, a parent would tell us about irregular visiting, or a counselor's letting her son "get away with murder" or coercing her son into playing baseball. These communications resulted in our calling in the counselor for consultation. Parent comments were behind 15 per cent of the project-initiated counselor interviews.

Half of the counselors attended weekly discussion or training groups, which were part of the project's consulting or supervising structure. Experienced group leaders (two clinical psychologists and a specially trained minister) were well oriented to program goals and notified the director of problems that appeared to need intervention. Most of the sessions were unstructured and followed a sensitivity-training or group-therapy format. Interpersonal-relations education was the training goal. Mostly, counselors explored their interaction with other group members and their boys. The sessions provided an arena for exploring skills of listening, self-disclosure, and accepting others. Sometimes we introduced structured group techniques designed to enhance the discussion of companionship problems.

Groups met from twenty-five to twenty-nine times. Sessions lasted about ninety minutes. At the end of each session, counselors filled out a brief sociometric scale for rating the behavior of every other group member. The six-point items asked about the group members' understanding, honesty, warmth, and assertion. This procedure allowed us to compute mean scores on these dimensions for each group member and every session. The mean scores were placed on a flow chart that displayed changes in the groups' perception of each counselor over time. Flow charts were updated after each session and given to the group members for their own use.

Sometimes this method of instrumented feedback was used by the group to discuss some undesirable change pinpointed in the flow chart. For example, if the group members were gradually losing trust in one of the members, this growing distrust would be displayed by a gradually decreasing function of the "honesty" variable on the chart. It was there for everyone to see and discuss. Frequently, an individual's pattern of scores for group interaction paralleled his style of interaction in the companionship. For example, a counselor's concern about being seen as distant and cool by his boy would be brought into sharp focus if his score on "warmth" was lower than those of other group members. Such dramatic evidence was hard to turn away from and usually brought aid through discussion or role playing or other forms of practice at disclosing emotions. Thus, at times, when interpersonal problems in the groups were reduced, interpersonal problems in the companionships also were reduced. In addition to individual scores, the flow charts contained total group scores for each variable. Thus, instrumented feedback from the sociometric scale provided visible group trends and individual patterns for the participants and leaders to use in their training task.

In order to get some idea of the group-process patterns for our training program, we combined the scores for all the groups. We compared the first half of training with the second half (about fourteen sessions in each half). The distribution of individual scores was quite wide, and significant differences did not occur between the two periods. However, the direction of change was similar for all variables: slightly higher scores for the second half of training. That is, trained counselors tended to be seen as slightly warmer, more honest, understanding, and assertive over time. An examination of scores by quarters showed the same pattern: second-quarter scores were higher than first-quarter scores, and fourth-quarter scores higher than first.

Collapsing the time periods into single scores revealed that counselors rated each other highest on honesty, then understanding, and finally warmth. Perhaps the increased quantity of authentic self-expression was the most visible aspect of the groups and was reflected in the higher honesty scores. Warmth was probably lower because of the rather constant low-level anxiety that characterized most meetings. But all mean ratings indicated that counselors saw each other as more honest, understanding, and warm than not. That is, mean ratings fell on the positive side of the scale. Our confidence in the validity of the scores was increased by an incidental finding. Counselors initially classified as outgoing during the project's selection phase were rated significantly ($p < .01$) more assertive in the groups, in comparison to those initially classified as quiet.

Over the two program years, we had a workable sampling of data from group sizes ranging from five to ten members. Without attempting to account for confounding variables such as systematic changes in the quality of group composition with group size, we computed scores on the three target variables for different group sizes. The counselor's experience of honesty, understanding, and warmth in the groups was highest when there were only five members. It decreased slightly and remained constant for group sizes six to nine. Scores became definitely lower once again with ten members present. The "assertion" variables decreased in a linear fashion from group sizes five to ten. This crude study suggests that an interpersonal-learning environment (for all male student groups) is best achieved when the group size is under ten. Groups of six to nine members seem to produce similar results.

When the program was two months old, we asked counselors in groups to do a "round robin" on companionship problems. Each counselor spent a few minutes outlining his concerns into a tape recorder, and our staff listened to the results. Here are some brief excerpts:

> At first I thought I was going to help consciously and in clear-cut ways. But it's not like that at all; it's really like an unconscious process that I can only take account of occasionally and then see its significance.

> The problem so far is getting a way to talk with him. We just can't seem to talk specifically to each other. I wish he could tell me what's bothering him specifically. Somehow, I'm not directing our friendship toward us sharing our feelings. Right now there's no promise of us ever getting that close.

> I expected more problems because this is a project for troubled kids. The project gave me a false impression by the way it's set up. I thought Sandy would be an introvert—but it's frightening how outgoing he is. You know, he monopolizes conversations and all that.

> Maybe it's not a bad thing that I can't find a problem. I'm just forgetting about it. You know, I was expecting something worse.

> Phil is just so damn withdrawn that I'm awfully frustrated. I just don't know him as a person. Maybe I'm causing it. Maybe I'm doing something bad.

Not all counselors experienced discomfort during the early phases of the companionship. However, as the excerpts demonstrate, our orientation and training did not altogether eliminate frustration and bewilderment. Counselors continued to expect quick intimacy and direct talk about problems. When these things did not come about, they attempted to bring order to their confusion by making psychological diagnoses to fill the void left by our unwillingness to outline the boys' problems. In some ways our counselors' reactions were similar to those of students learning to do psychotherapy in professional schools.

About a month before the companionships terminated, we again asked counselors in groups to describe their companionships so that we could have a tape-recorded transcript. This time the stories were different: fewer frustrations, lower expectations, greater acceptance of their boy's condition, and a more realistic conception of their roles. Here are a few representative excerpts:

So it's still the same problem: what should we do this time. Nowell is still reluctant to say what he wants. We're similar in not saying much. I've been curiously passive with him—really haven't given him what I should. But his damned mother contributes to the problem. You know, she pressures him to do what I want. And what do you think that does to him: he pulls back from me. He depends on her too much. It hasn't been very satisfying. Still, I've helped him become a little more independent— a little more willing to take for himself. He's used me.

My regret is that it took me so long to realize that Peter just needed a friend—and that's all I wanted to be. My big insight is that while I anticipated "real talk times" I didn't realize he wasn't used to talking . . . and neither was I. But Pete has become a lot less inhibited. He hasn't changed a real lot. I guess he has a little more confidence now because I let him do a lot of things on his own that he couldn't do at home. I also cared for him and that helped too.

[The companionship] hasn't been disappointing since I realized that Roosevelt isn't going to change spectacularly just because of my presence. Sure, I expected him to change a lot— but he hasn't. He hasn't gained insight, but he has gained a sense of steadiness. He could depend on me—so he got comfortable, and now he is dependable; constancy is important to him.

At the beginning I felt very inadequate. Sam didn't have any friends and I couldn't be everything to him. He doesn't have any now either, except in an organized way: he joined the Scouts. He is less interested in me now, maybe because of his interest in the Scouts. I'm less interested in him too. Maybe he couldn't have joined anything if he didn't have me to fall back on.

"Quiet" still holds for describing Wilt—but he's less quiet. Passivity was a problem for us all the way through . . . it was a pretty open relationship . . . [we] were able to get mad at each other near the end without feeling guilty. Wilt has more self-confidence now—no doubt about it. Now I take a back seat . . . sort of accompany Wilt. He's a pleasure to watch now.

We also asked counselors, after the training had terminated, to rate the usefulness of the groups. The questions were similar to those asked about the teaching-machine lessons. The initial open-ended question was responded to positively by 95 per cent of the participants. Responses appeared equivalent among all the training groups. Here are some representative examples:

At first I didn't enjoy them, but later I got to looking forward to the chance to explore my feelings and impressions.

Group was slow to start—but interesting to see how we all slowly changed.

Both exciting and disappointing, but I found it extremely valuable. My project experience wouldn't have been the same without it.

Frightening, but exciting and useful. Brand-new experience in working out feelings with people instead of just inside my mind.

After awhile I became thankful that [the groups] offered a chance to find out I was not the only counselor with problems with his boy.

Too early to calculate the final effect—but it seems I got somewhat more honest with myself, my feelings, my boy, my friends.

The following year, the question on the usefulness of the groups was asked with more structure: "Did they provide help in your relationship with the boy?" and "Were they useful to you personally?" To both questions the answer was "yes" about 90 per cent of the time. Comments were similar to those of the previous year. Those who answered "no" to the first question complained that the groups did not focus on the boys enough. In retrospect, we tend to agree. More structured intervention aimed at companionship problems could have provided needed support during the first two months. Here are a couple of comments:

> Didn't help that much with Steve. I needed more specific help. But they were great for my own life.

> They didn't provide a strong basis for getting to know my boy better, but they helped me become aware of others' feelings in general. Only helped me through some occasional support when I felt troubled with the companionship. They could have done more.

There was some tendency to confuse discomfort or tension in the groups with lack of usefulness; but, clearly, most counselors saw the groups as useful both to the companionships and to their other personal relationships. A comparison of the ratings for groups and teaching-machine lessons shows that group sessions were more often seen as useful (90 per cent versus 68 per cent).

Mechanics of Visiting

Counselors and boys had to solve some problems with transportation, scheduling, budget, and selection of activities. Fortunately, since some of the boys did not live near campus, about two thirds of the counselors had their own transportation. When possible, we assigned counselors without transportation to boys in accessible neighborhoods. A few counselors had to use busses often. They complained about the expense, so we increased their monthly allowance. Initially, transportation problems were not approached seriously enough by staff. With experience, it became evident that even minor chronic problems of transport could seriously erode a companionship over several months.

To provide boys with a sense of continuity, a visiting pattern of frequent and substantial meetings was needed. The one-hour minimum discouraged brief "drop-in" visits, and the two-visit-per-week minimum avoided lengthy lapses between visits. In the opinion of the counselors, our mandatory visiting schedule apparently was a success. When we posed the question at termination, eighty-five per cent of the counselors said that they would not change the two-to-three-visits-a-week requirement. The remaining 15 per cent wanted more (four to five) or fewer (one to two) visits per week. A few suggested all-day visits for excursions and overnight camping. Some thought that greater flexibility could be achieved through a monthly visit requirement (nine to eleven visits) instead of our weekly setup.

A few counselors and boys complained that the expense allowance (five dollars a month) was restrictive. Occasional conferences between boy, counselor, and staff member were used to work on the problem. The problem seemed connected to dyads with boys from low-income families. Apparently, these boys had few opportunities to visit public places or go on community explorations. They got "hooked" on excursions. On the whole, however, the five-dollar budget was not completely spent. The typical dyad spent $3.70 a month.

As mentioned earlier, the most common structural problem the pairs described was deciding what to do. They wanted more help from the project. We provided minimal assistance: a list of local things to do, some free tickets to sports events and concerts, and some special arrangements with the recreation department. The program rationale was to provide a context for boy-counselor collaboration. We wanted the boys to gain experience in giving and taking and living with the products of their decisions. Even the five-dollar expense allowance provided a vehicle for collaborative planning between the pair. Since bilateral decision-making was an unfamiliar task for most boys, they found the job difficult. Our staff disagreed about the level of autonomy *imposed* on the dyads. Some found the pleas for greater project involvement in structuring activities to be compelling, and they wanted to provide more organization or preplanned activity suggestions. But we settled on passing out a one-page list of suggestions and leaving the pairs to practice using their own resources.

At the end of each year, we asked the counselors for advice: "Please summarize your suggestions for making the project more comfortable and beneficial for you and your boy. Did we let you down at times?" Over half of the counselors had no specific suggestions but added comments such as "your job was done—my problems were within me," "hard to make important suggestions because it was a pretty good deal for Elgin and me," "No complaints or ideas—you were there when I needed support." The remaining suggestions and complaints were too heterogeneous for an orderly breakdown into content areas. Many of the specific suggestions were directed at small administrative matters. A fairly frequent suggestion involved more systematic staff-counselor contact on a one-to-one basis: ". . . just to talk things over and see how psychologists work." "Weekly interviews and professional hints would have made me feel more part of the larger project." A system for bringing pairs together for sharing activities was recommended: "Harold and I had a great time going to the zoo with another boy and counselor. We compared notes—it was comforting and 'loosening.' This should be done regularly throughout the project." A few wanted pairs brought together into larger monthly discussion groups. Here are some brief excerpts from other counselor comments: "Keep the salary low or even lower to get only sincerely interested students." ". . . better connection between project, parents, and counselors so parents can get help . . . feel like I'm dumping Mike into a hell he can't escape, which makes me feel awful because I can't do anything about it." "Don't even let us know that boys have emotional problems during the beginning as that could have been more damaging than helpful." ". . . emphasize right away how much we will be on our own so we don't flounder for two weeks." "Let us know that we might be paired with a professor's son, etc. It floored me because I was expecting a ghetto kid like me." ". . . continue companionships over the summer." "Find a way to make sure that the boy *himself* is really interested in the project. Sy got a false impression from his father."

Summary

Essentially, the project structure was geared toward serving research and program goals simultaneously. There was an attempt to create an effective, inexpensive, "exportable" program and to house a serious research design.

A dominant theme that shaped the program structure was our belief in the advantages of companionship autonomy. We wanted the pairs to be mostly on their own. Avoiding program structures that could not be reproduced in other settings was important. Our bias toward visitation consistency became a mandate for twice a week contact. Our bias against drop-in or "hello-good-bye" visits turned into a one-hour minimum visit rule. Leanings toward client-centered theory became structure through the withholding of diagnostic information from counselors, providing a minimum of activity advice, reducing the superordinancy or "expert" posture in counselors, and primarily in the systematic selection of those who seemed capable of providing more than everyday empathy, acceptance, and self-disclosure.

Here are some other project structures and their reasons for being: Matching boy and counselor pairs into dyad types (quiet-outgoing) was strictly a function of research interest. A strong motif in the orientation of counselors and parents was dyadic autonomy; it allowed the pairs to learn about each other *from* each other. Weaning counselors from their stereotypic role models of professional therapists was another theme in the orientation. Exchanging orientation instructions between parents and counselors was an attempt to establish trust, a demonstration of policy to share most of our rationale with all participants and to increase administrative efficiency. Visit Report forms were filled out after each contact by counselors and became a major vehicle for counselor supervision and research data. Dyadic interpersonal-relations teaching machines seemed a rapid inexpensive way of introducing students to elementary problems in two-person interaction before the companionships began. Setting up initial boy-counselor meetings without the presence of a staff member worked surprisingly well, saved staff manpower, and seemed to accelerate the acquaintance process. An option for any participant to change partners after the initial meeting was rarely used. Weekly group training for counselors was mostly unstructured interpersonal relations education by professional leaders. The groups also served as an adjunct supervisory device. A matched half of the counselors were not trained and served as controls for the study of training effects. Counselors were reminded to discuss the facts of termination one month before the official end; it was an easy subject to forget. Provision was made for the project's intervention in cases of difficult termination.

V

Initial Meeting
and Companionship
Activities

This chapter describes the "natural history" of eighty-eight companionships that existed over a span of eight months. The typical pair met about fifty times, and their average meeting lasted almost three hours. They met about twice a week. Each pair received a monthly allowance (five dollars for incidentals) and spent it at a rate of sixty-two cents a visit.

Our major view of the companionships was through the descriptions made by counselors. Boys and parents also gave us their observations—mostly after the companionships were over. Few questions were asked of boys during the companionships because we wanted them to be unfettered by the project's bureaucracy. For boys, the project was their counselor and little else. For counselors, the project was primarily their boys plus the inescapable forms that needed filling out after each visit. For us, the companionships were there to foster and study. The staff's task was to learn much and not intrude. Part of the task was met as we learned a little and intruded a little.

Methods for Studying Relationships in Process

Most of the findings in this chapter were generated by new instruments. These instruments can be modified for use with a wide variety of two-person relationships.

Visit Report form. We learned most about the companionship process through the Visit Report form. Besides providing information on activities, conversation topics, and feelings during each visit, this instrument aided our supervision of counselors and provided payroll data. It contained checklists, scales, and space for a brief running account of each visit. We urged counselors to complete the report immediately after a visit, while their memory was fresh. The report usually took twelve to fourteen minutes to complete. About once a week, counselors turned in the completed reports, and an assigned staff member carefully read them for signs of trouble and departures from program guidelines that might require intervention. When necessary, counselors were called in to discuss irregular visit patterns and other problems spotted in their reports. These staff-initiated interventions were infrequent.

The first component of the form is a check list of activities (see Table 9). More than one of the sixteen listed activity categories could be checked, but incidental activities were to be excluded. Our instructions* set the tone for response; for example, "By 'sitting down to talk,' we mean a definite and substantial conversation and not a brief chat while preparing to go out." The listed categories adequately covered 95 per cent of the activities reported; the "other" category was seldom used.

Another component of the form is a check list containing topic categories of conversation. Most of the categories were derived from unstructured counselor responses to earlier experimental forms

* A copy of the exact instructions is available from the author.

Table 9

Visit Report Form

Counselor ....

Boy ....

Date ....

Visit began ....   Total Expenses ....

Visit ended ....   Itemize:

Total Time [   ]   Visit No. [   ]

In box number one, please check activities for this visit. In box number two indicate those topics you *or* your boy discussed at length or even briefly (several minutes) during the visit. Add unlisted topics.

---

1. ACTIVITIES CATEGORIES

1. .... Active sports, games (ping-pong, fishing, baseball)
2. .... Quiet activities or games (cards, checkers, chess)
3. .... Spectator sports (watching ball game)
4. .... Hiking or taking a walk
5. .... A ride (not just transport) in auto, on bike, motorcycle or scooter
6. .... Working on a hobby (models, etc.)
7. .... A movie
8. .... Listening to records or radio; TV
9. .... Helping boy with homework
10. .... Having a meal together
11. .... Sightseeing: zoo, exhibit, campus, public place
12. .... Visit to boy's home (over one hour)
13. .... Visit to your own place
14. .... Visit to your friend's place
15. .... Sitting down to talk
16. .... Including a third person (or more)
17. .... Other: ....

2. TOPIC CATEGORIES	Boy's	Mine
1. School or school work		
2. Teacher(s)		
3. Mother		
4. Father		
5. Other family members		
6. Friend(s)		
7. Travels; vacations		
8. Skills		
9. Personality and behavior		

10. .... Your feelings about him

11. .... His feelings about you

12. .... Boy's role in home (duties, etc.)

13. .... Activities this visit or past ones

14. .... Plans for future visits

15. .... The project

16. .... Other: ....

3. Scan the topics you have checked above and circle the one which seems most prominent or important considering *either* the length of time spent on it or the degree of meaningfulness it seemed to have for your boy.

4. Write a brief running account of what you two did and talked about. Include your general observations. Please write legibly.

5. Check the *one* description (1–4 below) which comes closest to describing your boy during the visit. Then do the same for yourself.

	Boy	Me
1. NONPERSONAL: matter-of-fact; personal feelings not discussed	1	1
2. SLIGHTLY PERSONAL: a few feelings discussed	2	2
3. QUITE PERSONAL: some important feelings or thoughts revealed	3	3
4. VERY PERSONAL: deep personal feelings shared	4	4

76

6. Put an "X" in the *one* box between each of the eight opposite word pairs that comes closest to describing *your* general feelings or behavior during the visit ("C" stands for counselor).

Then put an "X" in the one box between each word pair that best describes *your boy's* feelings or behavior during the visit ("B" stands for boy). *Please don't skip items.* When you are unsure, just give us your best guess.

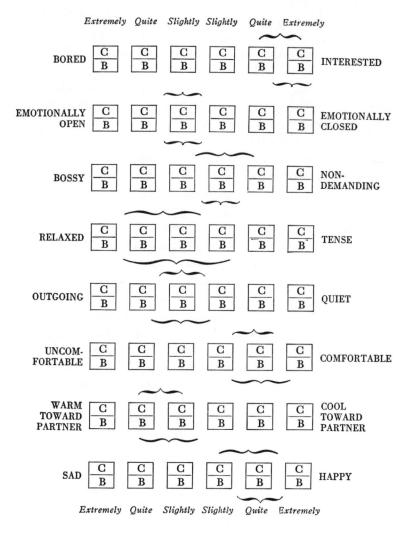

Brackets roughly indicate areas of response means for most counselors.

of the Visit Report. The written instructions asked counselors to avoid checking trivial topics.

As the table shows, counselors also were asked to describe what was said and done during the visit. Limited space kept the descriptions cogent.

The four-step scale (the component numbered 5) allowed the counselor to note the degree of intimacy he saw in the visit. As expected, the counselor usually rated himself and his boy on similar levels.

The final component of the Visit Report is a modification of the semantic-differential format. It contains eight dimensions relevant to a two-person encounter. Again, the ratings for boy and counselor were usually similar.

Counselors' Final Observations questionnaire. Questions about the companionship process were scattered throughout the omnibus questionnaire administered at the end of the program. Counselors were asked to look back and make general retrospective observations about their companionships. Most of the questions were intended to produce information useful to the administration of the program, but often the answers gave insight into the companionship process. (See Appendix E.)

Relationship Index. A simple ten-item scale was provided for boys and counselors to rate themselves and each other on interpersonal-behavior qualities of their companionship: openness, anger, fun, understanding, and control (see Appendix D). The language is geared to the boys' vocabulary and kept in the present tense: "I tell him all about myself." "I get angry with him." "I have fun when we are together." "I understand how he feels." "I try to get him to do what I want." The remaining items are identical except that "he" is substituted for "I." Boys and counselors responded to the scales privately but were free to discuss their ratings afterward.

"Story of My Companionship" form. This incomplete-story method is in a third-person format and contains the actual names of the interviewed boy and his counselor (see Appendix G). Some items refer to postprogram change; a few were inserted for continuity and the boy's comfort, but most are directed at the companionship process: ". . . *Dave* was a friend to *Billy* in a different way

than other people. Some of the ways he was different were————
————." *Billy* thought about if he wanted to be like *Dave* and decided
that—————." Almost all the boys were interested in this thirty-
five-minute task and seemed to have fun doing it.

Parent observations. About two months after the companionships began, parents were sent a note asking what they thought
of the program so far. It was an attempt to spot early problems
not evident in the Visit Reports. About three quarters of the parents
responded, and suggestions for change were practically nonexistent.
However, some of the notes did contain observations on boy-counselor interactions.

Initial Meetings

As mentioned in Chapter Four, the companionships began
well. We do not wish to imply, however, that the initial meetings
were without anxiety and interpersonal distance. Introductory
meetings were frequently tense and impersonal; but they rarely
required project intervention, and participants wanted to continue
regardless of their early discomfort. This picture comes from our
analysis of three Visit Report items.

The impersonal side of the four-step personal-versus-imper-
sonal-communication scale (see Table 9, component 5) was used
infrequently during the companionships. Counselors described
themselves and their boys as communicating impersonally during
only 5 per cent of the visits. The figure soars to 95 per cent for
first visits.

About 40 per cent of the counselors described themselves
and their boys as slightly or quite tense during the first session (see
bipolar scales in Table 9). The proportion of 40 per cent was
significant, since it dropped to only 3 per cent on the subsequent
visits. Anxiety seemed an appropriate part of the first meetings; so
the 40 per cent figure bolstered our confidence in the validity of
counselors' ratings on the Visit Report. We also discovered something special about the first visits of the fifteen dyads that broke up
before the official closing of the program: 70 per cent of the attrition boys were seen as tense, and 50 per cent of their counselors
rated themselves on the tense side of the scale. Thus, acquaintance

anxiety appears to be more common to companionships headed toward early termination.

Only 7 per cent of the five thousand visits we studied had boys rated as cool rather than warm; 3 per cent of the visits had counselors rating themselves as cool. In contrast, the initial visits showed 22 per cent of the boys and 7 per cent of the counselors on the cool side of the scale. Initial-visit ratings for attrition dyads were dramatically different: nearly 60 per cent of the boys and half the counselors were described as cool to some degree. Thus, for first visits, attrition boys were rated cool about three times as often as nonattrition boys; their counselors described themselves cool about nine times more frequently than nonattrition counselors.

The descriptions made by the attrition counselors agree with the quantitative findings: "He seems like a very nice boy, but he is extremely shy. I think he felt quite awkward from the moment we met till it was time to go (I know I did). We simply sat and said very little—showed me his room at his mother's insistence. We watched TV the rest of the visit. Seemed nonchalant when I said I'd call him next week." [Boy withdrew ten weeks later.]

Here is a first-visit description that is fairly representative of companionships that continued: "After I found the house, Jimmy, his mother, and I talked for a few minutes about the family's music skills. Then Jimmy and his sister started carving a pumpkin. We left her and sat on the porch and generally discussed our interests and plans for future meetings. Little feeling was communicated, and I led most of the conversation. It was kind of up-tight because we've got to know more about each other."

In sum, the introductory visits were usually accompanied by anxiety, impersonal communication, and the mutual desire to start a companionship. The meetings were typically satisfactory and clearly indicate the feasibility (or desirability) of initiating this form of companionship therapy without the customary intervention of an attendant professional "introducer."

Choice of and Change in Activities

The boys who joined our project seemed especially unpracticed at the give and take of collaboration in a dyad. Findings show that boys did find the companionships a place to be more of an equal partner with real power to determine the course of the pair through direct negotiation. Two of the most frequently discussed topics involved plans for future visits and current activities. The boys told us that most of the decisions were made either jointly or by them alone. An item from the boys' story-completion form drew information on the locus of choice: "Most of the time decisions about what to do were made by—————." Forty-six per cent of the boys' responses indicated that joint decisions were most common, 40 per cent said that the choice was most frequently their own, and 14 per cent said that the counselor usually made the decisions. These and other data suggest that the companionships were an active practice ground for boys (and counselors) to learn about collaboration. Apparently, the boys experienced forms of interchange usually unavailable to them in customary relationships or in the office of a professional healer.

Actually, the pairs were pushed toward collaboration by the project, since it imposed few rules and did not prescribe any type of activity. Their problem was what to do with the freedom—and it was a discomforting problem. Counselors complained about the difficulty of thinking up new activities or finding things they both could enjoy. They blamed their own limited imaginations or lack of initiative, their boys' fears or negativism or overassertion, and various other factors: "Mike was often afraid to make suggestions and made few. I ran out of ideas and it made me feel inadequate." "Peter was nonactive and I was too narrow-minded to think of enough nonathletic things." "Some of our interests were incompatible and I feared that things were too repetitious and maybe boring—but just talking seemed as good as anything else." Unfortunately, many counselors overemphasized the importance of "showing the boy a good time." Frequently, they were content to let their boys make unilateral decisions about activities. The boys had power in these companionships. They were often able to see their wishes become activity.

A few of the sixteen activity categories on the Visit Report form are obviously overlapping; for example, "visit to boy's home" and "quiet activities." Typically, counselors checked two or three activities per visit (2.5 to be exact). Percentage scores for each

activity category across an entire companionship were generated
by computing its frequency over the frequency of all activities
checked. For example, if a counselor checked the active sports category fifteen times and checked a total of one hundred activities
during the entire companionship, he would receive a score of 15 per
cent for active sports. This procedure allowed us to compare pro-
portions of activities between categories and among dyads. Percentage scores were also used to follow patterns of change over the
beginning, middle, and final periods of the companionships. Data
for each pair were divided into equal and consecutive thirds based
on their total number of visits. Figure 1 displays mean scores for
the three periods, along with mean scores for the three periods,
along with mean scores and standard deviations for the entire span
of companionships.

The existence of orderly patterns of activity suggests that the
companionships progress in a generally systematic fashion—as if
there were a predictable "natural history" for these types of friendships. We speculate that much of the orderly process of activity is
linked to a common decrease in interpersonal distance and an increase in emotional safety. Things like weather and final examina-
tions have undoubtedly affected our measures, but a closer look
at the findings will show that some major explanations can be
based on the development of intimacy between boy and counselor.
The associations we found between activities pursued and other
interpersonal processes appear useful as initial guidelines for companionship diagnosis or establishing better companionships. That
is, activity type and frequency can do some predicting of feelings,
behavior, conversation topics, and, perhaps, the therapeutic effectiveness of companionships.

There are eighteen curves in Figure 1; the first fifteen represent the frequency and flow of activities for all boy-counselor
dyads, and the final three describe some general parameters relevant to activities. Active sports was the most frequently checked
category. It encompassed many one-to-one-pursuits; playing catch,
kite flying, basketball, rowboating, swimming, table tennis, skate-
board riding, wrestling. About 15 per cent of all activities were
active sports. Since the average dyad indicated 2.5 activities per

visit, roughly one third (or about eighteen) of the visits included an active sport.

Sports-centered dyads. The dyads tended to engage in more active sports over time. The gain between periods I and III just reaches statistical significance ($p < .10$). Our correlational study indicates that dyads who chose active sports were not likely to go hiking or take walks or have lengthy visits in the boy's home.* These sports-centered dyads had meals together infrequently, took few rides, and rarely watched television or listened to records. They did not sit down to talk quite as often as other dyads. They liked to watch sports as well as play at them, and they attended the local games and watched the university teams practice more often than others. Counselors in these sports-centered dyads were a bit more outgoing and controlling, and their boys said they had slightly more fun when compared to others at the program's end. The final social-insight scores for all counselors show an inverse relationship to the frequency of active sports in the companionships. The inter-personal-closeness scale on the Visit Report also shows some negative correlation with the frequency of active sports.

Stay-at-Home Pairs. Visits in the boy's home comprised almost 12 per cent of all activities checked and occurred during 30 per cent of the visits. The typical dyad had fourteen lengthy visits (an hour or longer) in the boy's home during their fifty meetings. The frequency of such visits diminished over the program, especially the first two thirds (see Figure 1, pp. 85–87). The dyads who frequently stayed at the boy's home tended to spend their time talking or doing homework. They visited more often, seldom went sightseeing or to spectator sports or movies, and participated in active sports infrequently. We noticed that black boys and their counselors tended to stay at home less. This was especially true for black boys from low-income, large-family homes. We assume that they chose out-of-the-house activities to escape the intrusion of siblings and to try the many activities previously un-explored.

We failed to provide a category for those times when the

---

* Most of the reported correlations are at the .05 and .01 levels ($r \geq .21$, or $\geq .28$ for N of 88). Exact figures are available from the author.

boy's home was used for more than a starting point but for less than a lengthy visit. This error reduced the meaningfulness of the quiet activities category because counselors frequently used that category to describe intermediate-length visits (thirty to fifty minutes) in the boy's home. Apparently, the intermediate visits were frequent and involved comparatively quiet activities, such as playing a piano or guitar, carving soap, modeling clay, or "just loafing around a little." This category correlated negatively with hours per visit and generated a pattern of change that closely resembled the category "lengthy visit to boy's home" (Figure 1). When quiet activities were frequent, the dyad made few visits to the counselor's place and did not have many meals together or go for rides or include a third person. Unlike those dyads with many lengthy visits to the boy's home, these pairs did not stay away from active sports, spectator sports, or sightseeing. We cannot find a satisfying interpretation for these data. Assuming that most of the responses to quiet activities represent a visit of intermediate length to the boy's home, we can estimate that this activity occurred about eight times for the typical dyad. Combining this estimation with the lengthy visit findings suggests that the typical dyad had intermediate or lengthy visits in the boy's home during twenty-two of their fifty visits. They visited the counselor's place only six times. It seems fair to say, then, that the boy's home served as a headquarters for most dyads—especially during the first period (first third) of the companionships.

Walking and Hiking. Taking long walks and hiking through a park were prominent activities in the companionships. One of every five visits included a walk or hike for its own sake. The typical dyad took ten hikes. Those counselors and boys who hiked more had meals together more often. They participated in fewer active sports, saw fewer sports events, attended movies less often, and tended not to include a third person. This group of dyads happened to have more counselors who were assigned to the sensitivity-training groups. At the program's end, these boys described their counselors as having much fun (on the Relationship Index), and their counselors claimed a good understanding of their boys' feelings and rated the boys as expressing much anger.

A significant decrease in hiking or walking occurs between

FIGURE 1. Changes in activity patterns (eighty-eight companion-ships)

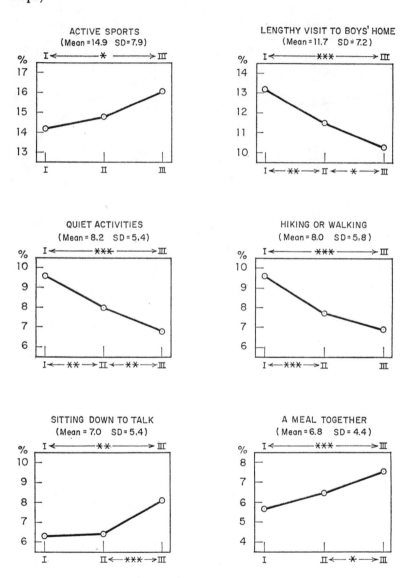

Asterisks denote significance of change between periods (I, beginning; II, middle; III, final) spanned by arrows: * = .10, ** = .05, *** = .01. % indicates proportion of all activities reported by counselors—approximately 2.5 activities per visit.

FIGURE 1.   Changes in activity patterns (eighty-eight companionships) (Cont.)

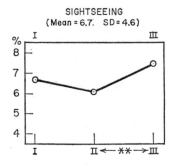

SIGHTSEEING
(Mean = 6.7. SD = 4.6)

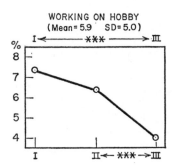

WORKING ON HOBBY
(Mean = 5.9   SD = 5.0)

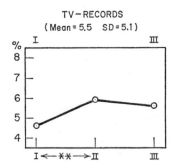

TV—RECORDS
(Mean = 5.5   SD = 5.1)

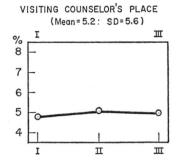

VISITING COUNSELOR'S PLACE
(Mean = 5.2: SD = 5.6)

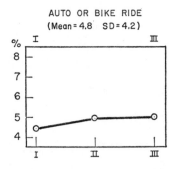

AUTO OR BIKE RIDE
(Mean = 4.8   SD = 4.2)

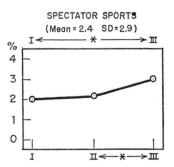

SPECTATOR SPORTS
(Mean = 2.4   SD = 2.9)

Asterisks denote significance of change between periods (I, beginning; II, middle; III, final) spanned by arrows: * = .10, ** = .05, *** = .01. % indicates
proportion of all activities reported by counselors—approximately 2.5 activities
per visit.

FIGURE 1.   Changes in activity patterns (eighty-eight companion-ships) (Cont.)

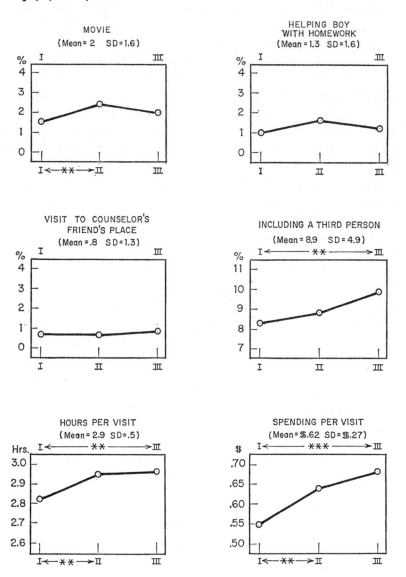

Asterisks denote significance of change between periods (I, beginning; II, middle; III, final) spanned by arrows: * = .10, ** = .05, *** = .01. % indicates proportion of all activities reported by counselors—approximately 2.5 activities per visit.

the beginning (I) and middle (II) periods of the companionships. Slight but significant increases over the same time span occur for watching television, listening to records, and going to movies. Apparently, some hikes were replaced by professionally prepared entertainment. However, hiking was still one of the most popular activities during the middle and final periods.

Conversation. Counselors were instructed to check the Sitting Down to Talk category only when a substantial conversation occurred. Most conversations centered around future activities, their feelings for each other, schoolwork, and family. Sitting down to talk represented about 6 per cent of all activities during periods I and II and showed a significant gain to 8 per cent during the final period (Figure 1). This gain may reflect an increase in closeness and comfort evident in the final third of the companionships. No other activity showed such a strong gain. The reduction in working on a hobby over the same period suggests a lessened need for structured or goal-oriented activity. The reduction could also be due simply to the "using up" of hobby interests. At any rate, the boys and counselors did have long talks more frequently as their relationships matured. The typical dyad sat down for long talks about eight times during their fifty visits. We are aware that these more deliberate conversations were not the sole source of meaningful talk within the dyads. Our study of the visit reports and recordings of counselor sensitivity-training groups has made it clear that brief and incidental interchanges were also occasions for important communication.

Our correlational study shows that dyads who sit down to talk more frequently tend to include third persons more often and have lengthier visits. The interpersonal-closeness scale on the Visit Report was also high for dyads who had many long talks. At the program's termination, counselors in these dyads said (on the Self-Disclosure Questionnaire) that they disclosed more about their personalities than counselors who had few long talks. These counselors also tended (on the Relationship Index) to describe themselves and their boys as open. They also described their boys as not attempting to control very much; their boys indicated some agreement, as shown by their low control scores on the Relationship Index. From these findings, we speculate that dyads who have long talks during, at least, one of four visits are more intimate; in addition, their visits are usually longer (over three hours), they are more self-disclosing toward each other, they include friends or siblings more often, and the boys make fewer gambits for control.

Lunch and Dinner. The category labeled "a meal together" was reserved for those times when the dyad "broke bread" together and was not used to record the frequent snacks that they shared. The typical dyad ate meals together about eight times during their fifty visits. Sometimes it was at the counselor's dormitory or fraternity; less frequently, at the boy's home or the counselor's girl friend's place or a public restaurant. In general, there was a gradual but significant increase in eating a meal together over the three companionship periods (Figure 1). The increase was probably a simple function of increasing friendliness or familiarity over time.

Boys and counselors who ate dinner together more frequently (one of four visits or more) were prone to go hiking more often. These pairs also visited the counselor's place more often. Since many of their visits involved outings, they tended to have longer visits and spent less time at the boy's home. The outings seem to have taken the place of active sports.

Sightseeing. Sightseeing activities (in San Francisco or Oakland or Berkeley) occurred somewhat more frequently during the final period, when visits to the boy's home and working on hobbies decreased (Figure 1). A typical pair went sightseeing about eight times. Those dyads that did much sightseeing (once every five visits or more) hardly ever remained at the boy's home. They also attended movies more than other dyads (once in eight visits or more), took a few more rides, and were less interested in sitting down to talk. Their visits were slightly shorter than average, and the counselors said that they were not self-disclosed with their boys. The boys described their counselors as hardly ever expressing anger. "Trained" counselors were underrepresented among the high sightseeing dyads. Although some of these trends are mild, the direction of findings points to the possibility that "on-the-go" dyads with a strong taste for sightseeing may prefer more formal or less personal contacts.

Hobbies. Almost all dyads worked on a hobby at some time during their companionships. We cannot explain the significant decrease in this activity during the final period. As mentioned earlier, the need for structured, goal-oriented activities may have decreased as the companionships matured.

The typical dyad worked on a hobby during seven of their fifty meetings. Those atypical dyads who spent more time with hobbies (once every six to seven visits or more) showed a few special characteristics: they tended not to include third persons, their counselors were somewhat more quiet or reserved, they seldom chose to watch television or go to the movies, and they were low on active sports.

Television and Records. The typical dyad watched television or listened to records six times during the fifty meetings. The significant increase from period I to period II is coincident with an increase in seeing movies and decreases in visits to the boy's home and hiking. We certainly cannot rule out the possibility that the more passive spectator activities became a source of interpersonal relief or relaxation for some after period I. If so, they were not a major mode of escape, since television and movies combined occupied a small share of the total activities.

A smaller subgroup of dyads ($N = 12$) used the television set or record player at almost twice the frequency of the typical companionship (one of five visits). This subgroup is interesting but difficult to characterize with precision because of its size; therefore, our speculation about it is tentative. Apparently, the boys in these dyads had less fun and felt less understood, less open, and more controlling when compared to the remaining boys (on Relationship Index responses). They also said that their counselors had less fun and attempted to control more often. Similarly, their counselors described themselves as more controlling and having less fun during the companionships. That is, the boys and the counselors did not actually report having little fun or attempting much control; they were simply lower in these respects than the very favorable descriptions produced by other participants. A larger proportion of counselors in this group lost access to a car or motorbike during the program, which may account for some of the greater use of television. An expected corollary is the subgroup's low score on the auto or bike ride category. Finally, this group worked on hobbies more than others and contained a disproportionate number of counselors who felt that their group training was not helpful to their companionships.

The atypically frequent use of television or records may be a product of less satisfactory relationships. If we could go back in time, we would certainly pay more attention to the heavy use of television or records as a warning of possible trouble.

Visiting the Counselor's Place. About 75 per cent of the boys visited the counselor's place (usually, a student cooperative, a dormitory, or a fraternity) during the companionships. The typical dyad made six visits. The pattern is very constant over all three periods (about once in every eight visits, or 13 per cent of all visits).

Visiting the counselor's place is not a strong predictor of other variables. The small subgroup ($N = 16$) high on this activity (one of five visits or more) had few visits in the boy's home, they had meals together more than other dyads, and their visits were longer. At the program's end, these boys described their counselors as particularly noncontrolling and rarely expressing anger, while their counselors described themselves as being open during the companionship.

Auto or Bike Ride. This category was checked only when the travel was central and not just incidental to getting somewhere. Almost 90 per cent of the counselors had access to cars, motor scooters, or motorbikes. The dyads went riding about once in every ten sessions, and there was little change in the frequency of this activity over the three periods.

Spectator Sports. Sometimes we were successful in getting free tickets to professional and college sports events. The slight rise in attending spectator sports during period III is probably a function of ticket availability. Nearly one fourth of the dyads never attended a sports event together. The typical dyad went three times, or about once in seventeen visits. Those who rarely or never went to sports events were prone to take walks or to have lengthy visits in the boy's home and seldom chose to participate in active sports. Spectator sports might have been a more popular activity if we had obtained more free tickets or provided a spending allowance of more than five dollars a month. As it stands, watching athletic competition was a minor activity in the life of the companions.

Movies. Although we did not actually prohibit moviegoing, we did discourage it, because we were afraid that it might become a habit for dyads who felt uncomfortable together. We communicated our concern to the counselors and suggested that they attend only one or two movies during the program. Half of the dyads went to a movie once or never. Typically, they went about once in twenty visits. A very small group $(N = 6)$ did not respond to our suggestion and attended movies at the rate of once in ten meetings, or about five times during the program. Counselors in this subgroup evidently became disenchanted with the program. Data on these counselors are unreliable because of the small sample size. Even so, they begin to suggest another warning sign for companionships in trouble. As the program closed, these counselors described themselves and their boys as having less fun and being less open with each other. Compared with other counselors, they reported small gains in their interest in children's behavior, in their own interaction with friends, and in mental health work. Vocational goals tended to change away from person-oriented professions. They described the sensitivity-training groups and the two-person programmed instruction on interpersonal relations as less helpful, showed fewer gains on the Social Insight Test, and were more frequently rated as rigid on the Adjective Check List. They spent more money and did more sightseeing than others. These weak but unidirectional findings do raise the possibility that more frequent movie attendance may be a product of a less satisfactory companionship.

Tutoring. Counselors seldom helped their boys with schoolwork; 40 per cent of the dyads never did homework together. It was their choice. A minority (about 10 per cent) did have something that vaguely resembled a tutoring relationship; they attended to studies approximately once in eight sessions. The typical dyad held tutoring sessions once or twice during the entire companionship. Homework was somewhat more popular with less mobile dyads.

Third Parties. Two thirds of the dyads never visited a friend of the counselor. Those that did usually made one visit during the program, had access to a car or bike, liked to take rides, and seldom stayed at the boy's home. Boys and counselors assessed as outgoing were more likely to visit one of the counselor's friends. In most instances, friend meant girl friend.

We had asked the dyads not to make a habit of including extra people in their meetings. Some counselors and boys felt hampered by our wish to minimize third persons, but they generally complied. About one in five visits included an extra person. Forty of the typical dyads' fifty visits were of a one-to-one nature. The inclusion of extra persons increased in frequency over time; during the final period, it occurred about once in four sessions (Figure 1). We isolated a subgroup that brought in others every third session (aproximately 20 per cent of the entire sample). In comparison with other groups, this group had few lengthy conversations, and the counselors reported that they knew little about what their boys felt and that they themselves did not disclose much to their boys. In contrast, their boys saw counselors as quite self-disclosing. These dyads rarely worked on a hobby and were low on the quiet activities category. They were also low on hiking and sightseeing and tended toward longer visits.

The function of third-person mediation is still an open and important question for companionship therapies. Obviously, much depends on whether the guest is a peer of the boy or the counselor. We feel that *some* intrusion is helpful, especially after the dyads are well acquainted and ready to be with each other in new interpersonal situations. The situation is too complex to establish an absolute frequency criterion for safe third-person intervention, but our guess is that it lies somewhere near once in three meetings—*after* the dyad is well acquainted.

Visit Length. One to four hours were the outer limits suggested for visit length. Any sizable deviations from those limits required permission from the project staff. Sometimes the dyads wanted to spend an entire day together, and we tried not to discourage these occasional long visits. However, we limited the counselor's pay to six hours per visit and asked the dyads not to make extra-long visits a habit. These restrictions were based on budget considerations and our assumption that a pattern of more frequent shorter visits was better than infrequent long visits. That assumption proved wrong (see Chapter Eight).

As the program ended, we asked the counselors whether we should change the limits on the number of hours per visit. Two thirds said "no," and many indicated that we should continue being lenient about the breaking of rules. Many that wanted change said we should extend the upper limit to allow all-day activities and weekend camping trips. Actually, the average meeting length was substantial: almost three hours. The mean length of visits increased after period I and remained quite constant thereafter. Outgoing counselors were significantly involved in longer visits. If the companionships were built around some goal-oriented activity such as tutoring or asking the boy to talk of his personal problems, the length of visits would have probably been much shorter—perhaps more like those fifty-minute therapy hours.

Spending. About two thirds of the dyads managed their activities at the prescribed budget level (five dollars a month), and many spent considerably less. The remaining dyads tried their hands at deficit spending and wound up in the red. Some of the boys and counselors complained about their skimpy allowance and offered details on its restrictive effects. A few sat down to negotiate with the project staff and sometimes were given additional expenses for special activities. Those without private transportation were given extra money for bus fare. In general, spending did increase significantly over time, particularly betwen periods I and II. The mean expenditure was sixty-two cents per visit and $29.91 (about three fourths of their allowance) over the entire companionship. The five-dollar-a-month maximum probably presented unfair restrictions to some pairs with special interests. But we suspect that the essential budget problems for most participants involved the making of joint decisions for spending their allowance in mutually satisfying ways. We welcomed these problems because their successful solutions required the learning of collaboration.

Summary

Because we wanted to limit our intrusion into the companionships, few questions were asked of boys until the program had finished. Most of our description of the companionship process came from counselors' reports made after each visit. Typically, dyads met twice a week for three-hour visits over an eight-month span for a total of 141 hours. They spent about thirty dollars of the forty allotted to them for incidental items.

A Visit Report form took counselors about thirteen minutes to complete after each session. The forms were turned in to the project office once a week and were carefully read by staff for signs of trouble. Visit Report forms contained check lists for activities, topics of conversation, and interpersonal-closeness scale, a set of items for describing feelings and behavior, and a limited space for a brief running account of the visit. Other observations on the companionship process were drawn from questionnaires given to counselors, boys, and parents after the companionships were completed.

Initial meetings were without incident but were frequently described as tense and impersonal and less warm than subsequent visits. Dyads destined for attrition appeared to signal themselves during the first visit through ratings of boy tension plus boy and counselor coolness. Because so many of the initial visits were satisfactory, we suggested the feasibility of initiating other forms of non-professional relationships without the customary professional intervention.

The companionships were an active practice ground for boys and counselors to learn about collaboration. Almost half of the decisions on what to do during visits were made jointly (most of the remaining decisions were made by boys). Boys had power of choice in the companionships and often converted their wishes into activity. Counselors reported between two and three activities per visit. Active sports and lengthy visits to the boy's home were the two most frequent activities—followed by quiet activities, walks, sitting down to talk, sharing a meal, sightseeing, working on hobbies, using the television or records, visiting the counselor's place, and going for an auto ride. Less frequent activities were going to sports events or to movies, doing homework, and visiting the counselor's friend. A third person entered the companionship about once in five visits. Changes in the frequency of activities over the three thirds of the companionship were displayed and discussed.

VI

Conversation,
Feelings, and
Termination

The procedure for structuring the boy-counselor interaction (Chapter Four) was designed to generate processes occurring in two forms of human relationship: psychotherapy and companionship. Our findings on activity choice indicate a considerable pursuit of collaborative activities and the sustained sharing of personal interests. These are essential characteristics of social companionships. In contrast to companionship, psychotherapy is usually based on the contractual expectation that patients will frequently disclose private feelings. The participating boys did not expect to discuss

96

private topics, but counselors were selected for their capacity to self-disclose, empathize, and show positive regard for the intimate communication of others. We hypothesized that the counselors' interpersonal style would draw much personal disclosure from their boys. Thus, our policy for structuring the relationships was intended to foster collaboration common to social companionship, while our selection and orientation of counselors was intended to foster the exploration of intimate topics common to therapy. This chapter discusses findings on interpersonal processes relevant to therapeutic change.

Conversation Topics

We asked counselors to check topics on the Visit Report only when those topics were part of an interchange that felt "significant," "meaningful," or "important"—even if the interchange was very brief. The use of a check list (component 2 of the Visit Report form) required much subjective counselor judgment, but we were willing to live with these impressionistic data because of their uniqueness and potential ability to predict. Most of the counselors checked between three and six topics per visit. The typical counselor described five topics per visit as important or meaningful. If that frequency seems high for a three-hour visit filled with various activities, it is because topic categories were frequently checked in pairs. A counselor discussing his own personality or behavior might create a climate where the boy would want to reciprocate.

The category list was developed from a smaller pilot study. The "other" category on the finished Visit Report form was used for about 10 per cent of the responses. Most of these were transferred to specific categories. Topics specific to the boy were listed with over twice the frequency (50 per cent) of topics specific to counselors (22 per cent).

Current and Past Activities. Current and past activities was the broadest and most commonly checked category—representing about 15 per cent of all interchange considered important; most of it focused on the present (see Figure 2). Talking about "now"

FIGURE 2.　Changes in topics of conversation (eighty-eight companionships)

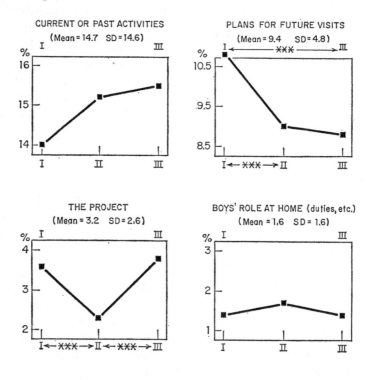

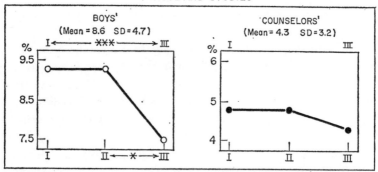

Asterisks denote significance of change between periods (I, beginning; II, middle; III, final spanned by arrows: * = .10, ** = .05, *** = .01. % indicates proportion of all topics reported by counselors—approximately five topics checked per visit.

FIGURE 2. Changes in topics of conversation (eighty-eight companionships) (Cont.)

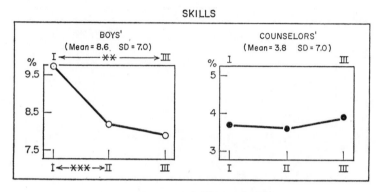

SKILLS

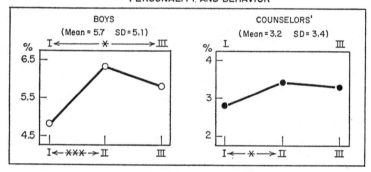

PERSONALITY AND BEHAVIOR

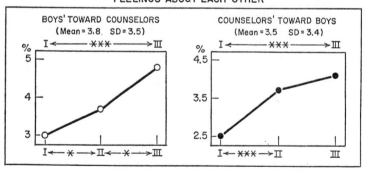

FEELINGS ABOUT EACH OTHER

Asterisks denote significance of change between periods (I, beginning; II, middle; III, final spanned by arrows: * = .10, ** = .05, *** = .01. % indicates proportion of all topics reported by counselors—approximately five topics checked per visit.

FIGURE 2.   Changes in topics of conversation (eighty-eight companionships) (Cont.)

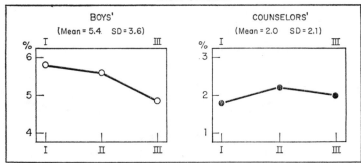

THEIR FRIENDS

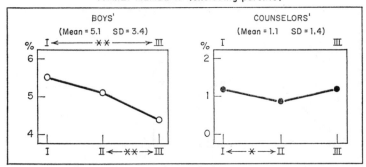

FAMILY MEMBERS (excluding parents)

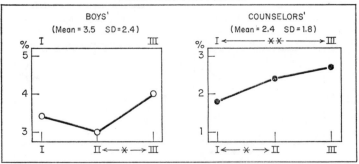

VACATIONS AND TRAVELS

Asterisks denote significance of change between periods (I, beginning; II, middle; III, final spanned by arrows: * = .10, ** = .05, *** = .01. % indicates proportion of all topics reported by counselors—approximately five topics checked per visit.

FIGURE 2. Changes in topics of conversation (eighty-eight companionships) (Cont.)

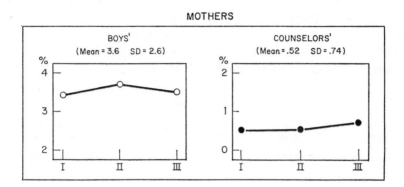

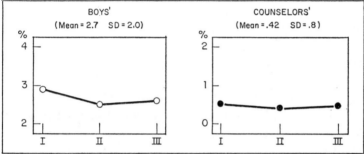

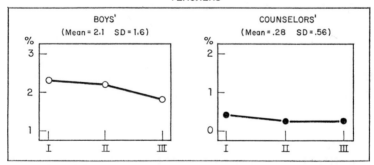

Asterisks denote significance of change between periods (I, beginning; II, middle; III, final spanned by arrows: * = .10, ** = .05, *** = .01. % indicates proportion of all topics reported by counselors—approximately five topics checked per visit.

can be just the opposite from being spontaneous when things at hand are used as a distraction from feelings at hand. Crowding the companionship with talk of current activities can leave little room for sharing personal thoughts. Our findings suggest that this occurred for some pairs. Those with very high scores on current and past activities checked few other categories. They seldom talked about significant others in their lives or about school and rarely worked on the boy's schoolwork. These counselors described their talk as less personal and less open. They went sightseeing and to movies more often than other dyads. We can imagine an almost rigid adherence to the mechanics of the present, but that is speculation beyond the data. High scores on this category could simply be a reflection of some counselors' response style. That is, the category is broad enough to be used as a "response wastebasket." Such an interpretation is weakened by the strong set of correlations with various indices of distance in the companionships—for instance, with low disclosure scores on the Relationship Index and the Self-Disclosure Questionnaire and a low score on the interpersonal-closeness scale of the Visit Report.

Future Visits. Almost 10 per cent of all meaningful interchange reported was about future visits. The typical boy and counselor discussed future activities during twenty-three of their fifty meetings. Here are some examples: "When we discussed next time, Stu took an 'I'll-do-whatever-you-want' attitude again. I insisted he tell me what *he* wanted. He said he wanted to see the go-carts run and wanted me to bring more of my stamp collection. His face lit up." "I was in the neighborhood and decided to drop in on Norman. He was doing nothing, didn't want to go out, didn't want me to stay, seemed very quiet, and said he would rather go out next time. But he kept saying 'no' to all my suggestions. I was surprised at his being so turned off and asked him why. He only shrugged and mumbled 'Nothing.' It was awkward talking of the future." "We discussed future projects and planned all sorts of things—building a rabbit cage, fixing his tree house, hiking in Tilden [Park], getting wood for my fireplace, seeing a basketball game, building a soap box racer . . . more than we'll ever do." Such planning talk decreased sharply after the initial period but still remained one of the most common topic categories (see Figure

2). The decrease was probably due to an increased familiarity with each other's habits. Some counselors and boys worried about their partners' desire to continue in the companionship—especially during the initial period. The high incidence of important planning talks during early visits may have stemmed from these concerns.

The Project. Talk about the project was much more evident during the beginning and end phases of the companionships. At the beginning, boys wanted to know how their counselors were chosen, why they joined, why the program existed. During the final period, they talked about vacation plans, the project's ending, why the program did not run throughout the summer. The typical pair had eight significant discussions about the project.

School. Commonly, the boy's school life was talked about more than the counselor's college studies. The typical dyad had twenty-one interchanges about the boy's school or studies, compared to eleven for the counselor. Discussions of the boy's school life apparently stimulated talk about the counselor's college life. (The two categories correlated significantly at $r = .59$.) Eventually, especially during the final period, significantly less attention was paid to the boy's school life. The strong positive correlations between these topic categories and the category labeled "teacher" support the internal reliability of the topic checklist. Dyads who were unusually high on these categories spent more time on the boy's homework than the remaining dyads. They also made more lengthy visits to the boy's home, spent less of their allowance, discussed their parents frequently, and tended to neglect conversation about their own personalities, behavior, and feelings about one another.

Skills. Erikson (1950) believes that the central developmental task for children like those in our project is the learning of productive skills: industry versus inferiority (p. 226). Children at this stage, according to Erikson, realize that their future lies outside the family and therefore begin to garner skills. They learn to win recognition by showing that they can produce things. We believe that this concern with taking on skill and displaying talent was, at least, one central event in the lives of our boys. The counselors were in a good position to teach and admire. Boys were eager to learn and demonstrate. Talking of the boys' skills was one of the most popular topics—especially during the first period. Typically, twenty-one of the fifty visits contained some meaningful interchange on boy's skill, although conversation on this topic decreased significantly over the companionships, especially after period I.

Counselors' skills were discussed less often (typically, about nine times). Ten per cent of the counselors never talked of them seriously. The correlation between conversation on boy and counselor skill was significantly positive ($r = .44$), which suggests that it was another reciprocal topic.

Personality and Behavior. The most reciprocal topic category was personality and behavior: talk of the boy's personality was likely to stimulate talk of the counselor's personality or vice versa ($r = .78$). Again, the focus was on boys almost twice as much as on counselors (typically, fourteen versus eight visits). This was an important topic category because it probably reflected talk aimed directly at personal problems. Much of it had a therapeutic flavor and focused on both boy and counselor:

> I told him the reason I didn't help him [across a stream] was because I thought he was doing ok and he wasn't asking for help. I told him, though, that I felt that he should be more independent and that I liked to see him doing things on his own and I did try to let him do things on his own. He said his mother "babied" him and though he tried to be less of a "baby" it was hard for him to do.

> Jay said that he found it very hard to ask me to help him with [his] homework. I told him, in great length, that I liked to help him and if he wanted help to ask me. I have a tendency to talk a point to death and was doing so with this one when Jay cut me short by saying "You're talking too much, Ron." In good humor I agreed and he went on to say that previously he would have been unable to criticize me, but now there was no need to hide.

> He shocked me at one point by commenting that I looked sad, which I was. This is a very new closeness for us.

The increases in the personality and behavior category over time are probably simple functions of increased trust and acceptance. If so, the significant change between periods I and II may offer clues about the development of closeness. Most dyads reached their peak of discussion on personality during period II and maintained it to the end. It takes, roughly, three months for most companionships to settle into close personal talk about each other.

Ten per cent of the dyads never had talks about the boy's personality that the counselor considered meaningful, and almost 25 per cent never had meaningful talks about the counselor's personality. These pairs tended to do more talking about school, studies, vacations, families, friends, and future visits. They spent more time watching television and working on hobbies. In contrast, those who talked about each other's personalities and behavior more than average tended to talk more frequently about their skills and their feelings toward each other. These dyads had a disproportionate number of counselors who were in the training groups. They rated the communication in the companionship as more personal, described themselves as disclosing much, and saw their boys as more angry and attempting to control more frequently. Their boys partially agreed by describing themselves as somewhat pushy and less self-disclosed. They spent more time together.

Feelings about Each Other. This category is related to the personality and behavior category (mean $r = .30$). As expected, scores for boys and counselors were strongly linked ($r = .70$). This type of interchange increased significantly over the span of the companionships, and counselors showed a sharp gain in expressing feelings about their boys during period II (Figure 2). Unlike the scores in preceding categories, the counselor and boy mean scores were quite similar on feelings about each other (typically, about ten times for the counselor and nine times for the boy). Here are some examples: "We both tried to 'make contact' several times, but didn't quite make it. I told Harvey that I wanted to be involved and interested, but couldn't seem to." "Brewster talked about the short time we had left together and said he hated to lose me because there was nobody else he could talk 'personally' to." "I said I got the feeling that I was bossy because he agreed with me a lot . . . and that I would like it if he were more willing to disagree or show anger when he felt it."

High scores on feelings about each other were associated with high ratings on boy and counselor expression of anger during the companionship; lengthier visits; higher scores on the activity

categories sitting down to talk, hiking or walking, and lengthy visit
to the boy's home; and lower scores on seeing a movie, watching
television, and sightseeing. High scores were also associated with
trained counselors, counselors' religious commitment, and counselors' self-disclosure to the boy. According to Visit Report data, 14
per cent of the boys and 18 per cent of the counselors never expressed important feelings about each other to each other.

Friends. The companions talked about the boys' friends more
than twice as much as the counselors' friends (thirteen versus five
times for the typical dyad). Every boy mentioned a friend in a
meaningful interchange at least once, but 25 per cent of the counselors never discussed their friends. Many of the boys expressed
problems in getting along with peer acquaintances or simply lacked
regular friends: "He talked of his imaginary friend 'Superfink'
for the second time (actually, Shelly's secret self)." "Bernie feels
that he is ahead of kids his age and prefers older boys . . . but he
can't keep up with them in athletic things, which causes some
problems."

Parents. Sixty per cent of the counselors said that they
never discussed their mothers in a significant way. In contrast, the
boy's mother was a meaningful part of the typical dyad's talk nine
times. Scores on this topic were positively related to the boy's self-
described disclosure score on the Relationship Index, the counselor's
retrospective description of how much he told the boy, and the
counselor's helping the boy with homework. They were negatively
related to talk about the boy's personality and behavior. Here are
some examples: "At the supermarket he told me what his mother
did and did not buy—and how she did things correctly. It seemed
to me that he felt she had to be right, or at least he wasn't about
to show his disagreement." "The most significant thing was Saul's
description of how he sees his mother's behavior as different from
other mothers. He almost said that it was hurtful to him."

Scores on significant talk about fathers show that it occurs
somewhat less than talk of mothers but retains the same large
discrepancy between boys' and counselors' fathers (typically, boy's
father = seven times, counselor's father = once). It appears that
the boys' fathers were frequent topics for those dyads who had the

habit of sitting down for long talks. In general, the boys' parents were popular subjects for conversation: one or the other parent was discussed approximately every third meeting. Talk of counselors' parents occurred about once in every twenty-five meetings.

Interpersonal Closeness. Counselors described the degree of intimacy in communication during each visit on a four-point scale of interpersonal closeness contained in the Visit Report (component 5 in Table 9). Since the counselors' ratings for their boys and themselves were identical most of the time, we combined them into a single score. Scores varied widely within dyads over visits. Mean scores offer a crude index of communication quality over the entire program. Three per cent of the dyads produced means close to the bottom of the scale (nonpersonal). These dyads reported only a few visits where important feelings or thoughts were revealed. Twenty-seven per cent of the dyads discussed personal feelings slightly during half of their visits. Over half (55 per cent) talked "quite" personally during one of four visits. The remaining dyads (15 per cent) generated means approaching the third step (quite personal); this group shared deep personal feelings during 20 per cent of their meetings.

The mean *combined* score for all dyads was near the slightly personal point (3.72, with a standard deviation of .72; see Table 9). Period I showed the lowest level of personal communication (3.64); the level increased during period II (3.77) and remained constant to termination. The increases between periods I and II, and I and III, were significant at the .10 level. Two previously mentioned topic categories (personality and behavior, feelings about each other) also produced significant gains between periods I and II. These findings support the notion that between two and three months of companionship are needed before personal communication becomes a habit.

Patterns of Feeling and Behavior

Eight bipolar items in a semantic-differential format filled the second page of the Visit Report form (Table 9). These items represented the major dimensions of feeling and behavior that appeared most meaningful to counselors during our pilot research. The items contained space for the counselor to describe himself and his boy.

Mean scores were computed for each item across all visits. For instance, a boy's mean score on the board-interested item usually used ratings from fifty visits and represented his counselor's continued assessment of the dimension over seven or eight months. From this, we can speak of interest level as a condition of the entire companionship derived from continued visit-to-visit descriptions.

We expected considerable mutual influence in the companionships, and out data suggest that it occurred. A bored counselor could engender boredom in his boy. Spending three hours with a boy in an anxious mood could stimulate tension in a counselor. On five of the eight dimensions, counselors' ratings of themselves and their boys correlated in the eighties (an r of $.28 = p < .01$). Since these correlations were done on mean scores covering the entire companionship period, it appears that the mutual influence went beyond single meetings—that the similarities measured were of general interaction styles within the companionships. Notions about counselor projection might also be used to explain some of the similarity in ratings. Another possibility is a strain-toward-symmetry hypothesis: "I want my boy and me to be close, to like the same things, and for him to respond to me as I do to him." Both of these response biases may be operating but seem to be weaker explanations than that of a real mutual influence of behavior and feeling—an influence that increases over time. The notion is supported by findings that show a significant increase in the similarity of boy-counselor ratings over the companionships; five of the eight dimensions (comfortable, outgoing, relaxed, nondemanding, and interesting) generate decreasing distance scores over the three time periods at the .01 level. Emotionally open became more similar at the .10 level, while the happy and warm dimensions remained constant.

Counselors were not prone to rating feelings and behavior during visits in an extremely favorable or socially desirable manner. The group means do indicate that most companionships were seen as more interesting than boring, more warm than cool, more comfortable than not. A composite of those items that could be aligned in a favorable direction was put together, and its mean fell near the "slightly" marker point, one third of the way toward "quite" favorable (see Table 9). Boy ratings were more favorable than those for counselors, especially in periods I and II (see "A Composite Favorability Score," Figure 3, pp. 111–113). Generally the rather favorable picture the counselors made reached its height during the final period. The self-descriptions of counselors remained constant in favorability during the first two thirds of the companionships and gained significantly ($p = .05$) during the final period. The composite favorability score for boys decreased between periods I and II as they were seen becoming more bossy and less interested, but the trend reversed and the curve reached its peak during period III. From our counselor's vantage point, the companionships appeared warmer, more open, and generally more positive during the final period.

The correlations in Table 10 create a pattern that supports the internal coherence of the counselors' ratings. For example, the item labeled "uncomfortable" shows its strongest negative correlation with relaxed and is also negatively associated with warm, outgoing, and open. Uncomfortable has a positive association with bored, sad, and bossy. Nondemanding-bossy, and quiet-outgoing are two dimensions with markedly lower boy-counselor correlation. These are probably the result of our initial matching process, which paired half the dyads into combinations dissimilar on a dimension that could be introversion-extroversion, reserved-intrusive, quiet-outgoing. Apparently, the lower correlations reflect the counselors' perception of discrepancy in interpersonal style. Counselors who characterized their boys as nondemanding were as likely to describe themselves as more outgoing and vice versa. This tendency was largely responsible for the lack of association between the combined scores for bossy and outgoing seen in Table 10.

Interest and Boredom. Boredom was a minor part of the companionships, according to counselors. However, they described their boys as significantly more interested than themselves during all three periods ($p < .05$). Interest slackened during the middle period, especially for the boys, but picked up again during period III (see Figure 3 for change curves on all dimensions). High interest scores for boys and counselors were positively associated with

Table 10

INTERCORRELATIONS OF FEELING AND BEHAVIOR SCALES

		1 Bored	2 Open	3 Bossy	4 Relaxed	5 Outgoing	6 Uncomfortable	7 Warm	8 Sad
Bored	1	(.82)[a]							
Open	2	−55[b]	(.81)						
Bossy	3	41	−20	(.36)					
Relaxed	4	−61	40	−53	(.83)				
Outgoing	5	−52	48	14	56	(.45)			
Uncomfortable	6	68	−45	53	−87	−57	(.82)		
Warm	7	−67	.60	−33	52	57	−67	(.84)	
Sad	8	54	−30	36	−50	−37	.64	−.68	(.85)

[a] Correlations in parentheses are between ratings of boy and counselor; for example, mean ratings for boy and counselor on bored correlated .82. Except for correlations in parentheses, boy and counselor scores are combined.

[b] r of .18 = p .10; r of .21 = p .05; r of .28 = p .01, for an N of 88.

FIGURE 3. Changes in feelings and behavior ratings (eighty-eight companionships)

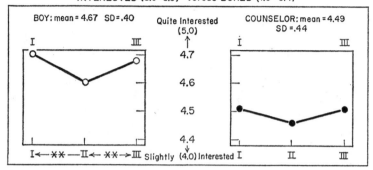

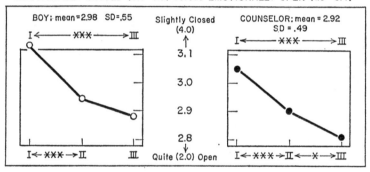

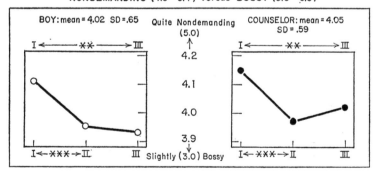

Behavior ratings are those of the counselors (see the sixth component of Table 9). "Bored": extremely = 1.0, quite = 2.0, slightly = 3.0; versus "interested": slightly = 4.0, quite = 5.0, extremely = 6.0. Asterisks denote significance of change between periods (I, beginning; II, middle; III, final) spanned by arrows. Composite favorability score is the mean of seven items arbitrarily aligned in a favorable direction: interested, open, nondemanding, relaxed, comfortable, warm, happy. Quiet-outgoing was omitted.

FIGURE 3.   Changes in feelings and behavior ratings (eighty-eight companionships) (Cont.)

TENSE (3.6-6.0) versus RELAXED (1.0-3.4)

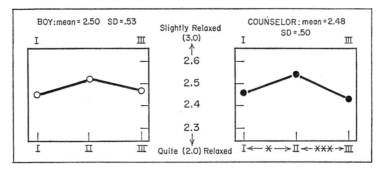

QUIET (3.6-6.0) versus OUTGOING (1.0-3.4)

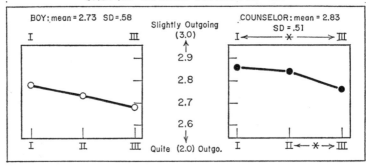

COMFORTABLE (3.6-6.0) versus UNCOMFORTABLE (1.0-3.4)

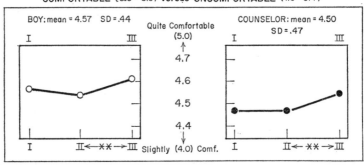

Behavior ratings are those of the counselors (see the sixth component of Table 9). "Bored": extremely = 1.0, quite = 2.0, slightly = 3.0; versus "interested": slightly = 4.0, quite = 5.0, extremely = 6.0. Asterisks denote significance of change between periods (I, beginning; II, middle; III, final) spanned by arrows. Composite favorability score is the mean of seven items arbitrarily aligned in a favorable direction: interested, open, nondemanding, relaxed, comfortable, warm, happy. Quiet-outgoing was omitted.

FIGURE 3.   Changes in feelings and behavior ratings (eighty-eight companionships) (Cont.)

COOL TOWARD PARTNER (3.6 – 6.0) versus WARM TOWARD PARTNER (1.0 – 3.4)

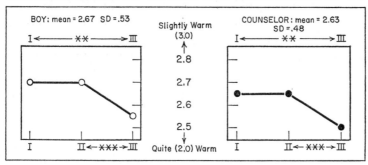

HAPPY (3.6 – 6.0) versus SAD (1.0 – 3.4)

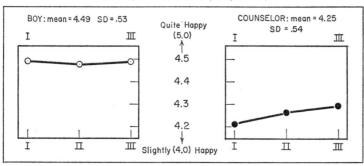

A COMPOSITE FAVORABILITY SCORE

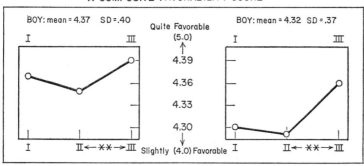

Behavior ratings are those of the counselors (see the sixth component of Table 9). "Bored": extremely = 1.0, quite = 2.0, slightly = 3.0; versus "interested": slightly = 4.0, quite = 5.0, extremely = 6.0. Asterisks denote significance of change between periods (I, beginning; II, middle; III, final) spanned by arrows. Composite favorability score is the mean of seven items arbitrarily aligned in a favorable direction: interested, open, nondemanding, relaxed, comfortable, warm, happy. Quiet-outgoing was omitted.

the counselors' description of self-disclosure, fun, and knowledge of each other's feelings in the dyad (Relationship Index). High interest was negatively related to the anger score on the same questionnaire, heavy participation in active sports, and meaningful talk of current and past activities. Interest was positively correlated with the frequency of activities over the companionship. In addition, high counselor interest was positively related with visits to the counselor's place, spectator sports, and sitting down to talk. It was negatively related with attending movies, watching television or listening to records, and the counselor's view of his boy's attempt to control.

Emotionally Closed versus Open. The feeling and behavior scale that showed the most consistent change over time was emotionally closed versus emotionally open. The counselors' mean descriptions of themselves and their boys was near the "slightly open" marker point during period I and moved significantly ($p <$ .01) toward the "quite open" marker by period III. Actually, most of the change occurred between periods I and II. At all three time points, counselors rated themselves slightly (nonsignificantly) more open than their boys. Openness correlated significantly with the following: the counselor's retrospective view of his experience of being known by the boy, his boy's disclosure, and his estimate of the boy's fun (all on the Relationship Index), his score on how much he told the boy (revised Self-Disclosure Questionnaire), the interpersonal-closeness scale, sitting down to talk, and talk about the boy's personality and behavior. Openness was negatively related to participating in active sports and using television or records as entertainment. According to Table 10, the least open companionships were the least warm; that is, the counselors' attribution of meaning for openness had much warmth in it.

The sharp rise in openness between periods I and II parallels similar gains in the topic categories "feelings about each other" and "personality and behavior." Once again, the findings point to the notion that intimacy in these companionships generally reaches its peak after two or three months.

Nondemanding versus Bossy. Those changes toward more openness and more meaningful talk about each other were paralleled by a significant increase over periods I and II in the demands counselors and boys made upon each other ($p < .01$). Greater closeness brought greater demands. Nondemanding-bossy was the most independent of all feeling and behavior items (see Table 10). Counselors tended to see one member of the pair as more bossy and the other as more quiet. The disparity between ratings on counselor and boy was greater than for any other dimension. Appropriately, the correlation between counselor and boy on this dimension was weakest.

Nondemanding scores were negatively related to the boy's self-description "I try to get him to do what I want." This finding adds some support to the validity of counselors' ratings. Nondemanding scores also correlate positively with the boy's experience of being known by his counselor, the counselor's experience of being known by his boy, and both of their ratings of each other's fun.

Tension. Counselors typically described the visits as "slightly" or "quite" relaxed. They rated themselves as less relaxed during the middle period. We cannot explain the change. High scores on tense were significantly correlated with the following Relationship Index ratings: boy's and counselor's descriptions of each other's anger, lack of fun, and lack of knowing each other's feelings. High tense scores were also associated with much participation in active sports, talking about the boy's teacher and mother, and the counselor's personality and behavior.

Quiet and Outgoing. Behavior during the visits was typically described as a little more than slightly outgoing. Quietness was associated with counselors' describing themselves and their boys as discussing fewer feelings and having less fun. Boys with high quiet scores said that they seldom tried to control their counselor. High quiet scores were negatively correlated with the interpersonal-closeness scale—suggesting that for counselors quietness meant less personal discussion during the visit. Counselors described boys as more outgoing than themselves. Both showed some move toward outgoing over the companionships. Those counselors who were placed in the "quiet" subgroup at the program's start rated themselves as more quiet throughout the companionships ($p < .05$).

Comfort. When counselors tended to rate visits as quite comfortable, their boys usually described themselves as feeling more understood and less angry on the Relationship Index. Counselors in these comfortable dyads said that their boys told much about themselves, had a lot of fun, attempted to control rarely, and "understands how I feel." These pairs played at active sports less frequently but checked more activities per visit than other dyads. The uncomfortable item correlated most negatively with relaxed and warm; most positively with bored and sad (Table 10). Ratings on boys and counselors moved significantly toward quite comfortable between periods II and III. Counselors described boys as more comfortable than themselves during all three periods.

Cool and Warm. Both mean scores on cool toward partner remained unchanged on the warm side during periods I and II but moved significantly toward quite warm for period III ($p < .01$). The pattern was similar to the previously described change toward comfortable. High scores on cool toward partner were associated with several Relationship Index scores: boys' view of counselors' anger, counselors' view of anger in their boys and themselves. Cool scores correlated negatively with the counselors' ratings of partners' openness, fun, and being understood. In addition, high scores on cool were positively related to participating in active sports and talking of current or past activities; they were negatively related to discussing counselor's family and boy's feelings toward counselor.

Happy and Sad. This item did not change much over the companionship. Some counselors protested that they had little idea of what it meant, yet most rated themselves as less happy than their boys. The intercorrelations on Table 10 suggests that happiness (for a counselor in a dyad) is mostly warmth, comfort, interest and relaxation—in that order. The item correlated with the Relationship Index scores in expected directions—negatively with anger, positively with being understood, and so forth. The pattern of correlations suggests that counselors saw the boy's mood and behavior as the major determinants of the dyad's happiness.

Composite Favorability. This score was made from all feeling and behavior items (except quiet-outgoing) aligned in a direction assumed to be favorable (see last set of curves and the note in Figure 3). We found a positive relationship between favorability scores and pre-post gains on counselors' self-described Adjective Check List scales for defensive ($r = .29$) and favorability ($r = .21$). Thus, we suggest that the favorable descriptions of visits made by counselors may be a partial product of their rating style. However, placing heavy emphasis on counselor style as a determinant of favorability in Visit Report rating data may be a mistake. Correlations of composite favorability with ratings of boys by other observers in other contexts give some support to the authenticity of socially desirable descriptions made by counselors. Here are some examples: high composite favorability is significantly associated with *low* Relationship Index scores (produced by boys) on anger and high scores on understanding. Favorability is also positively related with the parents' view of problem reduction in boys ($r =$ .28 with Problem List total scores). Also, favorability correlates moderately with gains in boys' popularity among classmates ($r =$ .30). It appears that when counselors describe the visits in favorable terms, the boys are also described in a socially desirable manner by themselves, their parents, and their classmates.

Patterns of favorability scores for counselors and boys were very similar ($r = .90$). Dyads high on favorability did not participate much in active sports, and their counselors thought that the project was less work than anticipated. They changed their fields of study more than other counselors did and became more interested in working with troubled people. The most favorable descriptions occurred during the final period. A significant gain occurred between periods II and III (Figure 3), much of this gain generated by strong movement toward the warmth and comfort poles.

Dyadic Distance. The total discrepancy between the counselors' descriptions of themselves and their boys on all eight feeling and behavior scales was computed for each visit. The mean score for all visits in a companionship was labeled "dyadic distance." Larger dyadic distance scores usually indicated less satisfactory relationships from the counselors' viewpoint. Companionships were described as more tense and cool, and less open when dyadic distance scores were large. As dyadic distance increased, counselors described themselves as more bored and unhappy and less outgoing, while describing their boys as less demanding. The "fun" items described by boys on the Relationship Index were negatively correlated with dyadic distance ($r = -.30$). As shown earlier (Table 10), counselors perceived much similarity between themselves and their boys; therefore, the dyadic distance measure typically expressed small amounts of discrepancy. But these small discrepancies did show promise as predictors of boy change measures based on parent and classmate observations. For example, boys in dyads with larger dyadic distance scores were described by parents (at termination) as improving less in their attitudes toward school and in their school work ($p < .05$) and relating to peers ($p < .01$). Parents also rated fewer pre-post improvements for problems with modesty and being upset by new situations (both at $p < .01$). Classmates of these boys in more distant companionships described them as becoming less hostile, less attention-seeking (both at $p < .10$), and less likeable ($p < .05$) from pre to post on the Peer Nominations Inventory. It appears that boys in dyads described as less symmetrical or more distant make fewer gains on their problems of withdrawal in other environments.

If small dyadic distance is a fair index of intimacy in the companionship and reduced withdrawal for boys at home and in school, we can say that the companionships grew measurably more intimate and more therapeutic over time. The mean dyadic distance score for all dyads was consistently and significantly reduced over the span of the project (difference between periods I and III = $p < .01$). This finding, combined with those displayed in Figure 3, creates a picture of developing companionships that increase in emotional openness, warmth, and ability to make mutual demands as the counselors perceive greater similarity of behavior and feeling over time. It is as if they were saying, "Our behavior and feelings became more alike as we gained in genuineness, warmth, and willingness to ask things of each other."

Termination

The decision to set a definite termination date instead of allowing companionships to close "naturally" was based on budget limitations, the inability of many counselors and boys to continue during the summer (because of graduation, summer camp, new jobs), and our assumption that a predetermined date would allow better preparation for the termination.

The thought of terminating the companionships gave us more concern than starting them. A few colleagues were especially worried about feelings of rejection and loss in the boys—particularly those without fathers in their home. Some planners of companionship programs for fatherless boys have worked on the assumption that a wholesome termination could bring about a therapeutic reliving of the earlier destructive loss. Our plan was to help participants prepare appropriate expectations for the ending at an early point in the companionships. We wanted them to have frequent discussions about their parting, so that it could become a useful and perhaps a less painful experience. The following instruction was part of a list given to all counselors during their orientation: "It is *absolutely necessary* that during the early visits you let the boy know that the companionship will end in June. If you neglect this point, the boy may not be prepared for the separation and he may feel badly let down." The time-limited nature of the program was also emphasized in the acceptance letter to parents: "Counselors and parents should be sure that boys know the relationships will end in June. . . . We do not want the ending to be a surprise." An additional reminder was sent to the counselors one month before the official close of the program: "It is now time to discuss thoroughly the ending of the project with your boy. If you plan to see, write, or call him after the first week in June, please be conservative with your promises. For most boys, the anticipation of parting is less uncomfortable than the disappointment of a broken promise. . . . If you feel the termination might be difficult, please contact us at once." If the counselor or the parents anticipated that the ending would be particularly difficult for the boy, the project was prepared to intervene—to confer with the boy, counselor, and parents and to extend the companionship if possible.

Extending companionships beyond the official termination date was rarely considered a necessity. However, some informal boy-counselor contact after the official ending was observed for 87 per cent of the dyads. Nearly two thirds had one or more additional meetings; some counselors wrote letters from other cities or kept in touch through phone calls. Departing counselors often left some form of remembrance—cats, dogs, hobby material. One mechanically inclined boy inherited a disassembled motor scooter. Despite our warnings, several counselors made firm promises to visit their boys during the summer and failed to appear.

Difficult and Easy Endings. A questionnaire given to counselors near the termination date contained the item "Do you think the ending of the project will be hard on your boy? yes——— no——— describe———." Responses were quite evenly divided: 54 per cent "yes" and 46 per cent "no." Varied explanations accompanied the responses. Those who said "yes" explained that their boys had few other friends, would miss the guidance, and still needed a father substitute or someone to rescue them from a drab existence. A few counselors thought that their boys would miss the opportunities provided by the project more than they would miss the personal relationship provided by the counselor. Many who agreed that the ending would be hard also predicted that their boys would successfully cope with the bad feelings—usually because they were well prepared for the loss. Here are some examples: "I seem to be the only friend with whom he can be assertive and masculine." "His father is no longer at home and I feel he wants older male guidance." "Eliot needs someone who gives him something to do besides watching TV all day in a stuffy, hot, boring room." "He will miss our activities. But, alas, *I* will not be missed very much."

Counselors who predicted that the ending would not be hard for their boys thought that the preparation had greatly reduced the problem or that the companionship was simply not close enough or important to their boys. Some counselors saw themselves replaced by new peer friendships. Summer trips and vacations were also seen as compensation for the ending of the companionship. Here are some quotes from counselors who described easier endings. "We've lived through the ending with long talks during the past two months." "We didn't get close enough to make our separating a painful thing." "He came to regard me just like another school friend." "He seemed a bit bored with me." "He has made lots of new friends lately."

In general, the "hard-ending" boys tended to be seen as more dependent or more emotionally involved with their counselors. This impression is bolstered by a finding from the counselors' final questionnaire. The "hard-ending" boys more frequently asked their counselors to "call, write, or visit after the project terminates" ($p < .01$). These boys, in contrast to the "easy-ending" boys, had spent more time with their counselors ($p < .01$), had counselors who told their boys how they felt about them more often ($p < .01$), and described their visits as more comfortable and interesting ($p < .05$). The "easy-ending" dyads produced lower interpersonal-closeness scores on their visit reports ($p < .05$). Boys in these dyads were described as more tense during visits ($p < .05$). It does appear that difficult terminations are most frequently associated with companionships that are emotionally close and comfortable.

Our attempt to gather systematic information from the boys' observations on termination was confounded because so many were still in contact with their counselors at the point of data collection. Those who did not anticipate further contact were almost always able to express some sadness or ambivalence during a structured interview (story-completion interview, Appendix G): "Very sad, like you're losing your brother." "Not real unhappy I guess, but kinda bad." "It didn't make me happy or sorry—sort of fifty-fifty." A few expressed relief: ". . . better, because I didn't get to see my other friends on Tuesdays and Thursdays."

A follow-up interview with parents (Appendix F) did not produce any accounts of severe reactions to termination. A couple of boys were seen crying after the last meeting, and several parents felt that the discomfort of termination was needlessly prolonged through the broken promises of counselors who planned summer meetings with their boys: "As June wore on and Ed failed to call, Jimmy seemed hurt but would not talk about it. He saw Ed on the street once (being unseen himself) but did not approach. A few weeks later, Ed did call to apologize for not visiting and told of the unexpected difficulties he was having in summer school and promised to visit Jimmy soon. He never did. It took away all the good things that happened in the companionship." Our attempts to orient counselors toward using great care in making promises to their boys obviously failed in some cases. In future programs, therefore, we believe that methods beyond ours (for instance, asking the boy and counselor to discuss termination with a staff member during the final stages of the companionship, or providing counselors with vivid descriptions of negative effects from broken promises in previous companionships) should be tried.

Willingness to Continue Companionships. At the closing of

the year, counselors were questioned on the dyads' feelings about continuing the companionships beyond the official termination date. Their responses broadened our view of the conditions surrounding termination. A clear majority of counselors described their boys as wishing to continue (85 per cent). Two thirds of the counselors said that they would like to continue (65 per cent). We divided the responses into four categories: both described as wanting to continue; both not wanting to go on; boy wanting to and counselor not; counselor wanting to and boy not. Then we did an impressionistic content analysis of the counselor's open-ended comments in each category. Here is what we found:

> *Both boy and counselor unwilling to continue* (11 per cent): Most of the comments pointed to the boy as being uninterested in his counselor—with frequent lack of interest also on the counselor's part: "[He] wants the things I buy him and not me—I'm frustrated." "Just didn't seem to want me any more, and besides I'm neglecting my girl friend and buddies." "He's just using me to please his ma." "We both prefer to spend our time with peers." "He only responds when I treat him like a baby."

> *Boy does not want to continue—counselor wants to* (2 per cent): In these cases the counselors saw their boys as very troubled and withdrawn and in need of more companionship.

> *Both want to continue* (65 per cent): The most frequent response (about 25 per cent) described the pair as wanting and needing more time to "finish the job" and develop the friendship. Almost as frequent were a group of comments simply stating that it was fun and they liked each other. Some wanted to go on beyond the close of the school year so that they could continue without homework demands and project demands (primarily, our rules about length of visits). About 15 per cent would prefer to meet less often—about once a week instead of the usual twice-a-week format imposed by the project.

> *Boy wants to continue—counselor does not* (20 per cent): Almost half of these counselors complained that the companionships were too demanding or caused strain: "I can't stand to see what his mother is doing to him." "Trying to do a whole range of things without a car is too much of a hassle." "John needs more love, attention, and time than I can give him." "[I] need a vacation from responsibilities." Remaining comments were mixed: "It was a job. Much of it got done. Now for something new." "Now he's

starting to make his own friends, so it's better for me not to get in his way." Often, counselors went out of their way to tell us that they did, however, want to visit their boys once in a while.

Summary

Conversation topics that appeared meaningful to counselors were recorded at the rate of three to six topics per visit. The pair talked about the boy's life twice as much as they talked about the counselor's. Frequent topics of conversation were current or past activities, plans for future visits, boy's school studies, boy's skills, boy's personality and behavior, boy's friends and family members (excluding parents). Less frequent topics were the feelings of counselors and boys for each other, vacations, parents, teachers, and counselors' family members. Patterns of topic change over the companionships were displayed and discussed. Correlations between topics were also discussed.

Intimacy of communication during each visit was assessed through a four-step scale ranging from nonpersonal to deeply personal. Mean scores moved toward greater intimacy at a significant level between periods I and II but remained constant between periods II and III. Since two topics-of-conversation categories ("feelings about each other" and "personality and behavior") also increased significantly over periods I and II, we suggest that it takes two or three months of companionship for personal communication to become a habit.

Eight bipolar items representing major dimensions of feeling and behavior were used by counselors to describe themselves and their boys during every visit. Boys' and counselors' scores were very similar, but the boys were usually described in more positive terms. The descriptions became warmer, more open, and generally more positive during the final period. Changes over time on each dimension were displayed and discussed in detail. Correlations with items from the topics-discussed and activities scales were described, along with variables from other sources. A composite favorability score correlated with independent measures of favorability produced by boys and parents. A dyadic distance score (total discrepancy between bipolar descriptions of boy and counselor) was negatively correlated with the "fun" score produced by boys on the Relationship Index. It also indicated that interpersonal distance decreased significantly for the group of dyads over the course of the companionships. The dyadic distance score was also negatively related to various change scores generated by parents and classmates and may be a predictor of less productive companionships for isolated and withdrawn boys.

Reactions to the termination of the companionships were extremely varied but in no instance traumatic for the boys. Some evidence suggests that the emotionally close companionships had more difficulty parting. Most of the dyads had some contact after official termination. Our initial concerns over the possible trauma and extreme feelings of loss due to termination were relieved.

VII

Change
in Boys

Most of the problems inherent in psychotherapy outcome research made themselves evident in our study of the companionships' outcome. In addition, we had to contend with extremely unstable subject matter: rapidly growing boys. Measuring behavior-problem changes in eleven-year-old boys is a treacherous business because they are in such an accelerated state of development that the quick appearance and disappearance of behavior problems is common (Levitt, 1971). In addition, the nature of our samples did not raise hopes for dramatic findings. Practically all the boys were mildly or moderately troubled; severe behavior problems were rare. We assumed that the more subtle, difficult-to-measure changes would be most characteristic of our less disturbed samples. Thus, we expected to miss much change in both our participant and control samples of boys. Hope for a thorough or even satisfying set of findings was small. Our satisfactions would have to come from breaking ground in an outcome research area where careful design is uncommon.

Most of our findings on change in the boys were drawn from observations made by parents (mostly mothers), classmates, and teachers during the third and fourth program years of the project. Data from both years were combined to provide a total participant sample of about eighty-eight boys for most variables. Seventy-four boys who also applied for the program served as the control group. (See Table 1 for details on the composition and matching of these two groups.) The follow-up control sample was composed of thirty-seven boys who participated in the third program year and were studied at three time points: pre (before the companionships began), termination (near the end of the companionships), and follow-up (about one year after the termination point).

Before combining the third- and fourth-year boys into a single large sample, we compared them for discrepancies. They were very nicely matched on most of the important variables. Both samples were evenly divided by grade (about 50 per cent from fifth and sixth grades) and almost exactly matched at the mean age of eleven years, three months. Racial characteristics of the samples varied by a few percentage points: 27 versus 29 per cent Negro boys. Socioeconomic status means were also similar at 2.5 on the Hollingshead Two-Factor Index (1957). Family religiosity for the two groups was close, with the bulk of ratings falling between very little and somewhat religious commitment. The fourth-year sample had more boys from broken homes ($p < .10$) and fewer first-borns and only children ($p < .05$). Pre Adjective Check List scores were very close, with no scale reaching the .10 level of significant difference. In sum, third- and fourth-year boys were very similar, and combining them seemed appropriate for research purposes. Control boys from the two years were even more closely matched than participant boys. This fine state of affairs concerning the symmetry of samples was largely the result of strict replication of selection procedures for the two program years.

To our knowledge, there are no controlled studies that have utilized pre, post, and follow-up assessment on the outcome of relationships composed of children and nonprofessionals. The few related studies, described in Chapter One, offer little encouragement for expecting results that show much positive change. Considering the strong possibility that our study of the unpartitioned sample would produce negative or mixed outcome findings, we prepared a rather complex design to help locate specific predictions of change and generate data pertinent to future researchers. Details in this chapter will not provide a simple answer to the question "Did it work?" Differences in boys, counselors, dyad types, companionship processes were found to be differential determinants of successful outcome. That is, the larger undifferentiated samples masked successful subgroups, and we were eventually able to find that companionships "worked" for certain boys, in specific situations, according to particular observer groups. Our attempts at global evaluation of the program produced mixed results.

Some of the earlier delinquency studies warned us not to expect positive findings with limited outcome criteria and undifferentiated samples. The monumental Cambridge-Somerville Youth Study remains a classic example of negative outcome research in the community mental health field (see Chapter One). It used boys' contact with the courts as a primary outcome measure. In a more recent controlled study, Tait and Hodges (1962) found that untreated control boys had fewer contacts with police than boys receiving an ill-defined form of therapy. Using similar criteria, Craig and Furst (1965) studied first-grade boys for five years and offered "no encouragement for the hope that child guidance therapy offers a means of materially reducing the incidence of serious delinquency." Of course, the big difference between our work and delinquency studies is the outcome measures. Delinquency research is usually limited to recidivism, but we were interested in a wider range of interpersonal behavior. Incidentally, delinquency programs commonly describe the parameters of their "treatment" in glib fashion. Length and frequency of contacts, duration of relationship, and therapy orientation are usually not described. Nevertheless, we assume that there was a series of contacts with a professional and that the impact of that contact was not measurable in terms of reduced recidivism.

Our use of multiple-outcome criteria and several observer groups to produce those criteria solved many research problems, and, of course, created new ones. The various observer groups (parents, teachers, classmates) agreed on some variables but did not agree on others. Such differences could be a real reflection of situational differences in boys' behavior; reduced aggression in the home, for instance, does not necessarily correlate with fewer fights on the playground. Another measurement problem that needed attention was the probable bias toward positive change in the eyes of parents. There seemed to be a tendency for both control and participant parents to describe fewer problems one year after the initial assessment. This appears to be a general phenomenon among parents of children in grade school. Shepherd, Oppenheim, and Mitchell (1966) questioned the parents and teachers of 6,920 children between the ages of five and fifteen. The majority had problems that were regarded as indices of "serious disorder": bed-wetting, violent temper tantrums, being afraid to go to school. The investigators matched fifty children in therapy with nontherapy controls of similar age, sex, and problem behavior. Two years later, a comparison showed that 65 per cent of those in therapy and 61 per cent of their controls had improved. Glidewell (1968) discovered the same phenomenon in his study of St. Louis school children. Here is his description:

> Of the 428 families who remained in the study for the full 2½ years, there were 107 who had no school mental health program available to them, and they consulted no' other mental health resources. The mothers of most of these families reported a reduction in the number of symptoms presented by the child in this study—80 per cent reporting a reduction during the first year, and 80 per cent reporting a reduction during the following eighteen months. The amount of reduction was only very slightly larger during the first period than during the second (p. 213).

These findings, along with those of Shepherd, Oppenheim, and Mitchell and the literature review by Levitt (1971), underline the difficulty of studying changes in childrens' problems from the observations of parents.

This chapter will also discuss a few findings based on observations of counselors. There is little or no precedent for studying measurement problems with student companions as evaluators of change in their clients. Since, unlike parents, the students in our study did not provide a major source of change findings on the boys, we can largely avoid the painful area of measurement problems with counselors. In the study by Holzberg, Gewirtz, and Ebner (1964), student companions to chronic mental patients appeared as a fairly enthusiastic group of raters. About half of the students reported gains in social behavior and personal appearance of the patients. Two thirds described gains in self-confidence, and 71 per cent indicated that the patients were conversing more freely by termination—remarkable improvement for long-term patients. We suspect that it is difficult for students to distinguish adequately between intimacy gains in the relationship and patient gains in other situations. We tried to provide a questioning format which emphasized the difference in changes outside and within the companionship. Our student counselors reported strong and frequent gains within the companionship process (see Chapter Five). The present chapter shows them somewhat less enthusiastic about improvement in other areas of the boys' lives.

This chapter also describes findings from four sets of data from teachers, classmates, and the participating boys. The first two sets are from teachers' and classmates' sociometric ratings. The ratings were obtained on all participants, their matched controls, and a stratified sample of random boys at two time points: before and after the companionships. Differences between the early and later ratings provided indices of change. We also gathered teachers' retrospective descriptions of change for the participant and control group. Of course, these descriptions had to be made at the end of the school year. Another set of findings were produced by the self-descriptions of participants. The participants were approached through structured interviews based on a story-completion device (a sequential set of sentence completions that paralleled the companionship phases). These four sets of observations allowed us to study (1) discrepancies between early and later teacher and classmate ratings of participants, matched controls, and randoms; (2) differences between teachers' retrospective descriptions of change for participants and matched controls; and (3) self-descriptions by participants about the companionship's influence on them.

Descriptions by Parents

Adjective Check List. The Adjective Check List (ACL) scales were developed from adult *self*-descriptions and require reinterpretation for use by parents who described their own children. Gough (1960) recommends the instrument for describing "others," but its application to children creates problems because of the differential in meaning of adjectives applied to adults and children. Since there are no instruments as highly developed as the ACL for children, and since we were also using other more appropriate instruments, it seemed worth the risk.

The ACL was filled out by parents (about 90 per cent mothers) on three occasions: prior to the companionships (designated as pre), again at the companionship's termination, and once again at a point approximately one year after termination (follow-up). The follow-up sample was composed of boys in our final program year ($N =$ about 40); the pre and termination sample was composed of boys participating in final two program years ($N =$ about 88). Thus, the follow-up sample is about half as large, creating weakness in our analysis of change from the time of termination to follow-up. This predicament could have been averted if we had delayed data analysis another year in order to collect follow-up observations for the boys in our final program. That was beyond our budget and patience.

A standardized self-report mean for adults is 50 for every ACL scale displayed in Figure 4, with a standard deviation of 10 (Gough and Heilbrun, 1963). After an informal review of the actual adjectives used by parents, I felt that standard ACL scale *names* were frequently not representative. Some were obviously inappropriate to the description of boys by parents. New names (in quotation marks) are shown along with the originals in Figure 4.

The entire ACL scales reveal only two significant differences in change patterns over the program year (pre to termination, I to II) between the full sample of participants ($N = 88$) and their controls ($N = 74$). Parents of participants gain more on rating involvement and describe their boys as becoming slightly more unmannerly; in contrast, according to parents, the controls became more mannerly.

The finding on rating involvement is not easy to interpret. Parents of participants used significantly more adjectives to describe their boys as the companionships ended. One clue to the meaning of this finding comes from two other scales, which showed

FIGURE 4.   Change patterns for parents' Adjective Check List ratings of participants (circles) versus controls (squares)

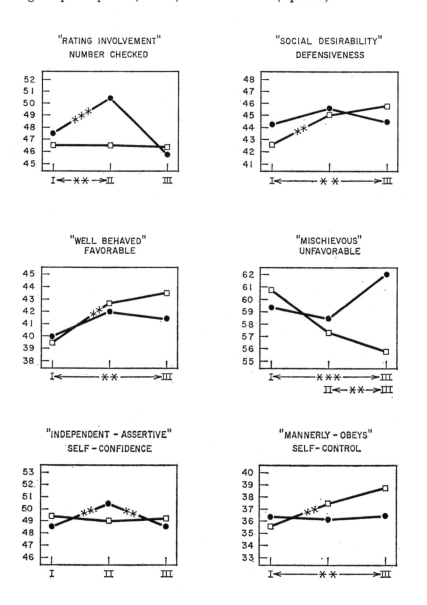

Asterisks denote significance of change between periods (I, beginning; II, middle; III, final) spanned by arrows: * = .10, ** = .05; *** = .01.

FIGURE 4. Change patterns for parents' Adjective Check List ratings of participants (circles) versus controls (squares) (Cont.)

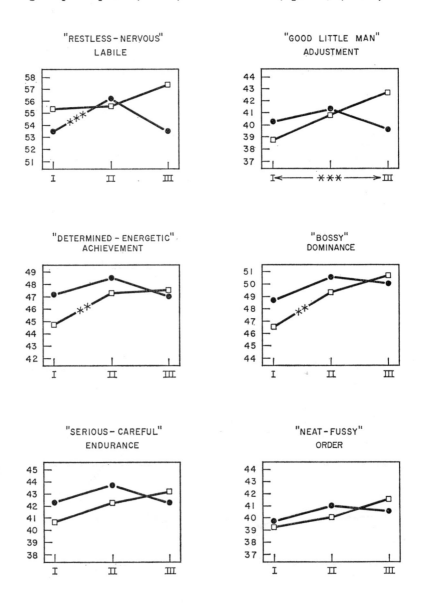

Asterisks denote significance of change between periods (I, beginning; II, middle; III, final) spanned by arrows: * = .10, ** = .05; *** = .01.

FIGURE 4.   Change patterns for parents' Adjective Check List ratings of participants (circles) versus controls (squares) (Cont.)

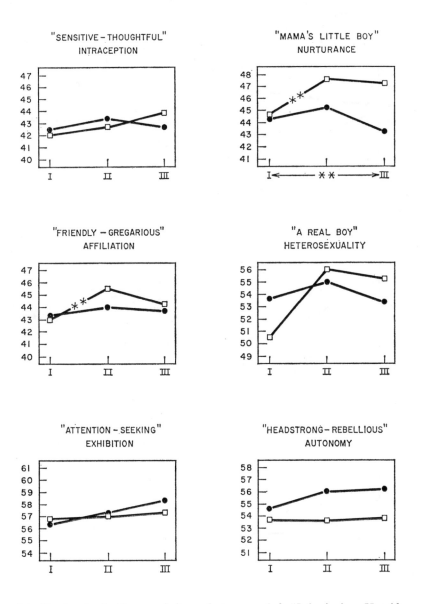

Asterisks denote significance of change between periods (I, beginning; II, middle; III, final) spanned by arrows: * = .10, ** = .05; *** = .01.

FIGURE 4.   Change patterns for parents' Adjective Check List ratings of participants (circles) versus controls (squares) (Cont.)

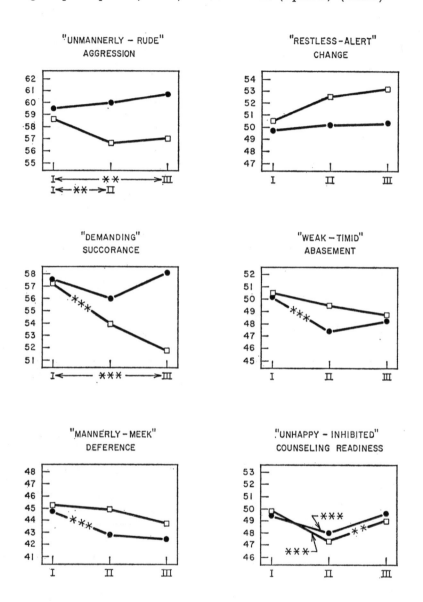

Asterisks denote significance of change between periods (I, beginning; II, middle; III, final) spanned by arrows: * = .10, ** = .05; *** = .01.

significant gains for participants over the same period: the independent-assertive and the restless-nervous scales. Thus, the additional adjectives used to describe participant boys at the program's closing suggest an increase in independence and restlessness. Here are some of the actual adjectives used with greater frequency to describe participant boys at the program's termination: *impulsive, adventurous, mischievous, enthusiastic, determined,* and *outspoken.* Adjectives used with less frequency were *modest, patient, reserved, serious, suspicious, unselfish.* The companionships evidently made the boys appear (or become) more active and autonomous. Correspondingly, they were also rated as becoming significantly less timid and mannerly. These changes could be evaluated as a "mixed blessing" by some parents.

Boys without companionships were described as becoming more gentle, reasonable, calm, and unemotional over the program year. Thus, according to parents, the companionships did nothing to reduce manageability problems. Indeed, the findings suggest that companionships impede the natural reduction of unmannerly, assertive behavior in moderately troubled boys—from their parents' viewpoint. The desirability of impeding unmannerly, assertive behavior depends upon parental values and the specific nature of the boy's initial problem. Apparently, the lack of change in this area for participating boys did not reduce their parents' positive estimates of the companionships' effectiveness. As will be seen, their written evaluations were mostly enthusiastic.

Only one statistically significant difference in change patterns was found over the postcompanionship period (termination to follow-up). The smaller follow-up sample of participant boys $(N = 37)$ gained on the item labeled "mischievous"; their parallel controls $(N = 34)$ produced lowered scores.

Seven significant differences in change patterns occurred over the entire research period (pre to follow-up, I to III) for the smaller follow-up samples. Controls $(N = 34)$ received higher ratings than participants $(N = 37)$ in the categories well behaved, mannerly-obeys, good little man, and mama's little boy. Mean scores for controls became significantly lower than those of participants on mischievous, unmannerly-rude, and demanding.

These ACL findings, along with the general trend of patterns on Figure 3, suggest that parents of controls progressively describe their boys as docile, well behaved, mannerly, and trouble-free over time. Once again, the findings show the controls becoming more manageable. However, since the initial ACL descriptions were taken during the application phase of the program, all of the parents could have been motivated to emphasize their boys' problems in order to enhance their chances for selection. Both participant and control parents produced descriptions low on favorability during the initial assessment. After the controls were rejected, the favorability of their descriptions increased. The original ACL scales on defensiveness and favorability show that controls gain significantly ($p < .05$) more than participants over the entire research period (see Figure 4). We must consider the possibility that the control group's scores were influenced by the parents' attitudes stemming from our denying their boys companionships.

The importance of the significant differences in change patterns between participants and controls was diluted by a further analysis. We compared the two groups on the absolute status of scores at each of the three test points. That is, we made static comparisons of participants and controls on each ACL scale at pre, termination, and follow-up. Testing for differences between the groups at pre yielded only one dissimilarity reaching the .05 level of significance: participants were higher on social desirability. An analysis at termination gave similarly skimpy results. Rating involvement was significantly greater (.05) for participants than for controls. Thus, it appears that the two groups were well matched on the ACL before the program started and remained quite similar at the termination of the companionships. A similar study was done one year later, at the follow-up point, with the smaller samples available. No significant differences were found. Most of the differences between groups were about two scale points or less; and these differences were rendered insignificant by the great variation of individual scores: standard deviations were typically around eleven points.

Thus far, the ACL evidence does not present a persuasive picture. It does not support the hypothesis that companionships improve boys in the eyes of their mothers—although the direction of change would be interpreted as improvement for boys who had been diagnosed as overcontrolled. Generally, the change in boys in the control group is in a direction that appears desired by their parents: more manageable, docile, and mannerly and less troublesome than participant boys. But the strength of change findings was diluted because the two groups were quite similar at each of the three assessment points: pre, termination, and follow-up.

Problem List. The Problem List for Elementary School Boys (PL) contains thirty-five typical schoolboy problems, with eight-step endorsement scales ranging from "never" to "always" (Appendix A). It was administered along with the ACL at pre, termination, and follow-up. Participants and controls were fairly well matched on the PL at pre, although controls were significantly higher on "His appetite is poor" and significantly lower on "He is modest—doesn't like to be seen undressed" (both at $p < .05$). Both groups tended toward a general reduction of problems over the program year. The total-problems score (a sum of the thirty-five items) in Figure 5 drops clearly, at first, for both groups. The drop for controls is significant at .05, but the similar change in means for participants misses significance because of the great variation in individual scores. Over the program period (pre to termination), controls had significantly reduced means on nine problems, compared to five problems for the participants (see Figure 5). Differences in change patterns *between* the two groups over this period occurred twice. Participants' means did not change much for "He must win at all costs" and "He is not sure of himself with people," while controls showed significant reductions for both problems.

Significant changes occurred less frequently for the smaller follow-up sample over the postcompanionship period (termination to follow-up). Participants were described as becoming significantly more moody: "He has mood swings—strong changes in feelings" and "He has sad moods." The latter item produced significant change-pattern differences between groups, along with "He becomes very jealous," which remained constant for participants and lowered significantly for controls.

The smaller follow-up sample was also used to study change-pattern differences between groups over the pre to follow-up (I-III) time span. Controls showed a significant reduction over the three assessment points on "He must win at all costs." Participants

FIGURE 5.   Change patterns for parents' Problem List ratings of participants (circles) versus controls (squares)

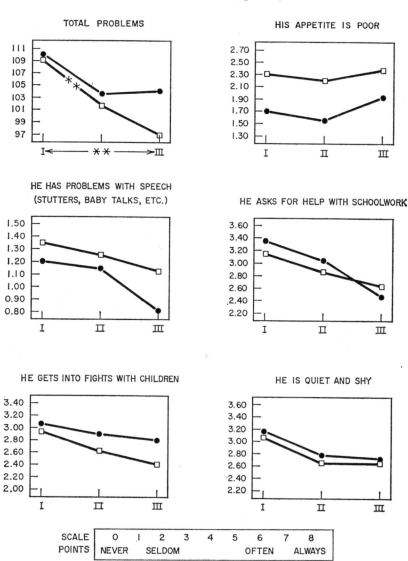

TOTAL PROBLEMS

HIS APPETITE IS POOR

HE HAS PROBLEMS WITH SPEECH (STUTTERS, BABY TALKS, ETC.)

HE ASKS FOR HELP WITH SCHOOLWORK

HE GETS INTO FIGHTS WITH CHILDREN

HE IS QUIET AND SHY

| SCALE | 0 | 1 | 2 | 3 | 4 | 5 | 6 | 7 | 8 |
| POINTS | NEVER | | SELDOM | | | | OFTEN | | ALWAYS |

Asterisks located directly on functions represent significance of change between time points: ** = .05, *** = .01. Roman numerals I, II, III designate the time points pre, termination, and follow-up. Asterisks spanning numerals indicate the significance level of differences in change between participants and controls.

FIGURE 5. Change patterns for parents' Problem List ratings of participants (circles) versus controls (squares) (Cont.)

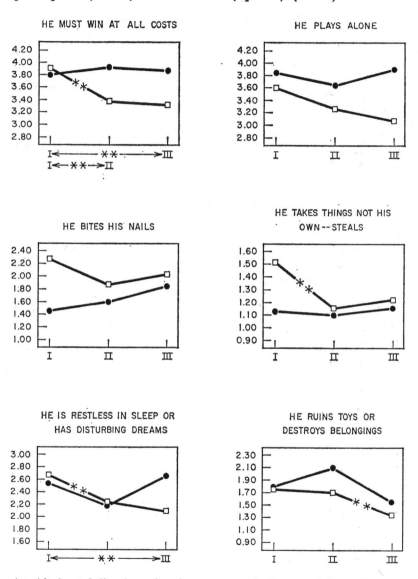

Asterisks located directly on functions represent significance of change between time points: ** = .05, *** = .01. Roman numerals I, II, III designate the time points pre, termination, and follow-up. Asterisks spanning numerals indicate the significance level of differences in change between participants and controls.

FIGURE 5. Change patterns for parents' Problem List ratings of participants (circles) versus controls (squares) (Cont.)

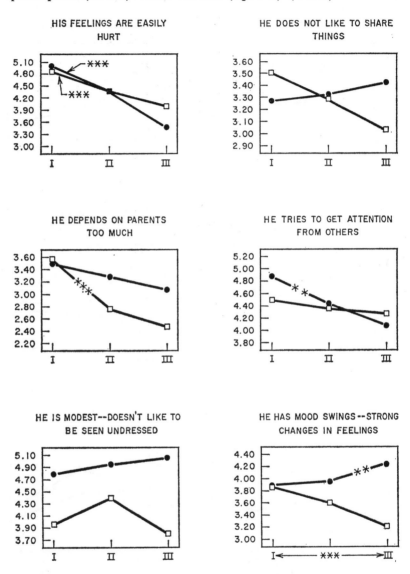

Asterisks located directly on functions represent significance of change between time points: ** = .05, *** = .01. Roman numerals I, II, III designate the time points pre, termination, and follow-up. Asterisks spanning numerals indicate the significance level of differences in change between participants and controls.

FIGURE 5.   Change patterns for parents' Problem List ratings of participants (circles) versus controls (squares) (Cont.)

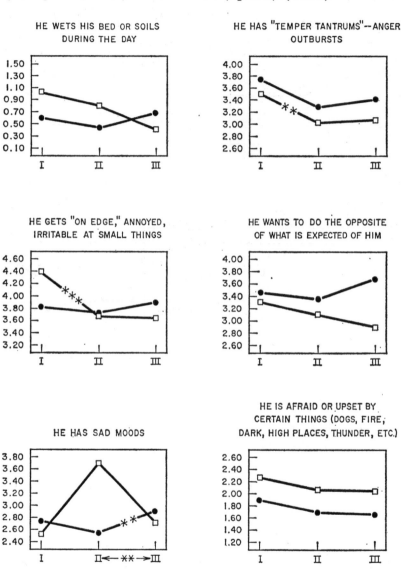

Asterisks located directly on functions represent significance of change between time points: ** = .05, *** = .01. Roman numerals I, II, III designate the time points pre, termination, and follow-up. Asterisks spanning numerals indicate the significance level of differences in change between participants and controls.

FIGURE 5. Change patterns for parents' Problem List ratings of participants (circles) versus controls (squares) (Cont.)

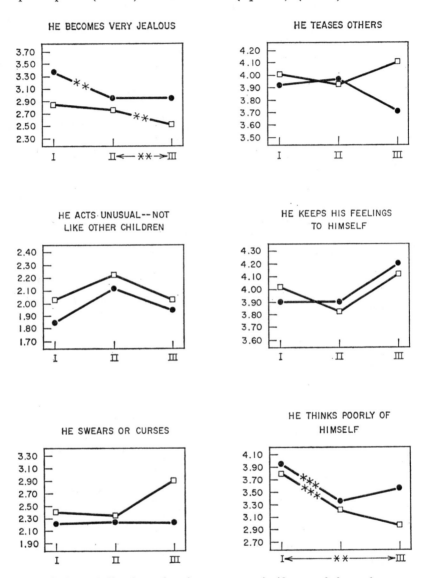

Asterisks located directly on functions represent significance of change between time points: ** = .05, *** = .01. Roman numerals I, II, III designate the time points pre, termination, and follow-up. Asterisks spanning numerals indicate the significance level of differences in change between participants and controls.

FIGURE 5. Change patterns for parents' Problem List ratings of participants (circles) versus controls (squares) (Cont.)

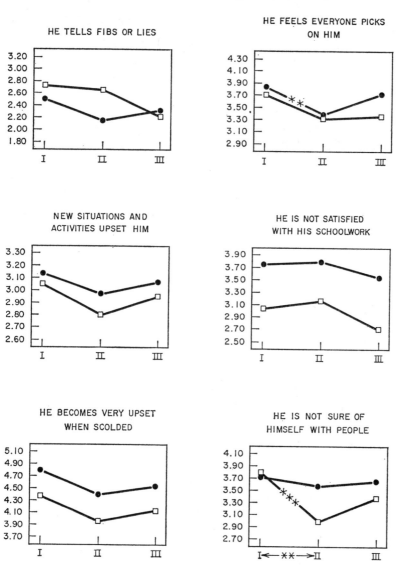

Asterisks located directly on functions represent significance of change between time points: ** = .05, *** = .01. Roman numerals I, II, III designate the time points pre, termination, and follow-up. Asterisks spanning numerals indicate the significance level of differences in change between participants and controls.

regained their earlier reduction on "restless in sleep or disturbing dreams," while controls had repeated reductions at II and III (see Figure 5). The two groups were similar at first on "mood swings–strong changes in feelings," but participants were much higher at the end. Both groups dropped sharply and significantly on "He thinks poorly of himself" over the program year, but afterward participants regained some of the problem whereas controls continued to show some reduction.

In general, ratings for the full sample of controls complemented the ACL changes for the program year. That is, some of the significant shifts in Problem List means were toward greater gentleness or docility: lower competitiveness, less stealing, fewer temper tantrums, less irritability. The PL also showed significant reductions in sleep problems, insecurity in relating to others, and dependency on parents. Both the participants and controls were seen as becoming less emotionally touchy ("feelings are easily hurt") and less troubled about their self-worth ("thinks poorly of himself"). Participants evidenced a significant reduction in jealousy and attention-seeking problems over the companionship year, two problems that could have been alleviated by the attention of our student companions. Finally, it appears that participants felt less "picked on" at termination when compared with pre assessment.

The clearest general statement about PL findings is that, amidst great variation, participants and especially controls tend to lose problems rather than gain them over time. Ninety-three per cent of the items did not yield significant differences in change pattern between groups over the program year, and 80 per cent of the items yielded nonsignificant differences over the entire research period. When differences occurred, they favored the controls. Frequently, participants and controls produced almost identical patterns of change for a problem (about one third of all items). The few significant PL differences between groups did not provide enough data to determine the effectiveness of companionships.

Adjective Check List and Problem List Combined. When we turn away from between-group change analyses for the ACL and PL and simply compare the status of groups at each of the three testing points, the differences are few. Combined, the ACL and PCL contain sixty items, which produced 180 participant-control comparison tests at the three time points. Less than 5 per cent of those tests proved statistically significant ($p < .05$). There were four significant differences at pre: participants had fewer problems with poor appetite and irritability, were more modest, and were described with greater social desirability. As the companionships terminated, participants still had fewer problems with appetite but told more lies than controls (companionships seemed to engender some secrets from parents). One year after the companionships terminated, the only ACL or PL difference was higher modesty scores for participant boys.

Subgroups. Parent ratings on the ACL and PL were also used to study smaller subgroups of boys based on specific characteristics. We could study these groups only over the program year because subdivision of the small follow-up sample left us with tiny groups unsuitable for statistical analysis. But the program-year analyses clarified some findings from the larger samples and gave clues about the types of boys that gained most from the companionships.

Participants with quiet presenting problems ($N = 43$) were compared with quiet controls ($N = 38$) on all ACL and PL scales, and no significant differences in pre to termination change patterns were found. A similar test was done for the outgoing participants ($N = 44$) and their controls ($N = 35$). The several significant differences that were found resemble findings from the entire sample, described in the previous section. Outgoing participants gained more on rating involvement, headstrong-rebellious, unmannerly-rude, and mischievous. Outgoing controls had increased ratings in the categories mama's little boy, mannerly-obeys, and mannerly-meek. It appears, then, that some of the differences observed earlier between the total samples of participants and controls were due partially to differences in the outgoing subgroups of boys.

The picture is clarified further by separate analyses of black and Caucasian subgroups compared with their matched controls. A subgroup composed entirely of Caucasian participants ($N = 60$) was compared with a similar group of controls ($N = 55$) for change patterns. Only one significant difference was found: Caucasian controls gained significantly more on restless-alert. A comparison of black participants ($N = 25$) and black controls ($N = $

19) revealed a number of differences: black participants gained more on independent-assertive, attention-seeking, headstrong-rebellious, and unmannerly-rude than their controls and showed a greater reduction on weak-timid, mannerly-meek, and "being afraid of or upset by certain things—dogs, dark, thunder." Compared with their controls, both our outgoing and black subgroups of participants are clearly seen as becoming more boisterous and troublesome over the program year. Outgoing and black controls became more manageable and mannerly in the eyes of parents. These change patterns are similar to those that emerged in the comparison of all participants and controls. Apparently, the patterns of change were heavily influenced by black and outgoing boys. Caucasian boys and those with quiet problems produced change patterns not much different from those of their control groups. Since both the quiet and outgoing subgroups had similar numbers of black, Caucasian, and Oriental boys (and, similarly, the black, Caucasian, and Oriental subgroups had similar numbers of quiet and outgoing boys), we cannot attribute most of the significant differences to a smaller subgroup of black boys with outgoing problems.

Boys who did not have a father or male guardian in their homes during the companionship were designated fatherless ($N = 27$). This subgroup was compared wih fatherless control ($N = 21$) and produced the largest batch of significant differences in change patterns. Fatherless participants gained on rating involvement, mischievous, and unmannerly-rude; their controls produced lower scores. The control group, but not the participant group, improved on the following items: well behaved, mannerly-obeys, good little man, serious-careful, sensitive-thoughtful, mama's little boy, friendly-gregarious, mannerly-meek; and PL irritability, being upset in new situations, acting "unusual," and ruining belongings. These significant differences once again show controls becoming more manageable and docile, with a reduction of boisterous qualities. These findings appear more dramatic when compared with those from counterpart subgroups of the remaining boys with fathers: participants ($N = 61$) versus controls ($N = 53$). There was not a single significant difference in change pattern between these groups. Obviously, fatherless participants and their controls were also making a major contribution to the differences observed earlier for the complete samples of boys.

There are, then, three subgroups that appear to account for the increase in troublesome ratings given to all participants: boys with outgoing problems, black boys, and fatherless boys. Incidentally, black, Caucasian, and Oriental subgroups of boys were roughly balanced on the fatherless variable: about 30 per cent had no father or male guardian in their homes. If our program were built around Caucasian boys with quiet problems (withdrawal, isolation) and intact homes, there would be fewer differences in overall ACL change patterns between participants and controls. Two patterns occurred for all three subgroups: fatherless, black, and outgoing controls showed strong gains in mannerly-obeys and clearly reduced scores on the unmannerly-rude scale. Unfortunately, our findings do not suggest a reason for the peculiar similarity of the three subgroups. The puzzle is further complicated by the dissimilarity between ACL and PL findings on the subgroups: Problem List findings showed few differences between the participants and controls of black, fatherless, and outgoing subgroups.

The entire set of findings based on parents "before and after" ratings resists neat interpretation. Several weak hypotheses are suggested. It may be that companionships activate fatherless, outgoing, and black boys to a point where they are regarded as more boisterous, unmanageable, and troublesome to their parents. Reports from parents during the program year repeatedly described an expansion of their boys' activities and sense of exploration. The egalitarian quality of the companionships, the emphasis on self-disclosure, and the bilateral decision-making taught many boys a new way of relating to adults. They were not asked to obey their counselors. Perhaps boys brought some of their new interpersonal style into the mother-child relationship. If so, we could expect parents to perceive their boys as more assertive, less timid, less mannerly, and in general less manageable.

Hypotheses considering the dynamics of the control group are most relevant because most of the significant ACL changes were produced by the parents of fatherless, black, and outgoing control boys on the Adjective Check List. Please remember that our control group was formed by soliciting the parents of rejected applicants to the project. We established matched pairs from our applicant sample, divided the pairs into groups, and designated them as accepted or rejected by a flip of a coin. The rejection letter contained an appeal for participation as a control subject. A majority of the rejected applicants agreed to serve as controls. So, although controls and participants were well matched on motivation, they were mismatched on the subsequent effects of rejection to the project. The applications of control parents gave evidence of two conditions: (1) They believed that their boys were troubled by psychological problems. (2) They were motivated to try new methods for alleviating those problems. Thus, we would expect control parents to seek other means of helping their boys after receiving our rejection notice. This was true to some degree; about 25 per cent of the control boys had contact with a professional person (school guidance counselor, social worker, psychologist, minister, or psychiatrist). Fifteen per cent of the participant boys had such contact. A larger proportion of fatherless controls received professional help: 45 per cent compared with only 7 per cent of the fatherless participants. Obviously, the lack of a father in the home and the denial of a project companionship caused mothers to seek professional help for their boys. The dramatic change differences between fatherless controls and participants may have been influenced by this professional help.

Observations during Companionships. Almost all of the informal parent observations that came to us about two months into the companionships noted some desired change. Parents were asked to write us a short note telling us "what you think of the program so far." The following excerpts from the parents' replies are representative of their observations regarding change in boys. They provide a picture of the change process not available from rating scales.

> We know so little about human personality and development, so it is hard to evaluate the extent of a single person's influence. But in the last two months, Nowell has shown a remarkable positive improvement. All of a sudden he doesn't see classmates hating him, and now he even likes some of them and

reports joining them in games which he formerly hated and/or shrank from. His counselor, Dave, enjoys college studies—so now Nowell is doing his schoolwork if not eagerly, at least willingly.

Sandy usually does not leave the house unless he has to. Ben does not have a car so Sandy now takes the bus to meet him. He takes the bus to go other places, too. I could never get him to do it before. . . . Sandy is getting confidence fast because of his new companionship.

Cary doesn't shy off in corners any more. He has been painfully shy. Now he talks back, doesn't *always* obey. It's not easy for me, but better maybe openly angry than silent for days on end. The change has come fast.

My wife and I believe that the project has already given Johnny more confidence and made him less dependent upon his other friends. In the past several years we have heard Johnny beg and bribe other boys to stay and play with him; yesterday he was very casual with a boy who threatened to take all his toys home and never return—the threat didn't work, and the boy stayed all afternoon.

Kent is working with Lennie in a most natural manner. . . . Lennie is more playful rather than so serious as usual. Now there is some sort of lightness in the air when he is around.

When your letter came, I asked Jerry what he thought of his counselor. He said he liked him. I asked him very much? He said, "Kinda like love, Momma." He has come in several times after being with Jim and said, "I'm so happy, Momma." . . . Jerry seems to be better adjusted now. He used to be sullen and jealous at times with his brother and sisters. This habit he has dropped altogether. He is more outgoing and contented. He has his own interests and has his mind on his own activities. He doesn't sulk as he used to.

He is less demanding at mealtimes when the family is together, less intent upon attention-getting and more tolerant of the older boys. . . . This is what Ernie has needed—to put someone first before himself.

There was so much praise and testimonial flavor in the parents' responses that our staff began to suspect that some were "putting in a good word to the counselors' boss." We also speculated that parents might be grateful for being accepted and simply say-

ing "thank you" with their praise. But there were also suggestions
and criticism from parents (about the range of activities, scheduling
procedures, counselors' political and religious views) that gave their
notes a ring of sincerity.

Many of the comments were general and did not refer to
the reduction of a problem: "getting better," "is more understanding," "learning to respect men." In addition, parents were describing some dimensions of improvement that would not be
detected by the structured scales and questionnaires. Such dimensions as "becoming more tolerant of others," "feeling more playful
and light," "feeling less hated by peers," "learning how to decide"
were probably not captured in our hard data. Some of the improvements that parents ambivalently described for quiet, withdrawn
boys might have appeared as changes for the worse in our formal
findings: "Now somewhat obnoxious and swaggers a bit." "Talks
back, doesn't *always* obey." "No longer washes up ten times a day
. . . has become messy and refuses to dress neatly." Of course,
similar changes might have been described by control parents. Our
request letter went only to participant parents, as a safety device for
checking on the progress of the companionships; obtaining change
data was a minor consideration.

Retrospective Views. Parents were asked to think back over
the previous school year and rate their impressions of the quality
and degree of change in several areas. The Retrospective Questionnaire began with items about school attitudes, schoolwork, peer
relations, and self-esteem (Appendix E). The items were attached
to seven-point change scales, with a "no change" midpoint. Almost all of the mean scores for participants and controls at termination and follow-up fell near the scale point that designated "a little
more" or "a little better." Standard deviations averaged 1.30 scale
points. There were no significant differences between the full
sample of participants ($N = 88$) and controls ($N = 74$) at termination. Similarly, there were no significant differences for the
smaller follow-up groups. In addition, no significant changes from
termination to follow-up were observed for participants or controls.

Both groups of parents, then, tended to see a little improvement in their boys' attitudes toward school, peer relations, schoolwork, and self-esteem at the project's termination and once again

one year after termination. Ratings for participants and controls on the four items are quite similar and approach a significant difference only in the case of the participants' higher rating on self-esteem at follow-up.

At termination, comparable subgroups of participants and controls were formed around the following characteristics: black–Caucasian, quiet problems–outgoing problems, fatherless–father in home. Differences in parents' retrospective ratings between participants and controls were studied for each characteristic. (A similar study was not possible for the follow-up point because subgroups were too small.) The only significant differences found at termination were for comparisons based on racial characteristics. Caucasian participants improved significantly more than their controls in their attitudes toward school ($p < .05$). Black participants ($N = 25$) were rated as more improved than their matched black controls ($N = 20$) on self-esteem ($p < .05$). A within-group comparison of participants showed black boys higher than Caucasians on liking school and on self-esteem ($p < .05$). Actually, our black participant boys were seen as gaining more than either their white counterparts or their matched controls on all four retrospective measures; but significance occurred only for the school and self-esteem items. These findings, combined with the previously discussed ACL and PL findings, suggest that companionships may have helped black boys to like themselves more; to show greater surgency; to become less timid, mannerly, and phobic; and to display more independence, assertion, and rebelliousness.

The fifth question on the Retrospective Questionnaire used the same seven-point scale to assess changes in the initial or "presenting" problem that motivated them to join the project (Appendix E). Frequently, parents were not specific or described something missing in their boys' lives. About one third of the descriptions could be categorized as interpersonal inadequacy: "Withdrawn and wanted to please adults *too* much." "Could not make friends and led a solitary life because of his intense competitiveness." Roughly one fifth of the responses described the need for a male adult: "Father's indifference and neglect leaves him without a man to identify with." "He's with girls or women 98 per cent of the time." Fifteen per cent described problems with self-esteem or self-confidence. Over 10 per cent mentioned problems in school—academically and with peers. The remaining problems varied: general irritability, insecurity due to divorce, overdemanding, sibling rivalry, nervousness, soiling, lacking in initiative, stealing, telling lies, tension stomachaches, self-pity, temper, concealing feelings.

At termination, the participants parents' typical response was "somewhat better." The controls were described as slightly less improved—a little better. The difference was not significant. Continued reduction of the initial problem was the mode for the follow-up assessment: participants were typically "somewhat better" and controls "a little better" (difference significant at .05). A closer look at the later findings showed that 91 per cent and 61 per cent of the controls of the participants were rated improved to some degree (a little to much better). Three per cent of the participants and 28 per cent of the controls rated their boys' initial problems as getting worse (little to much) by follow-up. The remaining responses were "no change."

Most of the participant parents cited the companionships and the counselors as important factors in their boys' improvement. One set of scales on the Retrospective Questionnaire asked about the counselors' contribution to any improvement described on each of the retrospective items. The scales ranged from 0 (none) to 4 (some) to 8 (very much). Most of the mean scores were very near 4.6, with standard deviations around .80. Counselors' contribution to improvement in their boys' self-esteem was slightly higher, at 5.1 (between some and much). The degree of improvement on an item did not correlate significantly with the amount of counselor contribution to that item. However, counselor-contribution scores did show moderately significant correlations among themselves. This finding suggests that parents tended to generalize the counselors' contribution across items; that is, if the counselor helped the boy with peer relations, he was also seen as helping the boy improve in self-esteem and the other categories.

Control parents cited various causes for improvement in their boys, who, of course, did not participate in the companionship program. Since our findings indicate that control boys improved at roughly the same rate as participants, it may be useful to quote the control parents in detail on the ostensible causes for improvement:

> "Our social worker suggested cub scouting, which has made him less nervous. I've helped too, by relaxing with him more." "Last year his introspectiveness was not helped by a teacher that did not understand. His new teacher appreciates him, which gives him confidence in making his way with other kids." ". . . no contact with adult males . . . divorced family. Now we have a male roomer! . . . helps a lot." "The soiling problem caused irritability, social insecurity, and poor schoolwork. [I] finally found a good proctologist, and things are going well." "Several months of psychotherapy did wonders." "[My] husband and I moved back together and spent more time with Harold." "[The] school psychologist wanted to try half-day classwork . . . showed marked improvement all around." "His first male teacher made some difference." "The boys' chorus requires two rehearsals a week . . . has been very beneficial." "[He has improved] because he is older. Twelve is a perfectly delightful age in a boy." "Transferred to a smaller class and an excellent teacher." "Spent six weeks with acceptant grandparents . . . without sibs or parents to fight with . . . vastly improved." "A lucky and particularly rewarding friendship with a classmate." "His father and I think that getting into therapy has changed Phillip considerably."

These examples suggest that control parents were actively concerned about their boys' psychological problems and, as mentioned, frequently sought other solutions after being rejected for participation in the project. Psychotherapists, significant males, and structured or task-oriented social activities were frequently mentioned causes for improvement. Participant parents did not list as many helpful interventions beyond the companionships. Perhaps the companionships were on their minds because the questionnaire came from our project, but the time devoted to companionships also precluded other possibilities.

An effort also was made to obtain global retrospective impressions of change from parents during the follow-up assessment. They were given a full-page chart containing two segments: one for the program year; the other for the follow-up year. Both segments contained the prefix "My son gets along with others" followed by five-step scales ranging from "much worse," to a midpoint "about the same," to "much better" (Appendix E). Instructions asked for general changes in the boys' personal relations—one year at a time. A space for open-ended written descriptions was provided for those who wished to elaborate on the meaning of their ratings. The five-scale points were assigned numerical values from -2 (much worse) to $+2$ (much better), and means were computed for both groups over both periods (see Table 11).

Participants' parents retrospectively rated more gains over the companionship period ($p < .01$) and, with marginal significance ($p < .10$), tended to describe more interpersonal improvement for the follow-up period. These findings are not well aligned with previously described findings from derived change scores or specific retrospective ratings. When parents were asked to pool all their impressions of interpersonal change into a single rating, the participant boys came out on top: 75 per cent seen as getting better (a little or much) over the companionship period, compared to 47 per cent better for the control boys. Ratings for the follow-up period also showed somewhat more improvement for participants than controls (86 per cent better versus 70 per cent better). Controls were rated as unchanged at about twice the frequency assigned to participants for both periods.

The most common change pattern involving both periods was repeated gains over the three assessment points. This pattern occurred for 59 per cent of the participants and 42 per cent of the controls. About one fourth of both groups produced a delayed-gain pattern. A repeated gainless pattern appeared for 20 per cent of the controls and 10 per cent of the participants. Gains-lost and gains-maintained patterns occurred infrequently for both groups.

We also asked the participants' parents, during the termination assessment, whether they still agreed with their decision to let their boys participate in the project. Almost all the parents answered "yes" (97 per cent). Their discussions usually expressed gratitude or described details about enjoyment received from the companionship or listed specific changes in the boys. "No" answers had discussions about "irresponsible" counselors who were often late or missed appointments or influenced boys to "talk back," enjoy motorcycles, or approve of campus revolt. When specific

Table 11

PARENTS' RETROSPECTIVE RATINGS OF CHANGE IN BOYS

Change	Companionship Period		
	Participants (37)	Controls (34)	*p*
	Per Cent		
Much worse (−2)	0	6	
A little worse (−1)	0	2	
About the same (0)	25	45	
A little better (+1)	59	38	
Much better (+2)	16	9	
Mean (−2 to +2)	0.92	0.42	.01

Change	Follow-Up Period		
	Participants (37)	Controls (34)	*p*
	Per Cent		
Much worse (−2)	0	5	
A little worse (−1)	0	2	
About the same (0)	14	27	
A little better (+1)	44	32	
Much better (+2)	42	38	
Mean (−2 to +2)	1.29	0.96	.10

positive change was mentioned, it was frequently about expanded interests, increased ability to collaborate, school improvements, or moving away from withdrawal habits: "Booker got interested in college life, sudying, football, civil rights, marches, and the kinds of things he will do when he gets older. [This project] would have been a great experience for me in sixth grade!" "My wife saw more change than me . . . but lately I've been amazed at his improved school grades." "[Our boy shows] unexpected maturity and willingness to pitch in with chores during our camping trip. . . . can't say [whether] the project is responsible or not." "One of the best things that's happened to Alan . . . don't think it is overstating it . . . values himself more and is peeking out of his shell."

Counselors' Retrospective Views

The counselors' perspective for viewing change was limited because they had no knowledge of the boys before the project began. Counselors' observations of change were obtained as the companionships ended. We asked them the following questions about their boys' problems: "Do you feel that your boy had some significant personal problem when he entered the project? Yes——. No——. If yes, please try to describe it in gross terms." "Has there been change in that problem? Check one box and describe below." A six-step scale was used, ranging from "none" to "very much."

Thirty per cent of the counselors said that they did not see a significant problem in their boys at first. Seventy per cent described a wide range of problems, which we placed in crude categories. A majority of those describing problems made reference to interpersonal difficulties. One of every four boys was seen as withdrawn, isolated, or severely concealed: "I don't think he trusts the world because he is not free to reveal anything about himself. He seems so withdrawn and yearning to believe someone likes him." "As far as I can tell, Dave has never had a meaningful relationship . . . no friends and was unwilling to talk about the problem or anything else." Twenty per cent of the problems were categorized as overdependence or chronic passivity: "Lewis either cried or became very moody when our visits came to a close. The same thing happened when he lost a game or when I asked him to build things by himself. He is insecure, always wanted me to initiate things and never got enough of me. What a drain!" Fifteen per cent of the descriptions were about hostility and aggressive behavior: "The guy was really afraid of losing control, because when it happened he appeared foolish and he knew it. After he lost his temper he claimed he didn't care." Another 15 per cent mentioned their boys' low self-esteem: "Stu was afraid of being himself: anger meant punishment, failure meant proof of his worthlessness . . . felt insignificant and unloved and daydreamed he was a strong man or a king." Other frequently mentioned problems were habitual lying, bizarre thinking, study problems, and physical complications such as asthma, impaired hearing, and skin disease. Almost one third of the counselors blamed the boys' families as the problem source: "a big brother that is capable of killing him," "confused, weak father," "mother's a real bitch," "family blatantly favors young sister." Overall, the counselors' descriptions suggest a population of mild to moderately troubled boys. Problem areas and frequencies were roughly similar to those described by parents and discussed earlier in this chapter.

Most of the counselors who described initial problems also reported some degree of improvement. Many of the 81 per cent who saw improvement described it as a small gain. More specifically, 62 per cent of those reporting problems saw very little, little, or some change in the problem. Much or very much change was indicated by 19 per cent. Here is the exact breakdown of response frequencies to our question on change in the boys' initial problems: none, 19 per cent; very little, 26 per cent; little, 16 per cent; some, 20 per cent; much, 12 per cent; very much, 7 per cent.

It was impossible to make direct comparisons with parent data on change in presenting problems because of scale discrepancies, but a rough comparison reveals some similarity. Participating parents rated 91 per cent of their boys as evidencing some degree of improvement, and the rate for counselors was 81 per cent. The no change rate of 19 per cent for counselors was higher than the 9 per cent no change or became worse rate for parents. Essentially, both groups described some improvement in most of the boys, and that improvement was typically modest or moderate.

Compared with parents, counselors described change more conservatively and more frequently in interpersonal terms. Here are examples of what counselors meant by "little," "some," and "very much" change: One boy initially seen by his counselor as "extremely introverted . . . frightened of people . . . clinging" was rated as improving a little. His counselor wrote, "At least now he recognizes and talks about his fears and shyness to me and others. That's progress, but he still slips back into hiding from discussion and gets on an intellectual plane." Another boy described as "super touchy . . . no confidence . . . unwilling to leave the house or admit any weakness" was rated as improving some. The counselor reported, "I think he has learned much from our being together and is now more confident. He can ride busses by himself, take out books from the library, buy things at the store, and meet new people without always feeling inferior." A boy seen as improving very much was initially described as "full of hostility and ready to fight when things didn't go his way. He was ostracized by his peers." His counselor was reticent to consider the companionship as the only change agent: "Maybe just spending time with me (or anyone?) was what he needed. He has become quite a leader among his friends and is respected (rather than feared as before). I've noticed change in his ability to participate in sports: he's now the best *team* player instead of the worst. I don't want to pat myself on the back—I just happened to be there when he grew better."

Another set of retrospective change questions given to counselors was identical to the set given to parents (described in the previous section). The counselors' mean ratings hovered around the scale point designating "a little" improvement in peer relations, self-esteem, and attitude toward school. The mean scale scores appeared equivalent to ratings of change for the boys' initial problems and were very similar to the mean scores produced by parents. We omitted ratings on change in quality of schoolwork because many counselors felt they had insufficient data. Both counselors and parents reported the greatest improvement in the area of self-esteem.

A final question asked counselors: "Would you say your boy has become more quiet, more outgoing, or unchanged?" Since many of the boys were initially described by parents as excessively quiet or excessively outgoing, we wanted to see whether there was measurable movement away from the extremes. Half of those boys initially classified as having quiet problems became more outgoing according to counselors—but the same was true for boys with outgoing problems. That is, 50 per cent of both groups were seen as becoming more outgoing. About 40 per cent of both groups were rated as unchanged, and 10 per cent as becoming more quiet. Since the primary observations were within the companionships, we assume that the counselors were usually describing changes in the boys' interpersonal stance toward their counselors.

Since it was impossible to obtain control data for counselor observations, the findings have limited usefulness. They do offer additional support to parent findings that show most boys improving in the area of their initial problem, peer relations, self-esteem, and attitude toward school.

Sociometric Descriptions by Classmates and Teachers

The *Peer Nominations Inventory* (*PNI*) is an empirically derived sociometric measure of adjustment in fourth-, fifth-, and sixth-grade boys (Wiggins and Winder, 1961). The initial items were drawn from interviews with 252 boys. A resulting sociometric scale was refined through several reliability and validation studies. Four of the five factors found by Wiggins and Winder were used in our project: social isolation, hostility, attention-seeking, and likeability. A factor labeled "crying" was omitted after our pilot research because several parents and teachers complained that it created sharp discomfort among boys who had crying episodes in the classroom.

Our own interviews with boys suggested another dimension common to perceptions in fifth- and sixth-grade classrooms. Boys frequently described some of their peers as "acting crazy," "does strange things," "different from everyone else." These descriptions of uniqueness, peculiarity, or atypical behavior influenced us to add a group of deviant items to our pilot study to see whether they would generate an independent factor. They did, and we grouped the three strongest items into a cluster labeled "atypicality," which was added to the original PNI factors.

The final revised PNI that was used to assess change in our samples contained five factors:

Isolation: "He plays all by himself a lot." "He is very quiet and shy." "He does not like to tell about himself." "Hardly any boys like to play with him." "On the playground he just stands around." "He doesn't have very many friends."

Hostility: "He makes fun of people." "When he doesn't get his way, he gets real mad." "If someone gets in his way, he shoves them out of the way." "He's just plain mean." "He says he can beat everybody up." "He likes to pick on little kids."

Likeability: "He is one of my friends." "He's a nice guy." "Many of the kids like him." "Some kids like him very much." "He has a lot of friends." "He's the kind of kid I like."

Attention-Seeking: "He's always acting up." "He wants to show off in front of the kids." "He tries to get attention."

Atypicality: "He does crazy things." "He does not act like the rest of the kids." "Sometimes he acts very strange."

The twenty-four items above were randomized and placed on a one-page form containing spaces to be filled in with names of all the boys in a classroom (see Appendix B). The format allowed the raters to scan all of the names and register endorsements for each item. Raters were instructed to focus on one item at a time and check the name of all boys who were appropriately described by that item.* Teachers administered the forms and also used them to supply their own endorsements.

Because it was necessary to maintain the anonymity of our subjects, all of the 1,200 boys in the fifth and sixth grades of Berkeley's schools were asked to rate each other on the PNI. Also, to reduce classroom disturbance, we asked the girls to rate the boys. Data analysis was confined to ratings made by boys, because the PNI was developed with boys as raters and we assumed that girls had less interchange with their male classmates and were consequently less capable of rating their characteristics. In addition, the large number of boy raters provided adequate data, and we preferred not to double our analysis task with the addition of girl rat-

---

* A copy of the exact instructions is available from the author.

ings. The 1,200 boys were scattered among forty-one classrooms. The ratings that we collected before and after the companionships were uniformly made at the end of successive school years, when classmates and teachers would be most familiar with our subjects. Since most classes remained intact between the fifth and sixth years, most of our subjects were rated by the same classmates and different teachers over the two assessment points.

We computed scores by determining the percentage of actual endorsements in relation to potential endorsements for each factor. For example, if twenty children rate a single boy on a six-item factor, that factor has 120 potential endorsements. If the boy actually receives twelve endorsements, his score will be 10 per cent for that factor. Teacher items were scored the same way except that the potential number of endorsements remained constant. Two inappropriate items concerning likeability were excluded from teacher scores: "He is one of my friends" and "He's the kind of kid I like."

There were no significant differences between the mean scores for all participants $(N = 87)$ and their matched controls $(N = 74)$ at the final assessment. The same was true for the initial assessment. That is, a comparison of both groups on all teacher and classmate PNI variables revealed no significant differences before the companionships began and no significant differences after the companionships terminated.

A change index was derived for every boy on each variable from the absolute difference between his early and later scores (raw gains). Mean raw-gain scores were compared between the participant and control groups, and no significant differences were found. Finally, we used "residual-gains" change scores (Manning and DuBois, 1962), which corrected for the effect of initial status on final status to compare the two groups. Once again, no significant differences were found between groups (Table 12).

The general direction of change for both groups was toward improvement. The nonsignificant differences between early and later scores showed a small reduction in isolation, hostility, and attention-seeking. Likeability means were slightly higher at the final testing. The only exception to the slight trend toward general improvement was seen in some minor gains in teacher-rated atypicality for both participants and controls.

Table 12

SOCIOMETRIC[a] CHANGE SCORES FOR PARTICIPANTS AND
MATCHED CONTROLS OVER THE PROGRAM YEAR

	Participants $(N = 86)$	Controls $(N = 74)$	t
Classmates' Ratings			
Isolation	5.5[b]	3.9	.72
Hostility	5.6	2.4	1.60
Likeability	17.6	19.3	.66
Attention-Seeking	8.9	5.6	1.45
Atypicality	9.9	7.2	1.14
Teachers' Ratings			
Isolation	4.4	4.5	.02
Hostility	2.8	1.4	1.27
Likeability	9.9	10.6	.30
Attention-Seeking	6.8	5.3	.75
Atypicality	5.7	6.0	.14

[a] Peer Nominations Inventory.
[b] Residual-gains scores.

We also compared several subgroups of participants with their matched controls for differences in PNI change. Only two significant differences were found. Quiet participants $(N = 41)$ and participants with fathers in their homes $(N = 60)$ improved less $(p < .05)$ on classmate-rated hostility than their matched controls $(N = 40$ and $57)$. Similar analyses between pairs of participant and control subgroups characterized as black, Caucasian, outgoing, and no father in home did not generate significant differences.

Apparently, according to the observations of classmates and teachers, participants cannot be differentiated from their matched controls. Both groups, however, were motivated to join the project

Table 13

Initial and Final Sociometric[a] Scores for Participants and Randomly Selected Boys

	Initial Scores			Final Scores		
	Participants $N=87$	Randoms $N=201$	t	Participants $N=86$	Randoms $N=196$	t
Classmates' Ratings						
Isolation	17	12	4.34**[b]	18	11	4.33**
Hostility	19	17	1.14 N.S.	20	15	1.69
Likeability	34	41	2.71**	37	43	2.10*
Attention-Seeking	27	20	3.08**	25	19	2.01*
Atypicality	23	15	4.64**	22	14	4.09**
Teachers' Ratings						
Isolation	8	5	3.53**	7	5	3.05**
Hostility	7	5	1.49 N.S.	6	4	1.24
Likeability	8	11	2.48*	12	14	1.12
Attention-Seeking	12	7	2.33*	11	6	2.86**
Atypicality	6	3	3.53**	7	4	3.45**

[a] Peer Nominations Inventory.
[b] ** = $p < .01$; * = $p < .05$.

and were described as moderately troubled by their parents. The diagnosis of moderately troubled was supported when we compared participants with a stratified group of "typical" boys at the early and later testings. To make up this typical group $(N = 201)$, we randomly selected three to six boys from each classroom (depending on size), excluding those previously selected as participants and matched controls. Their mean PNI scores are displayed in Table 13. The magnitude of t-ratios clearly shows that both classmates and teachers, at early and later testings, described participants primarily as isolated and atypical. The same characteristics can be applied to the matched control group because their means and standard deviations were quite similar to those of participants. Attention-Seeking was another significant problem for participants and matched controls over the school year. Classmates rated the participants as significantly less likeable than typical boys at both test points. Teachers described a significant difference at the initial testing only. The data do not distinguish participants as signficantly more hostile than typical boys, but there is a suggestive trend in that direction. These findings offer strong evidence supporting the definition of our participant and matched control groups as moderately troubled. Compared with typical boys, they are seen at both test points as isolated, atypical, attention-seeking, and less likeable. The direction of change from initial to final test point is toward very slight improvement for most of the PNI measures: eight of ten for the typical group, and seven of ten for the participants and matched controls. None of the changes were significant. That is, we have not been able to find any significant change for our major samples on the PNI. Obviously, these findings do not support hypotheses about the effectiveness of companionships in reducing boys' problems.

Teachers' Retrospective Change Ratings

With slight modification the parents' retrospective questionnaire (Appendix E) was made ready for teachers. Teachers were asked to think back over the school year and rate the quality and degree of change in the boys' attitudes about school, schoolwork, peer relations, and self-esteem. They used seven-point change scales, with a "no change" midpoint. At the end of the school year, teachers were given questionnaires for participants ($N = 84$) and controls ($N = 74$) in their classroom. They were also given questionnaires for one or two boys not associated with the project. A cover letter mentioned that some of the questionnaires were for participants and others for controls. They were instructed to designate whether they knew, did not know, or were uncertain about each boy's status as a participant.

The mean scores and standard deviations were very similar to those produced by parents and counselors. All of the means for participants and controls fell quite close to the fifth scale point, which designated "a little" improvement. Standard deviations ranged from 1.1 to 1.3. Here are the specific means:

Attitude toward
    School   Participants, 4.8; Controls, 5.0
Gets Along with
    Other Children   Participants, 4.8; Controls, 4.8
Quality of School-
    work   Participants, 5.0; Controls, 5.0
Feelings about
    Himself   Participants, 4.8; Controls, 4.8

None of the differences between participants and controls approached the level of statistical significance. Parent ratings on the same items tended to be higher by about one third of a scale point, but their overall descriptions are essentially similar. Thus, teachers, parents, and counselors seemed to be saying the same things about the boys they rated: "They improve a little."

Subgroups of participants based on race, intactness of home, and quiet-outgoing designations were compared with their matched controls. No significant differences were found.

The teachers appeared to have only minimal knowledge about which boys were in companionships. Of the participants' teachers, 10 per cent said that they knew of the boys' involvement in the project, 6 per cent said that the boys were not involved, and 84 per cent reported uncertainty. None of the controls' teachers said that their boys were involved, 14 per cent said the boys were not involved, and 86 per cent were uncertain. We conclude that biased ratings from teacher knowledge of participation played an insignificant role in our retrospective and PNI findings.

Observations by Boys

Throughout the program we deliberately avoided questioning the boys. After the companionships terminated, however, we conducted structured interviews with the boys to gather their impressions on the effects of the companionships and the companionship process. Besides direct questions, a sequential series of sentence-completion items were used (story completion). A content analysis of the responses provides some insight into the companionship's effect from the boy's perspective.

Some of the participants' ($N = 84$) impressions of dimensions affected by the companionship were captured by the following question: "Do you think a project like this can change boys in some ways?" Almost all (95 per cent) thought that it could. *Interpersonal change* was the most frequently mentioned area (49 per cent): "It can help kids learn to make friends by being around an older guy." "At first I used to do a lot of stupid things because I was shy and I wouldn't even say 'Hi' or anything. Now I make friends better." "If they don't have a father, it teaches them not to be scared of men."

General learning and awareness of others was the best label we could find for another frequently mentioned area of change (36 per cent): "I learned ways to do homework better." "Same way it changed me—by talking to [the counselor] and watching him, I learned about other people's feelings." "You can get started on something like developing film and going to college." "Now I know how other boys think who have older brothers."

Self-concept change was mentioned by 10 per cent of the boys: "For some people, it could make them feel more liked." "Makes you feel that you can be a better friend to people." "It can change their way of thinking about themselves—like they can do things good too."

Two further questions divided interpersonal change, the most frequently mentioned dimension, into areas of adult and peer relations: "Since you joined the project, has there been any difference in the way you are with adults? . . . Do you think your friendship with [*counselor's name*] had something to do with any change?" The word "adults" was replaced with "other boys" in the second question. Responses were sorted into categories describing (1) *more frequent or intimate contact:* "Sometimes I wouldn't like to speak to grown-ups. . . . Stuart showed me they really didn't mind kids that much, so now I talk to them more." "I guess I got more popular because I've gotten along better with other boys"; (2) *less hostility:* "I used to talk back and holler. I don't even talk back to the principal anymore." "I don't fight with other boys or tease them as much"; (3) *more hostility:* "It's gotten worse because I hate grownups." "Look at my eye [bruised]. I fight more and win a lot"; (4) *unspecified:* "Well, I just act better— people tell me so"; (5) *no change:* "Phil [boy's counselor] and I really learned to get along, but I'm the same with everyone else."

Roughly half the boys described some specific positive change: more contact, less hostile interaction (Table 14). They

Table 14

INTERPERSONAL CHANGE DESCRIBED BY BOYS

Change	With Adults Per Cent	With Peers Per Cent
More Contact	34	45
Less Hostile	10	15
Unspecified Gain	10	9
More Hostile	3	5
No Change	43	27

mentioned more specific positive change in their relations with peers (45 per cent) than adults (34 per cent). Most instances of change (95 per cent) were credited to the companionship: "We got to trust each other and then I started trusting some guys at school." "He would teach me how to do things and I would teach other boys. This is a good way to make friends." "At first I didn't agree, but he showed me how older people respect each other."

One of the story-completion items was designed to elicit the boys' impression of skills and knowledge they acquired: "When it was all over [*boy's name*] thought about whether he learned new things when he was with [*counselor's name*]. [*Boy's name*] thought that ————." Thirty per cent of the responses described the acquisition of social skills (such as increased ability to converse and to hear others' points of view). Athletic skills were the theme of 21 per cent of the responses, and academic gains accounted for 20 per cent. The remaining descriptions of acquired skills and knowledge were extremely varied; for instance, learning to cook, studying about New York, building a hi-fi set, doing carpentry.

This set of impressions from participants provides some information on how boys experience change resulting from structured companionships. Most evident is their focus on interpersonal gains. Nearly half specified improved relations with adults, and more than half described specific improvements in peer relations as a consequence of the companionships. About 10 per cent reported unspecified interpersonal gains. In sum, 54 per cent of the participants claimed improved relations with adults, and 69 per cent did the same for peer relations. Ten per cent saw the project as able to enhance self-esteem. Finally, the learning of social, athletic, and academic skills was frequently mentioned as a function of companionships.

Summary

Parents provided observations and ratings at four specific time points: before the companionships were initiated, during the companionships, at the program's termination, and about one year later. Counselors' views were obtained at termination only. Several approaches to measuring change were used for participant and control samples. The combined findings do not generate a cohesive picture of the companionships' effect on troubled boys. Discrepancies between initial, termination, and follow-up scores on the Adjective Check List (ACL) and the Problem List for Elementary School Boys (PL) were complex and largely unsystematic. Only eight significant differences were found for the 180 comparisons between participant and control groups at the three assessment points. A review of the change patterns for both groups revealed that most boys tend to be described with fewer problems as time progresses. Other studies suggests that this phenomenon may be common when parents rate their boys' problems over subsequent points in time.

Scores for control boys moved in a favorable direction more frequently than scores for the participant sample. Controls were described as becoming more manageable and mannerly while the participants grew more boisterous. This was especially true on the ACL patterns for black, fatherless, and outgoing subsamples of participants. We speculated that the companionships' emphasis on self-disclosure, bilateral decision-making, and general egalitarianism taught some boys new ways of relating to adults. The new behavior could have presented parents with some child-management problems, which were probably reflected in the less docile and more troublesome ACL ratings for participant boys. Overall, the change patterns created by ACL and PL scores failed to support hypotheses on the facilitating or retarding impact of the companionship program.

Almost all the informal parent observations that came to us about two months into the companionships noted some desired change. Parents' retrospective ratings at termination and one year later were less glowing but still positive. Participants and controls were typically seen as improving a little in attitude toward school, peer relations, schoolwork, and self-esteem. The self-esteem scores of participants were higher than the scores for controls at the follow-up testing. However, the level of significance was marginal: $p < .10$. Caucasian controls were described as improving more than Caucasian participants in liking school ($p < .05$), and black participant boys were rated as more improved in their self-esteem than black controls ($p < .05$). Black participant boys also gained more than Caucasian participants in liking school and self-esteem. Actually, black participant boys received (nonsignificantly) higher scores on all the remaining retrospective scales when compared with their controls and to Caucasian participants. ACL findings indicated that black boys reduced their phobias and increased their boisterous behavior much more than their controls ($p < .01$). These findings combined raise hope that similar companionships

can help Negro children to like themselves more, feel greater surgency, and become less timid, mannerly, and phobic while displaying more independence, assertion, and rebelliousness.

All parents described their boys' central problem when the
program began. Then they rated changes in those problems at
termination and follow-up. It seems that the companionships helped
alleviate some of these "presenting problems" such as interpersonal
inadequacy, withdrawal, low self-esteem, and poor schoolwork.
Typical changes for participants was "somewhat better" compared to
"a little better" for controls at termination. The difference was not
statistically significant. Both groups continued to show improvement
at follow-up (one year later), but the participants improved more—
and the difference between groups was significant at $p < .05$.
Ninety-one per cent of the participants were seen as improved at
follow-up, compared with 61 per cent of their controls. In most
cases participant parents cited the companionships as important
factors in the improvement.

Another set of global change ratings by parents was obtained
by means of a chart that asked for changes in the way "my son
gets along with others" over two periods. The participant parents
reported significantly higher frequencies of improvement over the
companionship segment when compared with controls. Participants
also received more improved ratings over the follow-up period, but
the differences were of marginal significance. Seventy-five per cent
of the participants improved in getting along with others over the
program period, compared with 47 per cent of the controls. Over
the follow-up period, 86 per cent of the participants were described
as improving, compared with 70 per cent of the controls. Almost
all of the participant parents (97 per cent) felt that joining the
program was a wise decision. If they had the chance, they would
do it over again. Some justified their attitudes by pointing to specific
changes.

Looking back in time, about 70 per cent of the counselors
said that they noticed a significant personal problem in their boys
at the program's start. Problem types and frequencies were roughly
similar to those described by parents. Most of the counselors reported improvement in the initial problem, but the typical gain was

seen as small. One of four counselors reporting improvement qualified it as "much" or "very much."

The combined findings from parents and counselors do not add up to an unqualified demonstration of the companionship method as an effective agent. Similarity of Adjective Check List and Problem List scores for participants and controls at the three assessment points do not provide satisfactory evidence for acceptance or rejection of the companionship as a psychotherapeutic device. But the retrospective data gave definite signs that support the usefulness of companionships—especially with Negro boys who are fearful, dependent, and in need of liking themselves more. Some encouragement about the program's effectiveness for all kinds of boys came from the parents' follow-up ratings. Two years after the programs began, the initial problems of participants were seen as significantly more improved than their controls. Even with the lack of sensitivity, masking effects, and biases of our systematic data, it is clear that the open-ended comments of parents were endorsements of the companionships as a therapeutic success.

Measures gathered from the classroom failed to detect important differences between boys participating in companionships and their matched control group. Sociometric ratings on a modified Peer Nominations Inventory were similar for both groups at initial and final testings. Patterns of change were also similar for both groups as measured by raw-gains and residual-gains procedures. Retrospective change scales given to teachers also produced similar means for both groups. Most measures tended to indicate mild non-significant improvement for most subjects in areas of isolation, hostility, likeability, attention-seeking(atypicality, attitude toward hostility, quality of schoolwork, peer relations, and self-esteem. Sociometric ratings made by peers showed quiet participants and participants with intact homes improving less than their matched controls, but the finding was not paralleled by teacher ratings. Both participants and matched controls appeared significantly more troubled than a stratified random sample of boys on all of the sociometric ratings (classmates and teachers) except for the hostility dimension. However, the random sample did not make significant gains on any measure. At the conclusion of the program, participants described the potential impact of the companionships, which were clustered into three dimensions: interpersonal change, general learning and awareness of others, and self-concept change. Over half described improved peer relations resulting from the companionship, and over two thirds described improvement in the relations with adults. Enhanced self-esteem, new social and athletic skills, and academic knowledge were also mentioned as benefits of the companionships.

VIII

Predictors
of Change

Perhaps companionships are effective mainly for specific types of boys, or perhaps they are most effective when counselors have special characteristics. Perhaps a particular element is needed in the companionship process if troubled children are to be helped by it. These possibilities became more important as our studies based on the undifferentiated total samples built evidence that did not generally support the effectiveness of all companionships. Earlier chapters described some findings from a few subgroups based on boy characteristics such as race, intactness of home, and quiet or outgoing presenting problems. The present chapter describes an extended set of small studies on subgroups based on particular characteristics of the boys and the counselors. Some of the subgroups were based on variables that did not allow comparison with our nonparticipating control sample; others were too small for serious statistical testing. Some variables could be studied only with correlational methods, but they are reported here along with the more rigorous data because of their possible value for future research and program development. In short, we have looked in many corners for clues of any strength that might lead to hypotheses about the effectiveness of nonprofessionals in therapy roles. We assume that even weak evidence can provide guidance in an uncharted research area.

The outcome measures used in the following studies are essentially similar to those described in earlier chapters on boy change: eighty-one variables generated by parent, teacher, and classmate observations over the school year. Derived measures of change based on differences between pre and post scores were produced by the residual-gains formula, which partials out the contaminating effect of a score's initial status on its final status (Manning and DuBois, 1962). This data treatment allowed us to compare change patterns between many subgroups whose initial scores were not well matched.

Boy Characteristics

Fatherless Boys. Nearly one third of the participants ($N = 27$) had no father or male guardian in their homes during the program. Their change patterns were similar to those of the fatherless control group ($N = 21$) according to teacher and classmate data, but mothers' observations produced several significant differences. Both fatherless samples were at first seen by parents as aggressive and autonomous; and both groups, especially controls, became more manageable. Mothers of fatherless controls reported significantly greater increases on mannerly-obeys,* mama's little boy, weak-timid, mannerly-meek ($p < .01$) and on well behaved, good little man, and serious-careful ($p < .05$). Conversely, fatherless participants had greater increases on assertive and headstrong-rebellious ($p < .05$). The participants' mothers also saw their boys as acting more "unusual" and showing little improvement in their capacity to cope with new situations ($p < .05$ on the Problem List),

* See Figure 4 for original scale names.

while teachers rated them as improving less in their attitudes toward school (.05).

Fatherless participants showed few significant differences when compared with intact-home participants, but the pattern of scores suggested that fatherless boys tended to move toward somewhat greater autonomy and self-assertion, and less self-control. They also played alone less (.05) and gave their counselors more fun (.05) than participants from intact homes.

A more dramatic or conclusive set of findings on fatherless boys could have been useful to the growing number of "big brother" programs that pair fatherless boys into companionships with men. Our companionships were more structured, with greater visit frequency, and less emphasis on discipline and control, but there are important parallels. All that can be offered is the strong suggestion that fatherless boys appear to use their companionships as a practice ground for testing their surgency and autonomy.

Quiet and Outgoing Problems. When the initial teacher, parent, and classmate ratings described a boy as withdrawn, timid, or isolated, we classified his problem as "quiet." "Outgoing" meant ratings higher on attention-seeking, aggression, rebelliousness, dominance. Most of the boys fit easily into these two categories, but some were borderline. It is a rough divison aimed at locating clues about the differential effects of companionships.

The evidence suggests that companionships have some effect in moving quiet boys away from their withdrawn, timid, nonaggressive interpersonal styles. Their problems were still of the quiet variety when the program ended, but increased aggression was seen by parents and classmates. A comparison of change scores for quiet participants ($N = 43$) and their matched controls ($N = 39$) showed parents describing participants as more eager to win at all costs, getting into fights more frequently, and gaining more in their self-appraisal ($p < .05$ for all items) but gaining less on independence and being sure of themselves with people ($p < .05$). Of the remaining nonsignificant comparisons, over two thirds showed more favorable gains for quiet participants over their controls.

Outgoing participants ($N = 45$) seemed not to reduce their

aggression as much as outgoing controls ($N = 36$). Participants moved less toward mannerly-obeys ($p < .01$), mama's little boy ($p < .05$), and meek-manerly ($p < .05$) according to parents. They also showed fewer reductions on the mischievous (.01), unmannerly-rude (.05), and headstrong-rebellious (.05) scales.

Differences in change between the quiet and outgoing participants were frequently a function of the initial division into problem types. Parents rated outgoings as improving more on problems with dependence, sadness, playing alone, and self-esteem ($p < .05$). The quiets also improved in these areas, but not as much as outgoings. Perhaps the small improvement seen in quiets was considered significant by parents: they rated their boys as improving markedly more than outgoings on the "presenting problem" described in their initial application ($p < .05$). Quiets were also seen as significantly more improved than outgoings in their capacity to do good schoolwork and were seen as less isolated in the classroom (.05). During the companionships, quiets said that they expressed more anger, while the outgoings (counselors) reported having more fun ($p < .05$). Most of the remaining nonsignificant comparisons (85 per cent) fell in the direction of greater improvement for the quiet boys.

In general, these findings suggest that withdrawn, passive, isolated boys do not become much more sure of themselves in the home, nor do they gain much independence from parents; but they do become more aggressive about winning, fight more frequently, and gain significantly in liking themselves. Companionships seem to relieve their specific "presenting problems," such as passivity, giving up easily, and low self-esteem. During the companionships, quiet boys claim to have expressed more anger toward their counselors. Companionships with nonprofessionals appear to hold promise as an effective therapeutic device for reducing passivity and low self-esteem in troubled boys. The general effectiveness of companionships for boys with outgoing problems is doubtful, according to our data. If anything, these boys become less manageable at home than their nonparticipating controls.

Severity of Initial Problem. The most appropriate general label for boys in the program is "mildly" to "moderately" troubled. The entire group produced initial means significantly above those of a random group of boys on most indices of pathology drawn from a balanced composite of teacher and classmate ratings. Participants and controls were divided into quartiles of problem severity, based on Peer Nominations Inventory scores generated by classmate and teacher ratings. The upper quartiles formed high problem-severity groups of participants $(N = 19)$ and controls $(N = 15)$. Their pathology scores are equivalent to the upper 3 per cent of a pathology-score distribution for the random sample. In short, our high problem-severity groups are significantly troubled, and a majority had quiet problems.

A comparison of significantly troubled participants and controls suggests that companionships are beneficial to boys with more severe problems. Participants gained much more on classmates' ratings of likeability $(p < .01)$ and parents' ACL ratings of independent-assertive $(.01)$ and bossy $(.05)$. Participants became significantly less self-abasing and had fewer problems with appetite, speech, and physical modesty when compared with controls $(p < .05$ for all items$)$. Almost two thirds of the remaining nonsignificant comparisons showed more favorable gains for the participants.

We also studied low problem-severity boys, whose initial pathology scores were in the first quartile. Change patterns for these mildly troubled participants $(N = 21)$ and their matched controls $(N = 19)$ were essentially similar.

These findings offer hope for the therapeutic effectiveness of companionships with significantly troubled boys. The high incidence of quiet problem boys in the sample and the previous findings on all quiet problem boys leads us to suspect that more severely troubled boys who are passive and isolated can gain much from similar programs. The direction of change for more troubled participants indicates that they make more friends in school, become more assertive and self-confident, and achieve greater self-esteem. Even though our samples were too small for a systematic study of more severely troubled boys with quiet problems, an informal matched-pair study of eight such participants and matched controls revealed that participants gained more in all eight pairings on some major outcome measures: teacher and classmate PNI scores, parents' Problem List improvement, parents' and teachers' retrospective gain scales. A contrast of these findings with the no-difference findings for mildly troubled boys emphasizes the probability that companionships are effective change agents for boys with more severe problems—especially quiet problems.

Black and White Boys. Negro boys comprised almost 30 per cent of our final research sample. Almost all of the counselors were white because less than 1 per cent of the Berkeley university students were black. Our difficulty in recruiting black counselors confounded the study of race as a predictor of boy outcome. That is, we ended up with two dyad types: racially similar (double whites) and dissimilar (black boys with white counselors). The general outcome picture is that black participants improve more than their matched controls and white peers, while white participants and their controls produce similar patterns of change. This section will focus on findings related to black boys and will consolidate findings reported at various points in earlier chapters.

Parents' ratings accounted for all of the significant differences between black participants ($N = 25$) and their controls ($N = 20$). Participants showed a marked reduction in specific fears (phobias) when compared with their controls ($p < .01$). They had lower scores on weak-timid and mannerly-meek ($p < .01$) and on good little man and mannerly-obeys ($p < .05$). They had higher scores on independent-assertive, headstrong-rebellious, unmannerly-rude, and attention-seeking. On the parents' Retrospective Questionnaire, black participants were rated as improving more than controls on their attitudes toward themselves—their self-esteem ($p < .05$). About 70 per cent of the remaining nonsignificant comparisons favored black participants.

A comparison of black ($N = 25$) and white ($N = 62$) participants expanded the picture. According to parents, black participants improved much more in problem areas of playing alone, fearfulness, and self-esteem ($p < .01$). These boys were also described as becoming more likeable and more hostile by classmates ($p < .05$). Their Hostility scores were primarily descriptions of boastful aggression. About three fourths of the remaining nonsignificant comparisons fell in the direction of less improvement for white participants.

Some finer-grained data analyses of the Parents' Retrospective Questionnaire data revealed that 76 per cent of the black participants were seen as improving their self-esteem "much" or "very much," compared with 44 per cent of the white participants and 39 per cent of the black controls. A similar comparison was made for improvement in attitude toward school; 61 per cent of the black participants received ratings of "much" or "very much," compared to 31 per cent for white participants and 39 per cent for black controls. Roughly two-thirds of the black participants' parents saw the counselors' influence as a very important element in their boys' improvement. This finding is complemented by the black participants' favorable ratings of their companionships: compared with white participants, they described themselves as having more fun, being more disclosed, getting more understanding from their counselors, and saw their counselors as having more fun ($p < .05$ for all items).

The overall picture is quite promising. The parents of black participants report some gains from the companionships that are not seen in black controls or white participants. We hypothesize that companionships reduce fearfulness, timidity, isolated play, and parent manageability in black preadolescent boys, and increase self-esteem, assertion, rebellion, and liking toward school. We would also expect these boys to be seen as more likeable and boastfully aggressive over time by their classmates. Black participants with white counselors apparently felt more open and understood and had more fun than white participants with white counselors. At least, we know that these cross-age, cross-race companionships can be effective. A further study using both races of counselors and boys will be needed to shed light on the differential effectiveness of all cross-race pairings.

Summary. Earlier, our findings on the entire sample revealed a particular theme in the ways participants changed. They moved toward more self-assertion, aggression, and autonomy. Without surprise, a similar theme cut across findings for subgroups based on boy characteristics. It was especially evident for subgroups of fatherless, passive-withdrawn, more severely troubled, and black participating boys. Fewer changes were found for subgroups based on boys with intact homes, mild or moderate problems were classified as "outgoing." Most promising were the findings for black participants and more severely troubled participants. Passive-withdrawn boys also appeared to make some important gains. For the present, these boy characteristics are the most predictive of therapeutic gains from companionships. Later in this chapter we will show that boy characteristics may not be the most effective variables for structuring companionships. Nevertheless, it would be very interesting to do a study contrasting more severely troubled, quiet, black children with a moderately troubled, outgoing white subgroup. Our hunch is that the first group would win.

Counselor Characteristics

The connection between characteristics of professional therapists and therapeutic change in their patients is poorly understood and remains as one of the most difficult research problems in clinical psychology. The same issue is becoming critical in community psychology research involving nonprofessional therapists in field settings. For us, a combination of (a) measurement errors in assessing counselor characteristics and boy change and (b) unattended intervening variables created weak expectations for precise or strong findings. That is why we were surprised to discover several trends connecting counselor traits with boy change. We have divided counselor characteristics into three sections: (1) training, (2) personal history and self-concept, and (3) interpersonal traits.

Training. About half ($N = 45$) of the counselors attended twenty-seven weekly "in-service" training sessions with professional leaders (see Chapter Four). The other half ($N = 42$) did not attend the training sessions but were matched with trained counselors on variables such as age, socioeconomic status, interpersonal traits, and academic major. Both groups took six lessons of an automated course on interpersonal relations and had twenty-four-hour emergency access to several professional consultants. Boys assigned to both groups of counselors were nicely matched on such variables as age, race, problem type, and intactness of home.

One of our studies related counselor training to the boys' retrospective ratings of their experiences during the companionship. Our training goals of increased empathy and self-disclosure might have been achieved, because group-trained counselors were rated higher on these qualities than counselors who were more self-directed. Specifically, boys with trained counselors, compared to boys with self-directed counselors, said that they knew more about their counselors' feelings ($p < .01$) and that their own feelings were better known by counselors ($p < .05$). These boys also rated their trained counselors as more self-disclosed and higher on "He tries to get me to do what he wants" ($p < .05$). These findings suggest that small-group training raises levels of empathy, disclosure, and assertiveness. Another, less likely, explanation is that training raised the counselor's frequency of metacommunication about disclosure and empathy: "I'm really trying to understand how you feel" or "I think it's good to let you know all about myself." These forms of metacommunication could serve a labeling function; that is, the counselors define themselves to the boys, and then the boys define the counselors on our rating forms. We estimate, however, that such forms of metacommunication occurred infrequently during the companionships.

Parents' gain scores differed for boys with trained versus boys with self-directed counselors. The ratings for boys with trained counselors showed larger increases in the categories bossy and attention-seeking ($p < .01$), smaller reductions in the categories headstrong-rebellious and unmannerly-rude ($p < .05$), and larger reductions in the categories weak-timid and mannerly-meek ($p < .05$). A similar trend was observed for the nonsignificant comparison between groups. Once again the major axis of the findings points to a dimension of assertion-timidity or aggression-passivity. Thus, our findings support a hypothesis holding that companionships with counselors effectively trained to empathize and disclose generate an increase in boys' assertiveness.

Backgrounds and Self-Descriptions. We can report with some certainty that the following counselor characteristics have little or no bearing on their therapeutic effectiveness with troubled boys: degree of financial support from parents, span of time between leaving high school and entering college, amount of participation in high school or college extracurricular activities, parents' socioeconomic status, religious belief and religious commitment, score on Chapin's Social Insight Test, total score and lie score on Jourard's

Disclosure Questionnaire, and all scales of the Adjective Check List. A few items, however, display some trends that might be worth another look in future studies. Boys with counselors who received higher levels of financial support from higher socioeconomic parents tended to gain a little less. The same was true for boys with counselors who score very high on Jourard's lie scale. The trend was reversed for boys with counselors who had great faith in the effectivenes of psychotherapy. These trends are without statistical significance and can only suggest that financial dependence, an admitted propensity for lying, and faith in psychotherapy are characteristics that deserve watching in studies of nonprofessional therapists.

The counselors' ages ranged from 18 to 35. Half were betwen 20 and 21. Our correlations suggested that older counselors (23 to 35) were with boys who gained less, according to parents, on problems with stealing, temper tantrums, bed wetting, and irritability. Correlations ran from the mid-twenties to the mid-thirties ($.27 = p$ of $.01$). Since almost all the counselors were undergraduates, those in our upper age range (23-35) were rather old and atypical for a college population. At any rate, we suggest some caution in selecting undergraduates above 25, and we consider age of college student as a worthwhile variable for further study.

On their application form, counselors were asked, "Would you describe yourself as more quiet, reserved, or outgoing?" On the basis of their answers, we classified about half of our counselors as quiet and the other half as outgoing. Boys with self-described outgoing counselors were seen as becoming more likeable by classmates; and they, in turn, attributed more likeability and less hostility to their classmates ($p < .05$). Their total score on the parents' Problem List also showed more problem reduction ($p < .05$) when compared with boys attached to counselors describing themselves as quiet. A simple self-description of quiet-reserved may indicate more than a lack of aggression or gregariousness. It could be a marker for a withdrawn, concealed, overcautious interpersonal style in some applicants. If so, we would speculate that such behavior does not produce therapeutic gains in clients.

Interpersonal Traits. GAIT (Group Assessment of Interpersonal Traits method) is detailed in Chapter Three. Essentially, it is a structured small-group procedure that uses sociometrics and professional ratings to measure samples of interpersonal behavior along several dimensions. Three scales were used as selection criteria for our counselors: understanding (empathy), open (self-disclosure), and accepting-warm. Since applicants who received lower scores on these variables were rejected, we are left with a restricted sample of medium and high scorers. The lack of a complete curve of scores clearly reduced our chances for finding statistically significant relations between counselors' GAIT scores and boys' outcome measures. We tried to remedy the situation by dividing the counselor sample into upper and lower thirds on each variable. The remedy was not very successful because the division did not create significantly distinct groups, especially on the accepting-warm scale. The remaining two criterion scales allowed somewhat more successful division and generated a few clues about their predictive potential.

Those in the high open group ($N = 26$) were typically endorsed as "honest, frank, emotionally open" by 99 per cent of the raters after the GAIT assessment session. The mean score for the medium open group was 73 per cent, a rather small difference. Low open applicants were not hired into the program. Boys with high open counselors gained more on the parents' composite adjustment index ($p < .01$) and showed a greater reduction in speech problems ($p < .01$) when compared with boys attached to medium open counselors. The high open group of boys also gained more on a real boy (ACL heterosexuality) and less on the irritability, mood-swings, and sadness items on the Problem List ($p < .05$ for all items). Counselors described these boys as less angry at termination (.05). At a lower level of significance (.10), they showed more improvement in their initial problems, felt less picked on, were rated as less attention-seeking by teachers and less hostile by classmates and teachers; and their counselors described themselves as having more fun during the companionships. Seventy per cent of the remaining nonsignificant comparisons showed more gains for boys with High Open counselors. This evidence suggests that boys improve somewhat more with high open counselors than with medium open counselors. We are encouraged to speculate that the differential change in boys would have been more dramatic if high and *low* open counselors were used to form subgroups.

The high open group of counselors tended to describe themselves on the ACL as more labile ($p < .05$) and saw human nature as more complex ($p < .05$) when compared with mediums. Highs were also rated more understanding and higher on counselor potential and therapeutic talent; and they were chosen more frequently as a learning partner during GAIT sessions ($p < .01$ on all items). They were also seen as less rigid and more disclosive of hard-to-express feelings ($p < .05$).

The high understanding group ($N = 28$) received endorsements from 94 per cent of the GAIT raters on "I feel he understands what others really mean." Medium understanders ($N = 28$) had mean scores of 67 per cent. Once again, the absence of low scorers on understanding (below 50 per cent) hampered adequate testing of the variable. Boys with high understanding counselors were seen by parents as reducing their problems with fighting, teasing others, shyness, and speech ($p < .05$ on all items). These boys also gained more on 65 per cent of the remaining nonsignificant comparisons. Parents also saw high understanding counselors as more helpful in reducing the boys' presenting problems ($p < .05$), and the counselors described themselves as less pushy (fewer attempts to control) during the companionships ($p < .05$). Compared with medium understanders, the high understanding group described themselves as lower on self-control (.01) and on autonomy and aggression (.05) on the ACL. They viewed human nature as more complex (.05) and were rated as less rigid, more accepting-warm, with more therapeutic talent and counselor potential, and were chosen more frequently as a learning partner (all at .01). High understanders tended to be more self-supporting (.05), which corroborates some earlier significant correlations between self-supporting counselors and boy improvement. Self-support may have something to do with the fact that these counselors changed living quarters frequently and pursued fewer hobbies. Finally, there is corroborating evidence that high understanding counselors are conceptually better at solving interpersonal-relations problems; with marginal significance (.10) they produced higher scores on the Chapin Social Insight Test.

The high quiet counselors $(N = 30)$ were endorsed as "a mild, reserved, quiet person" by 88 per cent of the raters. The low quiet group $(N = 28)$ had a mean score of 30 per cent and contained more outgoing and less reserved counselors. Unlike the preceding variables, the quiet-outgoing measure was not used as a counselor-selection criterion and produced two rather distinct subgroups. Quiet is roughly orthogonal to open and understanding; it correlates significantly and positively with accepting-warm and blue, and negatively with rigid. It is the most internally reliable of all GAIT variables (see Chapter Three). Evidence described later in this section suggests that interpersonal withdrawal may be a characteristic of high quiet counselors.

Boys with low quiet counselors (less reserved and more outgoing) became much less typical and hostile and more likeable $(p < .05)$ to their classmates than boys with high quiet counselors. Boys with low quiet counselors were also described as reducing their hostility more by teachers and as becoming more sensitive-thoughtful, neat-fussy, and serious-careful by parents $(p < .05$ for all items). With less significance $(p < .10)$, they showed less irritability and increased self-esteem (parents) and were less isolated (classmates). These boys were also more improved on almost three fourths of the remaining nonsignificant comparisons. During the companionships, low quiet counselors felt more understood by their boys $(.05)$.

Apparently, low quiet counselors did better with their boys —but what does being low on "mild, reserved, quiet" mean? First of all, it means a strong *tendency* to describe oneself as generally outgoing rather than quiet $(p < .01)$. It also means being *infrequently* endorsed as "sad, blue, and discontented" by peers and professionals during GAIT sessions $(.01)$. In general, and in comparison with high quiet counselors, low quiet counselors chose "person-oriented" academic majors; were seen as "self-disclosed" and "assertive" by peers during twenty-seven training sessions; produced ACL self-descriptions high on exhibit and labile and low on abasement, deference, and succorance; and maintained lower grade-point averages in high school (all at $p < .05$). With marginal significance $(p < .10)$, low quiets had more previous experience working with children, more extracurricular activities in high school and college, and higher ACL scores on self-confidence and lower scores on order. They also tended to use more adjectives to describe themselves. Admittedly, the findings present a complex picture of this more successful counselor type. Perhaps the low quiets can be characterized as rather undepressed, emotionally expressive, person-oriented, assertively independent individuals.

We also considered counselors' scores on "relaxed" as predictors of boy change. Because most applicants viewed GAIT as strange and challenging, the group atmosphere of assessment sessions was generally colored by a mild tension. About half the applicants were rated tense to some degree. Our staff observed many sessions and agreed that the large majority of applicants appeared tense. We assume that most raters saw most applicants as tense but that many raters extrapolated beyond the session when responding to the item "I see him as a relaxed, easygoing person." That is, we assume that the GAIT item labeled "relaxed" is confounded by a blending of observed situational behavior and prediction of enduring traits. In short, we are unsure about what is being measured. The relaxed category has the lowest split-half reliability (.44) of all GAIT variables. Findings suggest, however, that counselors low on GAIT relaxed seem to help boys improve more.

Counselors in the relaxed group ($N = 28$) had a mean score of 81 per cent, compared with 36 per cent for counselors in the tense group ($N = 28$). Boys with tense counselors were rated by teachers as becoming more likeable and less attention-seeking, temperamental, opposing, irritable, and bossy (all at .05); they were rated more independent-assertive by parents (.05). Their scores fell in favorable directions on 60 per cent of the remaining nonsignificant comparisons. Thus, our tense counselors seem a little more effective. Perhaps this group did less masking of tension during assessment sessions and less masking of other emotional expression during the companionships, but that is a farfetched assumption. Meanwhile, we must regard lower scores (below 50 per cent) on GAIT relaxed as predictors of more effective counselors.

The high blue (depressed) group ($N = 28$) were typically seen as "sad, blue, discontented" by 56 per cent of the raters. This was true for 10 per cent of those in the low blue group ($N = 29$). Boys with low blue counselors showed significantly more improvement on their presenting problem, according to parents ($p < .01$). Teachers saw them improving their attitudes toward school and getting along better with peers ($p < .05$). Counselors reported improvement in the quality of the boys' schoolwork (.05). About two thirds of the remaining nonsignificant comparisons showed more favorable gains for these boys. Low blue counselors were seen as less controlling by their boys (.05), and they tended to describe themselves as less controlling with boys (.10). These counselors also rated themselves as being more understood by their boys and as understanding their boys more ($p < .05$).

High blue scores seem to predict less effective counselors. This group received higher GAIT quiet scores (.01), were infrequently chosen as a learning partner by peers (.05), and, with marginal significance (.10), had academic majors and career goals that were object-oriented: chemistry, engineering, and the like.

Counselors in the high rigid group ($N = 23$) were typically endorsed as appearing "set in his ways" by 63 per cent of the raters, in contrast to 16 per cent for the low rigid group ($N = 26$). Boys with low rigid counselors became less sad and more likeable to classmates and had fewer eating problems ($p < .05$). They improved more on 63 per cent of the remaining nonsignificant comparisons—especially on the Problem List (parents), where they "won" on 80 per cent of the comparisons. These boys described themselves as less angry at their counselors. Rigid is not a strong predictor of boy outcome, but it seems to tap some enduring counselor characteristics. Low rigid counselors see human nature as more complex and changeable, describe themselves as less self-confident and dominant, claim less religious commitment along with their parents, were less close to parents during high school (all at .05), and tend to conceal less with friends (.10).

Summary. Although none of the predictors found can be used with great confidence, they do allow *some* confidence and appear to be the best prospects for current nonprofessional therapy programs and studies. If we were faced with the immediate need to find students for therapy roles, we would use the following selection criteria: (1) GAIT understanding scores about 75 per cent, (2) open scores above 80 per cent, (3) quiet scores below 40 per cent, (4) blue scores below 20 per cent, (5) rigid scores below 20 per cent, (6) relaxed scores below 50 per cent, (7) person-oriented vocational goal or academic major, (8) a view of human nature as complex and changeable. We would also consider (1) slightly higher self-confidence and slightly lower self-control scores on the ACL, (2) little financial support from parents, (3) low scores on Jourard's lie scale, (4) more than average faith in the efficacy of psychotherapy, (5) an "outgoing" self-description, and (6) a more typical age for college undergraduates—below 25 years (see Chapter Three for derivation of all these variables). The therapeutic talent and accepting-warm categories of GAIT could not be appropriately studied within our project design, but Chinsky (1968) and Rappaport and his associates (1971) found evidence suggesting that these variables may predict effective student group leaders for mental patients.

When our first- and second-order criteria are put in a capsule profile, they create a picture of an assertively independent, empathic, emotionally open, undepressed, and flexible young man who sees people as dynamically complex but wants to work with them professionally and believes that therapy is frequently useful. This profile may seem obvious to some and debatable to others. Assertive independence may counterindicate trainability; much self-disclosure could be a sign of uncontained lability or indiscretion; great flexibility could be a label for fluidity, instability, or lack of commitment; a dynamically complex view of people might mask the appraisal of man's enduring qualities; belief in therapy may be gullibility—and so on. Nevertheless, our findings offer some empirical strength to the criteria. At the moment, they are the best predictors of therapeutic potential we can offer.

Companionship Characteristics

To facilitate our major research tasks, we spent much effort on pairing boys and counselors into dyads that had comparable qualities. The pairs were quite similar in socioeconomic status, boy-counselor age discrepancy, and other structural characteristics. Process characteristics of the companionships were also quite uniform because we regulated visit length and frequency and spending money and provided counselors with general guidelines on their approach to the boys (see Chapter Four). We created some systematic difference in dyad types by arbitrarily pairing quiet and outgoing boys and counselors into four equal groupings. White counselors with black or white boys formed distinct dyad types, but our inability to recruit black counselors did not allow study of the four combinations. Findings on white-black and white-white dyads were presented earlier in this chapter. Some fairly distinct dyad types were formed on the basis of visit frequency, visit length, and other process variables described by the counselors.

Quiet-Outgoing Dyads. Counselors were ranked on a quiet-outgoing dimension, with a composite score based on direct self-report, observers' ratings of group performance, and the ACL Exhibit scale. Their rank was split halfway to produce a quiet and an outgoing group (see Chapter Four). Boys were sorted into quiet and outgoing groups based on parents' descriptions of their presenting problem, teacher ratings, and classmates' sociometric scores. These counselor and boy groups were well matched on a host of other variables. Finally, they were matched into four dyad types: quiet counselors with quiet boys ("double quiets"), quiet counselors with outgoing boys, outgoing counselors with outgoing boys ("double outgoings"), and outgoing counselors with quiet boys. We did eighty-one two-way analysis-of-variance studies on the boy outcome variables and dyad types (Table 15). Fourteen residual-gains outcome measures showed a significant relation to dyad types. They formed a striking pattern of sharp gains for both dyad types with outgoing counselors and markedly small gains for the double quiets. These findings were clearly supported by trends in the sixty-seven nonsignificant analysis-of-variance studies.

The outgoing-quiet dyads (counselors listed first) showed a few more strong gains but were not much different from the double outgoings (Table 15). These two dyad types with outgoing counselors showed superior improvement on parents' ratings of problem reduction in areas of attention-seeking, manageability, temper tantrums, and irritability, along with improved attitudes toward school and increased self-esteem. They also gained much more on classmates' ratings of likeability. The double outgoing boys were espe-

Table 15

Summary of Boy Improvement for Quiet-Outgoing Dyad Types

Significant Variables[a]	DYAD TYPES (Counselor-Boy)				
	HOMOGENEOUS		HETEROGENEOUS		
	Quiet-Quiet[b] N = 21	Outgoing-Outgoing N = 23	Quiet-Outgoing N = 22	Outgoing-Quiet N = 21	F[e]
Revised ACL (Parents)					
Less attention-seeking	4.9[c]	6.4	4.8	9.9[d]	2.85
Less unmannerly-rude	3.0	8.3	4.0	10.3	2.81
Problem List (Parents)					
Total problem improvement	(2.0)[f]	23.0	12.2	15.6	3.29
Plays alone less	(0.0)	1.9	1.0	(.3)	5.15
Reduced sleep problems	(0.3)	0.8	0.9	1.8	4.88
Fewer hurt feelings	0.5	0.6	1.5	1.3	2.76
Less dependent	1.2	1.7	1.5	(0.5)	2.96
Fewer temper tantrums	(0.3)	1.6	(0.7)	1.7	3.21
Less irritable	(0.5)	2.0	(0.7)	1.5	4.22
Increased self-esteem	(0.2)	1.2	1.0	0.7	5.81
Improved school attitude	(0.7)	1.9	(0.4)	1.4	3.12
Sociometric (Classmates)					
Likeability	(7.2)	21.4	15.3	25.8	6.20
Parents' Retrospective					
Improved schoolwork	5.1	5.3	(4.5)	5.9	4.01
Teachers' Retrospective					
Improved schoolwork	5.2	5.2	(4.4)	5.2	2.87

[a] From a two-way analysis-of-variance study with eighty-one outcome variables.
[b] Counselor is listed first.
[c] Score magnitudes increase with improvement.
[d] Outstanding improvement indicated by italics.
[e] Probability of .05 for $F = 2.80$ and .01 for $F = 4.01$ (d.f. $= 3 \times 80-84$).
[f] Markedly less improvement indicated by parentheses.

cially improved on total problem reduction (parents' Problem List); in particular, they played alone less, grew less dependent, and were less irritable. The quiet boys with outgoing counselors showed special gains in improved schoolwork, fewer hurt feelings, and reduced sleep problems. Once again our findings suggest that outgoing counselors are more therapeutic. Our findings on companionship process indicate that outgoing counselors typically had longer visits with boys when compared to quiet counselors (3.1 versus 2.7 hours: $p < .01$). They also spent more money and engaged in a greater range of activities per visit ($p < .05$). They rarely worked on hobbies and tended to describe less difference between themselves and their boys in their experiences of comfort and interest during visits ($p < .05$).

Boys in the remaining dyad types evidenced considerably less improvement—especially those in double quiet dyads. Double quiet boys showed especially weak gains in total problem improvement. Apparently, they still played alone frequently and showed minimal improvement in the areas of sleep problems, self-esteem, temper tantrums, irritability, school attitudes, and likeability (Table 15). In almost three quarters of the comparisons made between the four dyad types, the double quiet boys were the least improved. Counselors in these dyads tended to rate more difference between themselves and their boys on the feeling and behavior scales for each visit. They also described their boys as much more quiet and less comfortable than themselves. Outgoing counselors described only small differences in these areas. These findings bring to mind frequent complaints that we heard from counselors and boys in double quiet dyads: they described their partners as unwilling to take initiative, withholding personal feelings, and failing to "reach out." It was as if each was frustrated at the lack of a complement or contrast to his own quiet disposition. We began to refer to double quiets as "resentment factories."

Most of the gains for boys in quiet-outgoing dyads were larger than for double quiets but smaller than for dyads with outgoing counselors (Table 15). These outgoing boys with quiet counselors were markedly less improved in attitudes toward school and quality of schoolwork as rated by teachers and parents.

Clearly, the evidence on dyad types warns against pairing

quiet problem boys with quiet counselors. Outgoing problem boys do not do much better with quiet counselors. It is the counselor characteristic of outgoing that predicts most of the positive gains in both quiet and outgoing boys.

Frequency and Length of Visits. To study the effect of visit frequency on boy change, we formed high ($N = 28$) and low ($N = 29$) visit groups, averaging fifty-eight and forty visits during the program year—roughly ten above and ten below the typical visit total of fifty visits. Boys in the low visit group showed significantly more reduction than the high visit group in parent-rated problem areas of playing alone, feeling "picked on," expressing jealousy and disappointment, acting "unusual," and seeking attention ($p < .05$). Low visit boys were also described as becoming more likeable and less isolated ($p < .05$) and improved more on 87 per cent of the remaining nonsignificant comparisons. Why should the group of boys with forty visits do so much better than the group with fifty-eight visits? We have a few clues. In the first place, group-trained counselors tended to make fewer visits (68 per cent of the low visit and 47 per cent of the high visit group). Previous findings suggest that group training is linked to higher gains for boys. Counselors in the low visit group had slightly higher scores on the Jourard Self-Disclosure Questionnaire ($p < .10$), especially in disclosures about personal finances ($p < .05$). They were willing to disclose more to their boys about their personality and religious feelings ($p < .05$). They visited the boy's home more frequently and described themselves as more autonomous ($p < .05$). Finally, we observed a somewhat weak negative correlation ($-.13$) between visit frequency and visit length. In sum, the findings suggest that group-trained counselors who are more self-disclosing and more autonomous, spend more time visiting their boys' home, and have lengthier contacts with their boys make fewer visits over the program year as their boys improve more.

Longer visits also appear to be positively related to boy improvement. We formed two subgroups based on the upper and lower thirds of the visit-length curve. The long-visit group ($N = 32$) met for an average of 3.4 hours, while the short-visit group ($N = 27$) met for 2.7 hours. Boys in the long-visit group gained more on the parent-rated adjustment composite ($p < .01$) and on the good little man scale and on self-esteem ($p < .05$) and showed significant improvement on problems with stealing, phobias, temper tantrums, physical modesty, and shyness ($p < .05$). Teachers rated these boys as improving the quality of their schoolwork, and parents rated their counselors as influencing schoolwork improvement ($p < .05$). Finally, classmates and teachers saw them as becoming less isolated (.05). They did better than the short-visit group on 91 per cent of the remaining nonsignificant comparisons. Looking for clues about the characteristics of long-visit companionships, we found a slightly higher proportion of black participants in the long-visit group (34 per cent versus 24 per cent) along with more boys who saw their counselors as having fun ($p < .05$). Long-visit counselors talked more about their boys' behavior during visits, saw their boys expressing feelings about the counselors more frequently, rated visits as more interesting to themselves and boys, rated their boys as less demanding and experiencing more fun during visits, rated less difference between themselves and boys on the quiet-outgoing scale, and described themselves as lower on abasement and control on the ACL (all at $< .05$). There was also a slight tendency for the long-visit counselors to describe termination of the companionship as more difficult ($p < .10$).

We did not predict that visit length and frequency would be important factors in the effectiveness of companionships, but they proved to be variables worthy of further study in nonprofessional programs. The more successful low visit group maintained a pattern of slightly more than two visits a week (excluding vacations and final examination periods); the high visit group met almost three times a week. The more successful long-visit group typically met for 3.4 hours, compared with 2.7 hours for the short-visit group. That leaves us with a potentially successful pattern: visits twice a week, each visit lasting 3½ hours. More frequent and shorter visits are counterindicative of therapeutic gain in this study. Length of visits appears to be the better predictor, according to the magnitude of boy change. These findings are somewhat contaminated by associated variables that also predict therapeutic gains: counselor training and self-disclosure, along with race of boys. Nevertheless, if we had it to do over again, counselors would be asked to meet their boys no more than twice a week for minimum three-hour visits.

Conversation and Activities during Visits. We did not find much meaningful relation between boy outcome measures and the kinds of activities pursued or topics discussed (see Chapter Five for details about conversations and activities listed on the Visit Report). A few correlations in the high twenties ($p < .05$) linked positive gains (rated by parents) to sharing meals during visits; infrequent trips to the movies; frequent conversation about the counselor's skills; and infrequent talk of the boy's father, the counselor's mother, or the mechanics of the companionship program. With similar significance, teachers' and classmates' ratings of positive gains were associated with frequent automobile or bike rides; spending little money during visits; frequent conversations about the boy's mother and his role in the family; and infrequent talk about the mechanics of the companionship program. These varied findings are not easy to combine. Apparently, frequent discussion of how the program was administered is associated with less improvement as rated by parents and teachers. It could be conjectured that such talk carried an impersonal flavor—perhaps a sign of interpersonal distance. With a little imagination for help, we can see most of the findings suggesting interpersonally closer conversation and activities for more improved boys. The evidence is obviously scanty, but becomes more persuasive when combined with findings on boy-counselor feelings during visits.

Counselors' Views of Dyads' Feelings. Seven of the eight feeling or mood scales on the Visit Report had opposite-word pairs that could be aligned on a favorable-unfavorable dimension (Chapter Five). Ratings for all but the quiet-outgoing polarity were aligned into a composite favorability score. The following adjectives anchored the favorable extremes of the scales used in the composite: *comfortable, open, relaxed, warm, happy, close,* and *interesting.* Counselors rated themselves and their boys independently, but the typical boy-counselor description for each scale correlated positively around .90. Therefore, we combined each counselor's description of himself and his boy. The intercorrelations of the seven combined and aligned scales were all positive $(x = .53)$. The composite favorability score is a compiled picture of the counselors' evaluation of interaction over all visits.

Dyads with composite favorability scores on the upper third of the curve formed a high favorability group $(N = 29, x = 4.64)$, while those in the bottom third formed the low favorability group $(N = 30, x = 4.22)$. The mean scale scores can be translated into "somewhat" favorable for the high group and "slightly" favorable for the low group. A comparison of boy outcome measures for the two groups clearly indicates that the "quite" favorable descriptions of visit interaction by counselors are more significantly associated with therapeutic gains than "slightly" favorable descriptions. Boys in the high favorability group produced greater gains on parent, classmate, and teacher ratings. The following findings are significant at $<.05$: high favorability boys showed a much stronger reduction on the total Problem List score. Specifically, they were described as becoming less sad, irritable, opposing, upset by new situations, shy, and unsure of themselves. They lied less, teased less, fought less, and showed hurt feelings less frequently. These boys also were seen as growing less hostile and isolated by classmates and teachers. Almost 80 per cent of the remaining nonsignificant comparisons showed more gain for the high favorability group. At termination, they described their counselors as more disclosed, less pushy, and less angry; and they claimed that they felt less anger and were more understanding of their counselors' feelings. Similarly, their counselors described themselves and their boys as more disclosed and experiencing more fun. They also reported more understanding of feelings between themselves and their boys.

A correlational study revealed that every scale in the favorability composite was significantly and positively associated with many boy outcome measures (most correlations in the high twenties; $p < .05$). Visit descriptions of nondemanding, comfortable, warm, and relaxed produced the greatest number of significant positive correlations wth favorable boy outcome scores. The quiet-outgoing scale (excluded from the favorability composite) produced two significantly negative correlations $(p < .05)$ with favorable boy outcome: (1) the total score on the Problem List was reduced, and (2) classmates' likeability ratings were associated with quiet ratings—a finding that appears connected to the unsatisfactory gains for boys in double quiet dyads, reported earlier.

Because counselors' ratings of feeling and mood span the entire companionship, they are not legitimate early predictors. Actually, we have found that counselors' evaluations of visit interchange are strongly related to the therapeutic gains described by other observers. That is, when counselors view the entire span of companionship interchange as favorable, parents, peers, and teachers also see improvement in the boys. On the other hand, it does seem possible to use composite favorability scores (or individual scale scores) as longer-range predictors of boy outcome by computing them over an earlier segment of visits. Several scales are quite consistent over the entire companionship (happy-sad, interested-bored, and boy: tense-relaxed; see Chapter Six) and could be used as indicators for professional intervention in the form of consultation with counselors or even the replacement of counselors.

Companionship Attrition. The small attrition subgroup ($N = 15$) is composed of dyads who unexpectedly terminated their companionships at least three months before the predetermined ending date of the program. In many cases the ostensible cause for the premature termination was reported as a lack of cooperation by boy or counselor, a returning father, a counselor's academic pressures; but we had difficulty in determining a clear cause. In a few cases, boys or counselors actually moved out of the school district or left the area. After several attempts to order the attrition sample by pinpointing reliable determinants for the premature termination, we gave up and simply defined the entire sample as companionships that failed to keep intact for their expected life span. The typical attrition dyad met for nineteen visits (compared to forty-nine for the regular sample) and had fifty-two hours of contact (141 hours for the regular sample).

Since only two thirds of the attrition parents responded to our final questionnaires, systematic study of parent outcome measures was prevented. However, an informal review suggested a trend of smaller gains when compared to the sample of regular companionships ($N = 88$). This informally observed trend was supported by systematic findings from both teacher and classmate ratings, which showed the entire attrition sample gaining more on isolation, hostility, and atypicality and less on likeability ($p < .05$ for all items).

What are the factors generating lower levels of improvement for attrition boys? Do the unfinished companionships differ from equivalent early stages of the regular long-term companionships? Process variables from the counselors' Visit Report data and other companionship parameters provided some partial answers to these questions. We compared process variables for the first third of the regular companionships (approximately seventeen visits) with the same process variables drawn from the entire length of attrition companionships (x = nineteen visits). The comparison revealed that attrition dyads met for shorter visits ($p < .05$). Mean visit length for attrition dyads was extremely short (2.6 hours) and is similar to the short-visit subgroup (2.7 hours) described earlier in this chapter as improving little on a wide range of outcome measures. We also found that twelve of the fifteen attrition counselors were classified as quiet and that eight of the dyad types were double quiet (quiet counselor *and* boy). These frequencies are significantly above expectation. (Both quiet counselors and double quiet dyads were described as suspected counterindicators of boy improvement earlier in this chapter.)

The attrition group went to the movies much more frequently than the larger sample ($p < .01$). Attritions also pursued few activities each visit, talked less about the boy's mother and the boy's feelings toward his counselor ($p < .01$), and shared fewer meals ($p < .05$). Attrition counselors described themselves *and* their boys as feeling less warm and comfortable, and more closed and quiet, during visits ($p < .01$). While regular counselors described very little difference between themselves and boys, the attrition counselors rated their boys as significantly less warm and more closed than themselves ($p < .05$). Finally, the composite favorability score for attritions was lower—as was the boy favorability score ($p < .05$). Counselors in the regular sample tended to describe their boys a bit more favorably than themselves; this tendency was slightly reversed for attrition counselors. In sum, there are many process indicators to serve as warning signs of impending attrition: shorter visits, quiet counselors, double quiet dyads, a small range of activities and frequent movie attendance, few meals shared, low counselor ratings of warmth and comfort, and higher ratings on the dyad's being closed and quiet. Of course, we were not looking for this set of warning signs. Instead, we depended upon brief parental evaluations, which were requested two months after the companionships began. As it turned out, eleven of the fifteen parents of attrition dyads failed to respond—even after second requests. The no-response rate for the regular sample turned out to be 6 per cent. Clearly, the parents' poor response to requests for information is associated with companionship attrition. All of these early signals combined should be a strong predictor composite for attrition; in turn, attrition seems a pretty good predictor of less improvement in the boys.

Summary. Our study of dyad types based on the quiet-outgoing dimension did not really yield a single most successful type. Boys with both quiet and outgoing classes of problems were measured as improving more when paired with outgoing counselors. Outgoing boys with quiet counselors gain considerably less, but the group lowest in improvement was the double quiet sample. Thus, the best predictor of minimal improvement is a double quiet companionship. These findings are particularly relevant for withdrawn, isolated, or depressed boys entering a nonprofessional therapy program: They do much better with outgoing counselors. We cannot resist speculating that these findings on the lower productivity of double quiet dyads might generalize to many forms of helping relationships. The findings also indicate that companionships with lower frequency and greater length of visits are associated with more favorable boy improvement. Since visit patterns were largely a product of counselor and boy choice, they were not unadulterated variables; for instance, counselor-training groups appeared to influence visit frequency. Visit length may be the better predictor. The findings suggest that meetings twice a week, lasting at least three hours each, will benefit boys more than shorter and more frequent visits. Patterns of conversation topics and activities pursued did little predicting of boy outcome. The few topics and activities associated with boy improvement were interpreted along a speculative distance-closeness dimension. For example, frequent movie attendance and frequent discussion of an impersonal topic, such as the companionship program's administrative structure, were considered indications of impersonality and distance and were found to be associated with fewer outcome gains. However, the findings were scanty, and the speculation was long. Stronger findings came from the composite favorability score drawn from counselors' ratings of feelings and mood during each visit (collapsed into a single index). Boys in a high favorability subgroup gained much more than low favorability boys. We thought that a tendency toward positive ratings early in the companionship on scales such as happy-sad, interested-bored, and tense-relaxed might predict greater improvement in boys. The companionship quality of attrition (premature termination) was difficult to assess due to missing parent outcome data, small sample size, and the problem of adequately defining "internally caused" attrition. Teacher and classmate ratings of improvement were clearly lower for the attrition group. These "unfinished" companionships had other characteristics that appeared counterindicative of boy improvement: (1) a high incidence of double quiet dyads and quiet counselors, (2) shorter visits, (3) a small range of activities during visits, with frequent movie attendance and few meals shared, and (4) low ratings on the composite favorability score. We also found a high incidence of reluctance to fill out project forms among parents of attrition boys. Evidence of the reluctance was apparent while the companionship still existed.

IX

Impact on
Counselors

The few existing systematic studies of programs designed to use students in psychologically helping relationships report considerable impact on the students. Most companionships are capable of changing the participants' interpersonal styles or attitudes. A special companionship manufactured to help one of its members should be more capable of changing the "helper." We know that many joined our project hoping to acquire new interpersonal skills (see Chapter Three). In short, we expected to see change. So did Holzberg, Whiting, and Lowy (1964), who advanced the proposition that students serving as companions to hospitalized mental patients "undergo changes in personality that are not unlike changes observed and reported in psychotherapy—that is, student companions

after the companion experience perceive differently, think differently, and probably learn and feel differently."

In a pilot program similar to ours, Cowen, Zax, and Laird
(1966) studied changes in seventeen college students who volunteered for after-school day care of children with "manifest or
incipient emotional problems." The program was short: about
fifteen meetings. A comparison of pre and post responses to a
semantic-differential type of instrument suggested that the volunteers changed some of their attitudes as a result of participating.
Although the findings are weakened by the lack of control-group
data at posttesting, the trend suggests that students develop a
greater acceptance of troubled children, a disenchantment with
the school situation, a less glowing view of themselves, and a more
glowing view of the mental health field.

In another study, Scheibe (1965) noted changes in students
working in mental hospitals. The students were assigned to chronic
wards full time for eight weeks, received modest pay, and were not
the exclusive companions of individual patients. Three fourths of
the students were female. Once again, the pre-post changes in students showed an increase in positive attitude toward the people
they were trying to help—in this case, patients.

Apparently, the favorable shift in attitude toward emotionally disturbed people is a common occurrence for college students working in mental health projects. Scheibe's findings were
replicated by Chinsky and Rappaport (1970) and by Turner and
his associates (1967) with student companions in state hospital
programs. Self-descriptions of students changed in the direction of
greater surgency and confidence. They also perceived themselves
as better adjusted, more nurturant, and more self-controlled at the
program's end. Normality and mental illness were seen to be more
of a continuum as a result of the experience. A six-month follow-up
revealed that vocational goals tended to crystallize and a greater
number of students wished to enter the mental health field. This
last finding corroborates our own unsystematic impressions based on
communication with some counselors six to eighteen months after
they left the program. Unfortunately, we did not do an organized
follow-up study on our students. Their extreme mobility and our

other interests limited the collection of data to the beginning and termination of the program year.

Nancy Van Couvering (1966) noted changes in students who served as companions to juvenile delinquents for a school year. Black students showed more change in their self-concepts than white students. Deference scores for the black students dropped dramatically over the program year. They also decreased their self-control, adjustment, and endurance self-descriptions while showing strong gains on autonomy. Both subgroups of students showed a significant decrease in favorability and an increase in self-described aggression. According to Van Couvering, the shift in the black students' self-descriptions reflects their increased assertiveness, which was systematically observed by other students during training sessions. The other trend, for less socially desirable self-descriptions from all students, is more difficult to interpret, since a nonparticipating control group was missing; but it is similar to Cowen's finding of less positive self-descriptions from companions, along with a reduction of overidealistic views of institutional concepts. He postulates that the companions may have moved toward a more "healthily realistic" outlook.

Each of the programs above made different demands and provided different types of experiences for students, but all aimed at helping someone with emotional problems. While the results do not add up to a single pattern of student change, there is a trend for a more accepting view of emotional problems. It also appears that aggression becomes more acceptable and more a part of the students' self-concepts. Other studies have found that students working as therapeutic agents gain confidence and self-understanding and frequently reduce confusion about their career goals (Gruver, 1971). The picture is one of uniform student enthusiasm, with reports of increased knowledge about mental illness, greater introspection, and heightened academic achievement. In general, students appear very impressed with their expanded viewpoints and often claim the experience as a highlight of their college instruction. These findings are obviously rough because the programs lacked uniformity and research designs frequently (and understandably) lacked rigor. But, on the whole, these initial investigations clearly support the general notion that students who experience the role of psychological helper or interpersonal change agent can expect to find some important changes in themselves.

Initial Matching of Counselors and Controls

One of the defining characteristics of our control group was motivation to join the project. Good luck provided us with a control sample of students who were also interested in working with troubled children; about 90 per cent of the control group actually applied to the project but withdrew during the lengthy waiting period, which extended to five months for many (we recruited in May for October's program to allow some screening during the summer). Reasons for withdrawing were not studied, but applicants knew that there was a high rejection rate and we assume many took other job offers rather than wait for uncertain acceptance by our project. Regardless of the reasons for withdrawing, the control group's initial motivation to work on the project is an important characteristic that parallels the counselor group and makes them more comparable.

In order to enlarge the control sample, a few additional (nonapplicant) students were recruited through the following paragraph in our project announcement: "If you are interested in our work but cannot spend the required time, we invite you to fill out the application and participate as a member of the 'control' group which will help us assess changes that may occur in our counselors. This would involve filling out questionnaires now and again at the end of the spring semester."

About 20 per cent of the original control group was trimmed away in the process of matching them with the counselor group. Matching was based on quiet-outgoing self-descriptions (a combination of the ACL exhibit score and a pertinent question on the application), vocational goal, age, and socioeconomic status. The two groups looked quite similar: mean age was within half a year; marital status, mobility, grade-point averages, and high school and college activities were almost identical. There were some initial differences that should be considered in assessing differential change between the two groups: counselors described themselves as more self-disclosing—especially to peers around the areas of personality and money. They also had higher scores on ACL heterosexuality (Gough and Heilbrun, 1965) and more frequently chose person-oriented academic majors. Counselors' mothers had more education, while their fathers were less committed to religion. The Social Insight Test scores (Chapin, 1942) were also somewhat higher for counselors (see Chapter Three for more details on these differences). But, in general, the two groups were quite similar. The many parallels in self-description, attitudes toward human nature, family background, academic status, and interest in mental health work provided a meaningful control group with which to compare changes occurring in the counselor group who worked in our project.

Personal Changes Described at Termination

We asked counselors and controls to report increases or decreases in several classes of interest. Table 16 shows the differences

Table 16

CHANGES OF INTERESTS FOR COUNSELORS AND CONTROLS

Change of Interest in	Counselors $(N = 88)$	Controls $(N = 43)$	p
Children's Behavior	7.0[a]	6.1	.01
Working with troubled people	6.3	5.4	.01
The way you interact with friends	7.6	7.0	.05
Your own feelings and behavior	7.1	6.8	N.S.
Your field of study	6.4	6.1	N.S.
Political issues	6.3	6.3	N.S.

[a] Of a nine-step scale starting from "decreased greatly" (1), to "no change" (5), and ending at "increased greatly" (9).

observed between counselors and their controls in order of increasing similarity. Because most of the controls had initially applied to work in the project, we assume that their interest in working with troubled children was generally similar to that of the counselors. Therefore, the significant gains in interests shown by counselors appear to be the result of participation. Increased counselor interest in children's behavior, in their own interpersonal behavior, and in working with troubled people could be the signs of readiness for reappraising career goals. For example, nearly half of the controls described "no change" in interest toward children's behavior, compared to only 7 per cent of the counselors.

The final three items on Table 16 are not significantly disparate between groups. However, counselors who attended the interpersonal-training groups tended to indicate a greater increase than controls in interest toward their own feelings and behavior ($p < .10$). Incidentally, group-trained counselors who reported very sharp increases in interest toward personal feelings and behavior were described by their fellow group members as especially good understanders of others' feelings ($r = .52$). The "political issues" item was inserted as a test for response set. Since it was unlikely for the project to influence the political concern of students, any great change in the counselors' political interest (as compared with controls) would cause us to suspect a "strain-toward-change" bias in their response styles. As seen in Table 16, counselors and controls reported identical means. This finding brings greater confidence to the significant differences found in other areas of interest. Incidentally, about 75 per cent of both groups said that their political interest had increased. We assume that much of the increase was due to the heightened political activity on campus during the program.

An accessory question given only to participating counselors asked whether being a companion had had any effect on the interest areas discussed above. The five-step scale ranged from "no effect" to "great effect." Two thirds of the counselors said that the project experience had influenced their thinking about study majors. Most described the influence as slight or moderate; 10 per cent were strongly influenced. The project had considerable influence on counselors' interests in working with troubled people; only 15 per cent described themselves as unaffected by participating. Ninety-one per cent of the counselors said that the project had affected their interest in the way they themselves interacted with friends;

and one third of these said that the influence was strong. The project's most pervasive impact on counselors' interest was in the areas of *children's behavior* and their *own feelings and behavior*. Almost all said that the project was responsible for some change, and about half of the counselors described the impact as strong.

When asked whether they had experienced changes in any other areas, about 40 per cent of the counselors chose to comment that the project had increased their interest in areas of race relations, social action, studying psychology, going into therapy, parent-child relationships, and families in general. The most frequently mentioned area of influence was interpersonal relations—especially with peers or, more specifically, girl friends. A close second was the project's effect on attitudes toward self—personal worth, life goals, "growing up." Next came cross-race relationships. White counselors who were paired with black boys often felt that they now "wanted to become more familiar with black people and their way of life." Interest in a number of very specific things (such as building another program for grade school children with high school companions, or studying the bureaucracy of research projects) also was stimulated by the project. The amount of project influence was usually rated as "much effect." The "slight effect" category was never used.

Counselors and controls were both asked whether there were changes in their extracurricular activities, religious commitment, quality of schoolwork, manner of relating to friends. Items asked for "yes" or "no" answers, with room for additional comment on the quality of change. The two groups were almost identical in reporting no change in their religious commitment (which was slight at the project's start) and small increases in their extracurricular activities. A question on change toward a quiet or outgoing interpersonal style had more of the counselors describing a shift toward outgoing, but the difference between groups was not significant. A later analysis of counselor and control subgroups initially classified as either quiet or outgoing did produce a significant difference: quiet counselors saw themselves as becoming more outgoing than did their matched quiet controls ($p < .05$); outgoing counselors and controls tended to report no change. We also found that the program's demand of time and energy seemed not to interfere with the counselors' progress as students; they reported academic gains similar to those reported by the control group.

About 9 per cent of the counselors and the controls started to see a professional therapist or counselor during the year. At the beginning of the year, 6 per cent of the counselors and none of the controls were in therapy or counseling. Our extrapolation from the university's mental health service intake records indicates that about 9 per cent of the male students start therapy each year. We assume that the project experience was unrelated to starting therapy, since the rates for counselors and controls were similar.

One item asked: "Did your experience on this project serve, in any way, as an influence on your thinking about future involvement in some type of mental health work?" About half of the counselors said "no"; the other half described some increase in their desire for involvement in mental health work. The controls also were asked about future participation in mental health work; only 5 per cent described increased interest.

Another question, directed solely at counselors, asked: *"Since you have been with us,* have you decided to apply for work in the Peace Corps, Vista, or any other interpersonal, mental health, or person-centered program? Were you accepted?" Thirty-six per cent had applied; and 14 per cent were presently thinking about such work. Sixty per cent of the counselors who did apply told us that they had been accepted; 14 per cent were rejected; the remainder had applications pending. These figures may be conservative, since our subsequent informal contact with former counselors revealed that interest in mental health work sometimes crystallized months after the counselor had left the project.

We found no differential change in study major between the two groups, even though the evidence indicates that counselors move closer to mental health work. Ninety per cent of the students did not change their major, and were unlikely to, since three fourths of them were graduates, seniors, and juniors. Another factor reducing the possibility of finding a significant counselor shift toward more "person-oriented" majors was that most of them were already there: 57 per cent were studying within the social sciences.

One of the more important findings was the significant

difference betwen counselors and controls on the item asking about change in "the way you interact with friends." Three fourths of the counselors described better or more frequent relationships with peers, compared with 45 per cent of the controls. Here are some typical counselor comments: "I feel I now *relate* more than just *react* to friends." "The project has helped me to be more direct, personal, and curious with people." "Somehow I have become less concerned about the ideas they express and more tuned in to the feelings behind the ideas." Only 22 per cent of the counselors said that they did not change in this area, compared with half of the controls. The coded responses for the two groups were significantly different ($p < .01$).

We also asked the counselors: "If you were starting over again, what would you do differently (if anything) to improve your relationship with your boy?" Here are some very representative responses: "Worry less about what he thought of me and try harder to be myself in as honest and open a way as possible." "I'd more readily tell him of things I liked and disliked in general, about him, me, and our companionship." "First, be more open with myself." "Have less preconceptions. Be frank about my motives for seeing him and my affection for him." "Be myself more—honest— not try to 'treat' the boy, but be a friend."

The final question, directed at counselors only, asked: "Has the project affected you in some way that we did not ask about?" Nearly half answered mainly with some elaboration of a previously asked question on relations with others. Many of the responses described a profound impact by the project. A few comments described negative experiences and point to the ways students might change in an unwanted direction: "I got a feeling of inadequacy from not being able to keep things moving—most visits started out trying to figure out something to do."

Changes between Initial and Final Assessment

The Adjective Check List (Gough and Heilbrun, 1965), the Self-Disclosure Questionnaire (Jourard, 1962), the Philosophies of Human Nature Questionnaire (Wrightsman, 1964, 1968), and the Social Insight Test (Chapin, 1942) were administered to counselors and controls on two occasions: before the companionships started (pre) and near their termination (post). The ACL is more suspect of reflecting a social-desirability response set at the initial testing than the remaining instruments because it was given soon after the GAIT sessions and before the applicants received their acceptance or rejection notices. The remaining instruments were administered to accepted counselors and controls after the notices had been mailed. However, the initial pattern of normally favorable scores (see Chapter Three) does not support a response-set hypotheses.

Self-Description Changes on Adjective Check List. The tone of counselors' ACL self-descriptions became less favorable at posttesting. Controls produced a similar pattern, but on a smaller scale. Counselor change was seen by a significant decrease ($p <$ .01) in the use of favorable words and a trend ($p < .10$) toward using more self-critical words. Their scores on the defensive scale dropped significantly ($p < .01$), and they chose many more adjectives to describe themselves at the program's end ($p < .01$). In addition, counselor scores lowered on affiliation, self-control, adjustment, endurance, nurturance, intraception, and order (all at $p <$ .01). Lower scores on deference and achievement also occurred with slightly less significance (both at $p < .05$). Two scales increased significantly ($p < .01$): autonomy and aggression. A similar pattern of change was produced by the controls, but there were only two instances where the magnitude of change was clearly significant: decreased favorability and increased succorance (both at $< .05$). Significant differences in the magnitude of change between counselors and controls occurred infrequently because both groups were headed in the same direction and displayed much variability. Nevertheless, it is apparent that counselors changed their self-descriptions more than controls. Of the twenty-five ACL scales, counselors changed significantly on fourteen, compared with only two significant changes for the control group ($p < .01$).

One important difference between counselors and controls occurred on the ACL item labeled "change." Counselors reported increased needs for change, spontaneity, and risk-taking, while controls reported a decreased need. The difference in movement is significant at .05, and the difference between groups at posttesting is significant at .01. Counselors decrease sharply from pre to post-testing on order ("cautious," "logical," "rigid"), while controls remain the same ($p < .05$).

Findings from the previously mentioned programs using student workers show some correspondence to the ACL changes found here. Holzberg's finding that a change toward greater toler-ance of aggressive behavior in companions (Holzberg, Gewirtz, and Ebner, 1964) may be similar to the increase in self-ascribed aggression for our counselors. Students in the program reported by Cowen, Zax, and Laird (1966) changed descriptions of "myself" toward the less pleasant and good side of the rating scale after their short experiences as companions. The investigators regard the change as one toward more realistic self-definition. The changes Van Couvering (1966) found offer some striking duplications of our findings. Both her students and ours decrease significantly on ACL favorability, nurturance, and affiliation while increasing on aggression. Van Couvering's subgroup of black students shows further changes similar to our ACL findings: a significant move-ment toward less deference, self-control, adjustment, defensiveness, order, and endurance, accompanied by a significant gain on auton-omy. When findings from Van Couvering's student groups are combined, they create a pattern of eleven ACL changes (compared with our fourteen). Each of the eleven changes finds exact parallel in our findings. Since Van Couvering's project was closely modeled after ours in selection procedure, training, number of visits, length of relationship (seven to eight months), and student population (Berkeley males), we could conclude that the similar findings on change are a product of similar program experiences for both groups of students. Perhaps the weekly sensitivity-training groups used by both programs were a factor in the reduction of defensive self-rating. Scheibe's (1965) students showed a minor increase in ACL defensiveness, but the change was not significant. His findings also suggest an increase in the students' surgency or self-assertion, which appears in Van Couvering's and our findings as increased aggression and autonomy.

More clarity is brought to these ACL findings when we cast them within the factor structure found by Parker and Megargee (1967). Their factor analytic study of the ACL produced a primary factor labeled "positive vs. negative evaluation," which closely resembles a factor found by Scarr (1966): "social desirability." It contains the categories defensiveness, favorability, self-control, adjustment, endurance, order, intraception, nurturance, and affiliation; and (reflected) unfavorability, autonomy, aggression, and succorance. Our counselors changed significantly toward negative evaluation on a dozen of the thirteen scales in this factor. The weakest significant change was on the number-of-unfavorable-adjectives scale ($p < .10$), suggesting that most of the movement was toward reducing favorable words instead of increasing unfavorable words. Since this factor accounts for most of the counselors' ACL change, we can be more definite in concluding that students systematically reduce their favorable self-descriptions after participation in the project.

Another factor, labeled "emotionality vs. stolidity," contains the categories change, order (reflected), lability, heterosexuality, and counseling readiness (reflected). Counselors moved significantly ($p < .01$) toward the "emotionality" pole. Their performance through both factors shows that counselors come to appraise themselves as less stolid (or more emotional) and less socially desirable.

Changes in Self-Reported Disclosure to Others. Almost all the initial self-disclosure scores were lowered by counselors and controls during the final testing (Figure 6). Once again these students seemed to be describing themselves in a less favorable light at the project's close. The reduced self-disclosure scores could be seen as (1) an artifact of the questionnaire upon repeated testing, (2) a product of feigned openness during the initial testing, (3) a result of greater self-awareness, or (4) a true index of lowered self-disclosure over the school year. Perhaps all of these possibilities influenced the findings. If the counselors did feign openness, it was not motivated by a desire to enhance their chances for selection, since the Self-Disclosure Questionnaire was administered *after* they were aware of being selected. The controls also took the questionnaire after they had officially switched status from applicant to paid control subject. The possibility that lowered scores might be a true index of reduced self-disclosure left us unconvinced until we examined the pattern of "target person" self-disclosure scores

FIGURE 6.   Changes in self-reported disclosure to several target persons for counslors (circles) and controls (squares)

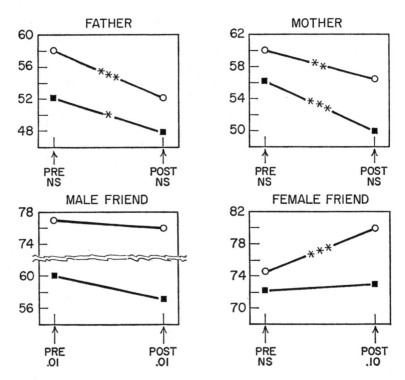

Asterisks indicate significance level of change from pre to post: * = .10, ** = .05, *** = .01. "Pre" and "post" indicate significance level of difference between the two groups at either pre or post.

(Figure 6). Both groups showed a significant trend toward disclosing less to parents over the year. There was no such trend for reduced disclosure to peers (pals and girl friends). Thus, these findings indicate that our students tell less about their feelings and thoughts to parents over the college years. Such a hypothesis is easy to believe; therefore, we consider the lowered scores primarily an index of true change. Since counselors and controls evidence similar change, we regard it as a phenomenon uninfluenced by the program.

The counselors' sharp increase in disclosure to their girl friends, however, may have been influenced by the program, since such an increase does not occur for the nonparticipating controls. The mean score for controls remained stable over the year, while the counselors' mean rose sharply and significantly ($p < .01$). As an earlier retrospective finding had shown, many counselors felt that the project had increased their interest in the way they related to girls. Perhaps learning how to get close to a troubled boy helped them get closer to other people who can be troublesome to them— such as college females. Being in the sensitivity-training groups also may have helped counselors share more with girl friends; trained counselors gained more than any other subgroup on disclosure to female friends.

In general, all the disclosure scores of counselors were higher than those for controls both at pre and post. Both groups came from the larger population of project applicants with one important exception: counselors survived the group-assessment process (GAIT), where nearly one third of the applicants failed to meet standards that included high scores on open ("He appears honest, frank, emotionally open"). Controls were not screened by GAIT, and their lower scores on the Self-Disclosure Questionnaire may reflect this fact. In detail, the mean general disclosure score for controls went down slightly from pre to post ($p < .10$). The significantly higher counselor scores remained very stable. Without exception, both groups reported the least disclosure to father and mother at both time points. Jourard (1962) and Weigel and Chadwick (1966) also found that male college students tell less of their current thoughts and feelings to parents than to peers. These convergent findings are less than startling, but they do offer some support for the internal coherence of Jourard's questionnaire.

Neither group changed much on the disclosure content scales: attitudes, tastes, studies, money matters, personality, or body. The rank order of mean scores describes a continuum from disclosing least about the concrete-personal to most about the abstract or less personal.

Counselors gained slightly on the lie scale—an index of admitted lying. The mean score for controls dropped ($p < .10$). Thus, the counselors said that their lying habits were similar at pre and post, while the apparently more concealed control group tended to claim a reduction in lying.

Philosophies of Human Nature Questionnaire. Final scores on the Philosophies of Human Nature Questionnaire were quite similar to the scores produced at the time of application. Working on the project did little to change students' values about the nature of man. Their views of the trustworthiness, resoluteness, complexity, independence, and goodness of others remained very stable. Counselors continued to describe people as quite trustworthy. Their mean scores on the category labeled "trustworthy" were higher ($p < .10$) than the control group's scores at all testing points. Thus, controls said that they trusted others less and reported telling less to others on the Self-Disclosure Questionnaire.

Compared with controls, the counselor group showed an insignificant tendency to describe people as more variable and independent and possessing less strength of will. Otherwise, our study of changes in attitude toward human nature indicates little project influence when all counselors are compared with all controls. A more detailed look at specific subgroups revealed that some attitude change did occur, but it depended upon initial student characteristics and situational factors within the project. These findings are discussed later in this chapter.

Social Insight Test. Not much happened on the Social Insight Test. Both groups gained about the same at posttesting. Counselors' gains were somewhat more consistent and appeared modestly significant ($p < .10$). The mean score for counselors at the time of application (25.9) is close to that of college students in general (see Chapter Three). At termination, the counselors' mean score moved up to 27.1, which is close to the mean for graduate psychology students: 27.4 (Gough and Heilbrun, 1965).

Changes in Quiet and Outgoing Counselors

We designated counselors as quiet or outgoing on the basis of a balanced composite score of self-description and others' observations. A rank ordering based on the composite score was split in half to form the two groups. The quiet counselor had a lower score on ACL exhibit, described himself as "quiet or reserved" in social situations, and was rated as a "mild, reserved, quiet person" by peer and professional observers during a structured group selection session (Chapter Three). The outgoing counselor tended to be the appropriate opposite on all three variables. At the time of application, quiet counselors had significantly lower scores than outgoings on all ACL scales comprising the extroversion-introversion factors found by Scarr (1966). We found several other significant differences between the two types of students: outgoings chose more person-oriented academic majors, saw human nature as somewhat less complex, and were more set in their ways according to staff and student observers in the group selection sessions. Interestingly, the staff predicted that more quiet counselors would turn out to be the best counselors, but the student observers chose outgoings. Students also saw outgoings as more understanding and open, while the staff said that they were less warm than quiets. The students turned out to be better predictors, since boys with outgoing counselors were measured as improving more frequently (see Chapter Eight). In our study of differential change between these two groups, we were able to measure more movement for the outgoing group. However, the findings that follow may strike some as indicating more important changes in the lives of our generally less responsive quiet counselors. Both groups showed more movement than their closely matched nonparticipating controls.

The two groups were matched on age, socioeconomic status, academic major, and the self-description components of the previously mentioned quiet-outgoing composite. The twenty-four quiet controls seemed to do a lot of changing during the year without participation in the companionship program. Since they too were applicants, it may be that they were ready to try new things—ready for change. However, the forty-three quiet counselors were measured as changing a little more. On the retrospective questionnaire, quiet counselors reported significantly greater gains in curiosity about the way they interact with friends, while also describing significantly more improvement in their actual relationships with friends and more interest in children's behavior ($p < .05$). Other significant changes occurred on the ACL. Quiet counselors sharply increased their scores on the aggression scale—moving toward self-descriptive words such as "forceful" and "argumentative" and away from "shy," "mannerly," "reserved." Similar gains occurred on the item labeled "number checked" which could reflect a movement toward "surgency and drive, and a relative absence of repressive tendencies" (Gough and Heilbrun, 1965, p. 5). In all, quiet counselors changed significantly (.05 or better) on seven scales, in contrast with two for the quiet controls. Counselors also reduced their scores on order, favorability, intraception, nurturance, and endurance—as if they became less "good" and less compulsive in some ways. One retrospective question asked students whether they had become more quiet or more outgoing during the year. Quiet counselors described themselves as becoming significantly more outgoing when compared with controls ($p < .01$).

As we measure it, quiet counselors felt themselves becoming more outgoing, surgent, aggressive, forceful, and perhaps less in need of order and control. Findings based on pre-post shifts plus retrospective questions point in similar directions. The changes are essentially movements away from passivity toward self-assertion. At the project's close, these quiet counselors said that they were more interested in people and related to friends better than when they joined the project. Since the matched control group did not show change of such magnitude, we can entertain the hypothesis that quiet students lose some of their reserve and move closer to people after participating in a project like ours.

The forty-five outgoing counselors changed significantly ($p < .05$) on thirteen ACL scales, compared with two such changes for their twenty matched controls. Outgoing counselors reduced their scores on scales that were heavily loaded on a social-desirability or positive-evaluation factor (Scarr, 1966; Parker and Megargee, 1967). They increased significantly ($p < .05$) on a set of ACL scales that suggest gains in surgency, self-exploration, and self-assertion: number checked, change, autonomy, and aggression. In short, the self-descriptions of outgoing counselors became more outgoing and more self-critical over the project year. Outgoing controls moved somewhat in the same direction, but not significantly.

Some discrepancies in change between outgoing counselors and controls were large enough to be significant. They generally underline the findings discussed above. The counselors' modest gain on lability was contrasted by the controls' sharp loss; the difference in change magnitude was significant at .01. Here are the other strong discrepancies followed by the significance levels: counselors reduced their self-control and deference scores, while controls increased theirs (.05); counselors gained much on autonomy, and controls lost a bit (.01); counselors gained on aggression, and controls remained constant (.05).

On the Self-Disclosure Questionnaire, both groups decreased disclosure to parents. However, the counselors still tended to disclose more and produced significantly higher general disclosure scores at posttesting ($p < .05$). Controls disclosed much less about their studies at the program's end, while counselors remained the same; the difference in change is significant at .05. Once again counselors said that they lied more and controls claimed that they lied less. Outgoing controls did not tell their girl friends more over the year, but counselors did; the gain is significant at .01. Our confidence in this Self-Disclosure Questionnaire is limited because we suspect that very high scores are produced not only by those who disclose a great deal but also by those who lie a great deal. Still, the consistency of some findings suggests that initially high-disclosing outgoing counselors learn to disclose even more because of their program experience.

Outgoing counselors gained modestly on the trust scale of the Philosophies of Human Nature Questionnaire, while controls lowered their scores (difference: $p < .05$). Both groups gained insignificantly on the Social Insight Test.

Compared with their controls, the outgoing counselors became much more interested in working with troubled people (.01) and learning about children's behavior (.05). They also moved toward person-oriented academic majors more often (.01) and said that they related to friends better (.05) than did outgoing controls.

Both retrospective and pre-post discrepancy measures describe outgoing counselors as changing more than their controls. It appears that outgoing counselors grew more self-critical, self-assertive, and closer to friends; and became more interested in working with troubled people, learning about children, and studying person-oriented majors in school. Many of the changes in the outgoing group were paralleled by the quiet counselors, noticeably along the dimension of surgency—self-assertion versus passivity-withdrawal. Quiets seemed to reverse their reserved interpersonal styles, while outgoings appeared to become even more of what they were. Thus, even though outgoings change more in relation to their controls than do quiets, the shift in direction displayed by quiets makes their gains look more pronounced.

A direct comparison of change measures between quiet and outgoing counselors produced few significant differences—fewer than either group showed in contrast to its set of matched controls. Outgoing counselors gained more than quiet counselors on the trust scale of the philosophies of Human Nature Questionnaire ($p < .05$). They also gained slightly more on disclosure about their personalities, improvement in schoolwork, and movement toward person-oriented academic majors ($p < .10$). On a direct retrospective question, quiet counselors described themselves as becoming more outgoing with much greater frequency (.01). Fellow participants in sensitivity-training groups rated quiet counselors as gaining more than outgoings in their ability to affect the group. Even though outgoing counselors were described as more open and assertive during both halves of training, the difference between outgoings and quiets narrowed considerably over time. These ratings by peer participant-observers support the self-descriptive data, which describe quiet counselors gaining in self-assertion and perhaps gaining more visibly than their outgoing counterparts.

Changes in Trained and Self-Directed Counselors

Some significant differences between our trained and self-directed groups (see Chapter Four) did appear. We are confident that the initial characteristics of the two groups had little to do with the differences found. The groups were closely matched on age, quiet-outgoing classification, academic major, vocational goal, high school grade-point average, self-description profiles (ACL), Social Insight Test scores, experience with and confidence in psychotherapy, and Self-Disclosure Questionnaire patterns.

The findings suggest that the group sessions made a considerable difference in counselors' openness to peers—especially girl friends. (All of these findings are significant at the $< .01$ level.) Trained counselors were also willing to disclose more to peers about physical matters, sexual attitudes and activities, and thoughts regarding their own personalities than were counselors who did not attend groups. Group training may have retarded the sharp decrease in disclosure to parents that we expect from college males. Decreases in the trained group were insignificant and markedly smaller than those produced by the self-directed counselors.

In addition to becoming more disclosed with their peers, trained counselors were also assessed to be more open with their boys. They disclosed much more regarding religious views than self-directed counselors. They also reduced the discrepancy between how much they were willing to tell their boys and how much they actually told their boys over the year. Being in the groups also appeared to extend an existing interest in ways of interacting with friends. The differential in increased interest between groups might have been larger if self-directed counselors had not taken the programmed instruction course on two-person interaction.

ACL changes can be interpreted as indicating greater surgency and use of aggression for both groups. A reduction in social desirability or positive evaluation also occurred for both groups. Not too much can be made of the trained counselors' larger gains on the Social Insight Test because the difference was of modest significance $(p < .10)$. Still, it is something to remember because this is the second instance where the Social Insight Test has produced a meaningful finding (it previously showed a significant correlation with the GAIT understanding score, described in Chapter Three).

At first we were puzzled by the significant difference in scholastic improvement reported by the two groups. Trained counselors tended to describe no change or slight decreases in quality of schoolwork, while self-directed counselors generally reported gains. Did attendance in a weekly self-exploration group interfere with schoolwork by using up the good part of an evening, or demanding emotional energy at the expense of studies? We cannot tell. The findings can be partly explained by a measurement artifact: the grade-point average of trained counselors was significantly higher at the initial assessment $(p < .05)$, so that the self-directed counselors had more room for improvement. But we must still consider the possibility that the demands for personal exploration made by the group sessions retarded the academic studies of some students.

Characteristics of Boys

Obviously, the needs, ideas, and interpersonal styles of the boys had considerable impact on the counselors. Could the impact be systematically traced to some general characteristic of the boy, or would the many impinging influences make such measurement improbable? The latter is probably true, but we thought it worth a starting effort and formed subgroups of counselors characterized by specific traits of their boys: mildly troubled versus moderately troubled, quiet versus outgoing, fatherless versus with fathers, Negro versus Caucasian. Rather than solid findings, we gathered a few clues about how various kinds of boys might influence the lives of their student companions.

Mildly versus Moderately Troubled. Some initial observations from parents, teachers, and classmates were combined to form a composite index of problem severity, and boys were ranked according to their composite scores. The rank order was divided into quintiles, and boys within the first and fifth quintiles were designated "mildly" and "moderately" troubled. Counselors with moderately troubled boys $(N = 19)$ described themselves as becoming significantly more outgoing (.05) than counselors with mildly troubled boys $(N = 20)$. In addition, among those counselors who attended group sessions, those with more troubled boys reported receiving much more help from the group training. In brief, these findings point to the possibility that students in companionships with more troubled boys may change toward being more outgoing or less reserved, feeling that people are not always in control of their own behavior, and seeing people as complex and changeable.

Fatherless versus Intact Homes. About one third of the boys who completed the program were fatherless (no father currently living in the home). We expected them to make an especially big impact on counselors because they were more aggressive and presumably able to elicit more fatherly behavior from adult males. We either thought wrong or were unable to measure differential effects, because the two groups showed few significant differences in change patterns.

Black and White. The final study of counselor change dependent on boy characteristics also yielded little. The major finding is that Caucasian students in companionships with Negro or Caucasian boys changed in similar ways. About 30 per cent of the companionships were Caucasian counselors with Negro boys; the remaining 70 per cent were mostly "double Caucasian" companionships. Our early plans for studying the four permutations of black-white companionships never materialized because black students were scarce and few black students could be recruited. We did manage to form a few companionships composed of black counselors with Caucasian boys or black counselors with black boys, but there were not enough for adequate study. Moreover, those subgroups of companionships we managed to study (black and white boys with black counselors) had poorly matched groups of counselors, which hampered the research; age, socioeconomic status, and interpersonal style as measured by the Group Assessment of Interpersonal Traits (GAIT) were initially different for the two sets of counselors. Change scores were essentially similar for the two groups, with two exceptions: the majority of counselors with black boys did acquire a strong interest in black studies and cross-race relations. At the project's end, they had applied to similar programs with much greater frequency than those students paired with white boys ($p < .01$).

Summary

We found a few studies of students working in experimental mental health programs, but they were not strictly comparable to ours in intensity, setting, or length of contact. Their findings combined suggest that students who work in therapy roles can expect to become more critical when describing themselves, crystallize career goals, learn to tolerate more aggression in others and themselves, gain self-confidence, and develop more acceptance of psychological dysfunction. We found similar and additional changes in our counselors.

Counselors described significantly more change than nonparticipant controls on a retrospective questionnaire and between the initial and final assessment instruments. They gain much more interest in children's behavior, working with troubled people, and their own interpersonal relationships. On the average, counselors said that the project had "much effect" on their enhanced interests. Working on the project also appeared to improve the ways most counselors (75 per cent) related to their friends (compared with 45 per cent of the controls). They claimed that the program helped them to become more concerned, direct, and sensitive to feelings in their friendships. We considered these reported changes as by-products of the counselors' attempts to be genuine with their boys. Only a few students found the project a negative experience.

Differences between the early and later self-descriptions were much greater for counselors than for controls. Counselors changed significantly on over half of the twenty-five Adjective Check List scales; controls changed on two scales. Counselors became more self-critical or less defensive. They sharply lowered scores on twelve of the thirteen scales forming a social-desirability factor. Strong gains for the counselor group occurred on the autonomy and aggression scales. Counselors increased on the need-for-change scale (spontaneity and risk-taking) as the controls decreased. The discrepancy was significant. The two groups also differed significantly on the need-for-control scale. Counselors reduced their scores while the control group remained constant. These ACL changes support the hypothesis that students in the program became less defensive and more self-critical, autonomous, aggressive, and exploratory.

Self-Disclosure Questionnaire scores for counselors were consistently higher than scores for the control group. This may be a result of the counselors' successful screening on the Group Assessment of Interpersonal Traits sessions, which assessed self-disclosure. The Self-Disclosure Questionnaire showed both groups becoming much less disclosed to parents, and maintaining constant disclosure to male friends. Controls were also constant in disclosing to girl friends, while the counselor group showed a sharp significant increase. There were no differences in change between the two groups on the Philosophies of Human Nature Questionnaire and the Social Insight Test.

Differences in change between the quiet and outgoing subgroups of counselors were fewer than between each of these groups and their matched set of controls. Both subgroups of counselors said that they became more outgoing, but the shift was dramatic for the quiet counselors. Their fellow group members in the sensitivity-training sessions also described quiets as gaining more than out-goings in self-assertion and openness over the program year. We see the differences in change as more than a measurement artifact produced by initial discrepancies. Quiets also reported a greater increase in curiosity about the way they interact with friends. Out-going counselors gained much more interest in working with troubled people and became more involved with person-oriented academic majors than quiets. Outgoings also gained more on dis-closure to girl friend, accompanied by an increase in their attribution of trustworthiness to human nature.

The weekly training seems to have influenced the counsel-ors' self-disclosure behavior. Trained counselors gained significantly more than the self-directed group on several self-disclosure scales. They also showed less discrepancy between what they "would tell" and "did tell" their boys. Training also appeared related to greater interest in the process of relating to friends and in the counselors' current field of study (mostly social science). A modestly significant gain on the Social Insight Test occurred for the trained counselors. Since the quality of schoolwork increased more for self-directed counselors, we entertained the possibility that attending group ses-sions took energy away from the counselors' studies.

A comparison of counselors with "moderately" versus "mildly" troubled boys showed that those with the moderately troubled boys changed more toward being outgoing or less reserved and found the training groups more useful. Perhaps having more to cope with caused these counselors to become more assertive and seek more help from the training groups.

Spending the year with a black or white boy seemed to have similar impact on the counselors. Counselors with black boys ac-quired a strong interest in black life and cross-race relations. They also applied to similar programs with much greater frequency than those counselors who worked with white boys.

X

Summary, Speculation, Suggestions

Our goal has been to provide research contributions to the bright future of companionship therapies. We have found specific classes of boys, counselors, dyads, and companionship process that show promise as predictors of therapeutic gain. The project has already generated procedures for locating troubled schoolchildren, a format for structuring companionships, devices for assessing companionship process, and a systematic method for selecting therapeutically talented nonprofessional counselors. This chapter summarizes our findings, discusses their implications for community mental health work, offers a set of recommendations for program development, and reviews major administrative procedures—beginning with our strategy for obtaining research samples of troubled children.

224

There was no way to avoid compromise in selecting a single sample of troubled children to meet both research and program requirements. We wanted to optimize administrative ease by selecting boys who could adapt to the program, but we also wanted to enhance our research with a fairly homogeneous and representative sample. Community mandate limited our choice to young *boys* in trouble (Chapter One). The final sample was composed of mild, moderate, and a few more severely troubled boys able to function in regular fifth- and sixth grade classrooms. They were 10 and 11 years old, and one third were from broken homes. Almost three fourths were white, one fourth black, and the rest Oriental.

We decided against a pure "clinical" sample because it seemed that more severely troubled boys would create havoc in lightly supervised companionships. We were wrong. Counselors working with high pathology boys did not require more supervision; furthermore, these boys appeared to gain more from the program than mildly troubled boys did (Chapter Eight). Companionship programs need not shy away from disturbed children equivalent to our high pathology subgroup. Nonprofessionals can cope with them, and they benefit from companionship. Another advantage in working with more troubled children is that their vivid problems are more available to change measurement.

Preadolescent boys were chosen because their problems are not complicated by the physically induced crisis of adolescence, they are developmentally ready for learning the one-to-one collaboration forced by the companionships, and are old enough to enjoy a wide range of activities with a college student.

Most school systems do not have an accurate accounting of their emotionally troubled children. We found classroom sociometric assessment to be an efficient tool for locating our sample and studying change. Wiggins and Winder's Peer Nominations Inventory is an excellent device (Chapter Two). Teachers were able to administer it to all of Berkeley's fifth- and sixth-grade classes. Parents were also used in our selection process. All parents of fifth- and sixth-grade boys were sent project descriptions and applications. About 14 per cent applied, and 8 per cent were accepted. When parent descriptions and sociometric ratings agreed in describing a boy as troubled, we accepted him into the program. We estimated the final sample to roughly represent the most troubled 15 per cent of the fifth- and sixth-grade boys. We have detailed the procedure and described some problems in this format for large-scale screening of troubled children in Chapter Two. The use of multiobserver groups—parents, teachers, classmates—worked quite well. We recommend it to workers requiring large groups of troubled children.

Mental health researchers do not enjoy much trust from communities. We hoped to make ourselves more believable by disclosing details of our goals, project structure, and research needs in an announcement distributed to 1,250 parents. We promised to avoid deception and to apply much effort in selecting the best counselors for their children. Actually, we were asking parents to take the chance of submitting their troubled children to an experiment with untutored therapy agents using an unproven format. The response was gratifying. Our first set of announcements brought in formal application requests from about 25 per cent of the parents. Besides being pleased, we were also surprised that one of four parents showed serious interest in a project clearly advertised as limited to emotionally troubled children. We cannot be sure, but it seems that the heavy response was facilitated through trust engendered by the disclosures in our announcement. However, trust in the program could open the door only for those already interested. The great interest displayed by parents suggests that we may be underestimating community acceptance of experimental therapy programs using nonprofessionals. Of course, our findings are limited to the Berkeley community and may not be representative. But if they are—if similar levels of acceptance are found in other communities—the implications for national mental health planning will be profound. We could be moving into a period where nontraditional community-therapy programs will provide the major source of help for troubled children —and troubled adults.

The large number of applicants helped our research. After the boys were selected, we sorted them into matched pairs based on problem characteristics, grade, race, home situation (Table 1). The pairs were randomly split and assigned to control group or participant status. About half of those designated as controls volunteered for future assessment. Thus, our control group was matched on initial motivation to join the program but unmatched on inclination to volunteer for future assessment. They also differed from participants in being denied a companionship. This rejection factor appeared to harm our subsequent attempts to measure change (Chapter Seven). Our final research sample contained seventy-four controls and eighty-eight participants. They looked like a fairly representative cross section of troubled boys with moderate problems. Parent descriptions characterized the boys as unmanageable mischief makers who demanded attention, created disorder, felt restless, and lacked friends (Table 2). Teachers and classmates described them as more isolated, attention-seeking, and atypical and less likeable than a stratified random sample of two hundred boys from the same classrooms. Thus, all the observer groups saw our samples as troubled. Chapter Two contains detailed descriptions of various sample parameters, including family characteristics and problem frequencies.

The selection procedure (and program structure) was kept intact for two successive program years. We were tempted to correct mistakes and modify some procedures for the second research year, but resisted for the benefit of combining samples. In retrospect, the advantages of running pilot programs become more evident. The pilot work allowed us to develop instruments, program formats, and an overall research design that could be used without change for two program years. Combining parallel research for two years allowed us to test reliabilities and provided us with a sample large enough for partitioning into many subgroups. These subgroup studies turned out our most important boy outcome findings.

Speculations on GAIT

GAIT is probably the most important instrument to come out of our project. It was used to select counselors. The procedure is detailed in Chapter Three, and related findings are described in Chapter Eight. Essentially, GAIT is a prototype group-assessment method that utilizes successive sets of dyadic interaction as performance samples for subsequent rating by participants and outside observers. The primary variables are understanding (empathy), openness (self-disclosure), and acceptance—warmth, which combine to form a therapeutic talent composite. Client-centered theory has influenced us to consider these qualities as requisites for effective nonprofessional therapeutic agents. The scales are modestly to moderately reliable, and some evidence for validity has come from our work and the work of others (Chapter Three). Because of GAIT's potential for use in a variety of applications requiring the selection of interpersonal competence, we are planning further work on upgrading reliability and testing its validity.

Besides selecting college students as therapeutic companions, GAIT may well have other potential uses as a selection device. Some of the qualities we consider important for therapeutic applications seem needed for work in cross-cultural settings. It would be interesting to study the effectiveness and attrition rates for Peace Corps or VISTA volunteers who score high and low on GAIT criteria. The Job Corps has expressed interest in exploring GAIT as a method for selecting counselors to work in a residential training center. In addition, GAIT could be refined for use as an adjunct screening device to complement academic-achievement criteria and letters of recommendation for applicants for advanced education in clinical and counseling psychology, psychiatry, pastoral counseling, and psychiatric social work. Such applicants are often selected with the use of data that have little relation to their intended work in therapy situations. The addition of a structured group-assessment procedure would add complexity and expense to the already overburdened selection committees—but if it really worked, the advantage would be enormous.

GAIT also might be of use to nontraditional mental health programs that emphasize the training of paraprofessionals. The selection criteria for trainability seem related to our criteria for therapeutic talent. At minimum a good candidate for therapy training should be open to new experience and possess good listening skills. It would also be interesting to see whether low scores on GAIT rigidity would correlate with successful learning in a thearpy-training program. There are some parallels in the readiness for therapy training and the readiness for receiving therapy. With some fanciful thinking one could imagine using something like GAIT as a diagnostic aid for those seeking therapy. It might help by providing firsthand samples of interpersonal performance problems or providing evidence for the advisability of group versus individual therapy.

In addition to these potential selection functions of GAIT, it might also have use as an instrumental feedback device for group psychotherapy, encounter groups, and sensitivity training. Providing individuals with organized feedback on how a group perceives them along such dimensions as empathy, openness, rigidity, outgoingness, and warmth may accelerate interpersonal learning.

Another possibility is suggested by the research of D'Augelli and his associates. They found the GAIT therapeutic talent score to be a significant predictor of personal-exploration levels in training groups. Their use of GAIT to predetermine group composition and subsequent group interaction stimulates the exciting possibility of ensuring the effectiveness of small-group processes—especially those "one-shot" or weekend groups common to growth centers. We have started to explore such feedback with clinical psychology graduate students at UCLA. Finally, procedures like GAIT show promise as research tools for pretesting and posttesting of experimental treatments in small-group settings. Of course, the effects of repeated administration would have to be studied first, and the scales might need modification to enhance the measurement of change.

Companionship Structure and Process

Our final program format proved to be an inexpensive, fairly simple package that appears easily exportable to a variety of settings (Chapter Four). It can be condensed or expanded without much sacrifice. The actual companionships were quite autonomous and consistent. Intrusions by project staff were rare. A mandatory pattern of visit length (one to four hours) and frequency (two to three per week) was established to ensure visitation consistency and avoid "hello-goodbye" contacts. Our client-centered bias influenced some program structures: counselors were denied diagnostic information about boys, advice about companionship activities was kept to a minimum, attempts were made to reduce any "expert posture" in counselors, and counselors were selected by criteria important to client-centered theory. Other program structures involved (1) matching boys and counselors on quiet-outgoing characteristics and race as a means for enhancing outcome research; (2) sharing the project's detailed rationale with parents, counselors, and boys as an attempt to establish trust and increase administrative efficiency; (3) requiring a structured Visit Report from each counselor for each contact, to provide a vehicle for supervision and a source of research data; (4) administering automated interpersonal-relations instruction to all counselors before starting companionships; (5) setting up initial boy-counselor meetings without the presence of a staff member or parent: (6) weekly small-group training for half the counselors, allowing additional supervision and systematic study of training effects on outcome and process; (7) written reminders urging counselors to discuss the facts of program termination at early dates; (8) full-time phone consultation available to counselors for emergencies; (9) a provision for extending companionships in cases of difficult termination (utilized on only two occasions). Chapter Four describes the project structures in greater detail and elaborates on their rationales and some problems encountered. In general, the program machinery operated smoothly, engendered trust, and allowed systematic investigation to proceed without dehumanizing the research subjects.

The Visit Report form typically required about thirteen minutes of the counselor's time after each contact. We found it an excellent device for supervision and gathering data on companionship parameters. Visit Report data showed the average pair meeting twice a week for three-hour visits, 141 hours of contact. Initial meetings were without incident and described as tense, impersonal, and less warm than subsequent visits. The satisfactory descriptions of first visits suggests that similar programs can dispense with the customary introduction by a staff mediator. Companionships doomed for attrition signal themselves in first visits through ratings of interaction that lacks warmth, accompanied by high levels of tension in boys. We wanted companionships to foster much collaboration between counselor and boy. It occurred. Almost half the decisions about what to do during visits were made jointly according to counselors.

Surprisingly, most of the remaining decisions were made by boys. Our strong orientation warnings to counselors about not offering boys "mock choices" may have fostered the high frequency of decisions made by boys. Typically, two or three activities were chosen for each visit and usually involved active sports or lengthy (over an hour) visits in the boy's home. Quiet activities were common; so were walks, sitting down to talk, sharing meals, sightseeing, working on hobbies (mostly things like photography or model building), watching television, listening to music, visiting the counselor's place, and going for a ride. With less frequency, the pair attended spectator sports or movies, did homework, or visited one of the counselor's friends. The interaction was one-to-one about 80 per cent of the time. A third person entered the companionships about once in five visits. Activity patterns over time are displayed in Chapter Five.

Typically, counselors mentioned five "meaningful" conversation topics for each visit. Of course, they were not mutually exclusive topics. Most of the conversation was about the boy's life; about half as much was directed at the counselor's life. Most of all, the talk was about current or past companionship activities, plans for future visits, the boy's studies and skills, the boy's personality and behavior, and the boy's friends and family members. With somewhat less frequency, counselors and boys discussed their feelings for each other, vacations, mothers, fathers, and teachers. Changes in conversation patterns suggest some general trends related to intimacy and are displayed in Chapter Six. Counselor ratings indicate that there was a significant movement toward discussing "deep personal feelings" between the first and second thirds of the companionship, and we concluded that it takes roughly six weeks for personal communication to become a habit.

Counselors tended to describe their own feelings and behaviors positively but used even more favorable descriptions when viewing their boys. The descriptions became more positive during the last third of the companionship—especially along dimensions of warmth and openness. Interpersonal distance (as measured by discrepancy between descriptions of counselor and boy) also showed a marked decrease over the entire companionship period. This counselor distance score was negatively related to the boys' rating of "fun" during the relationship and to various boy outcome measures. These associations are detailed in Chapter Six, along with a discussion of correlations between activities, conversations, feelings, and behavior.

Terminating the companionships stimulated a wide range of reactions. Some evidence suggested that the emotionally closer pairs had more difficulty parting. In most cases, there was some contact after the program officially ended. We started with some serious concerns about the effects of termination on boys, but after careful scrutiny the concerns were relieved. Sadness and a sense of loss occurred frequently, but we were unable to locate serious problems.

Measures of the conversation, activity, and feeling processes listed above are associated with boy outcome. Strong associations occurred for only a few process variables, but the general configuration of findings gives reason to believe that companionship process holds much evidence for the causes of therapeutic change. Process is certainly difficult to pin down, and our initial attempts have only scratched the surface. With refinement, the study of interpersonal process should lead to a new era in the delivery of therapeutic services where controlled relationship parameters will be used to raise the probability of obtaining precise change. Coupling some free speculation to the trend of our findings produces a vision of humanistically oriented behavior modification programs using prescribed "doses" of interpersonal stimuli to desensitize some complicated dysfunctional habits like inability to collaborate, intimacy phobia, or even low self-esteem. Relegating such fanciful thoughts to the science fiction category is no longer appropriate. They have become real possibilities within the current mental health revolution, which demands innovation in therapeutic processes.

The well-publicized demand for innovation has generated a confusing rush of novelty interspersed with a few careful starts. A common reaction to the rapid proliferation of untested procedures has been the call for serious research. Thus, investigators of therapy process are finding new freedom in their ability to execute research. These events have allowed us to structure relationships and study process with real "clients" and "therapists." Obviously, our prototype procedures and scattered findings must be viewed as an "early example" of therapy process research in field settings. We have detailed process investigation in this book as a hopeful contribution to those workers searching for the links between dyadic interaction and therapeutic change.

Effects on Boys

Companionships were measurably effective for specific classes of boys and counselors in structured relationships with particular characteristics. When specific classes of boys, counselors, and companionships were gathered together into one large unpartitioned sample, the findings were mixed. Before discussing the most effective kinds of companionship, it may be helpful to focus on the unpartitioned sample and outline some problems inherent to global research on heterogeneous client and counselor populations.

At first glance, our group of troubled boys might appear to be sufficiently homogeneous for a study of companionship effects: most were moderately troubled as described by parents, teachers, and classmates. They were motivated to enter a "mental health" project, were in their tenth or eleventh year, and were capable of functioning in the fifth and sixth grades of public school. In our project, the cross-section sample studied alone would have masked particular classes of boys that later appeared to benefit significantly from companionships. Similar subgroups were embedded in the unpartitioned group of college student counselors. They were self-selected and then systematically screened. The data in Chapter Three indicate that they were homogeneous on many variables; but we eventually found specific classes measured to be more therapeutic with boys. The need for more specificity also applied to companionship qualities. Companionships were governed by a list of public rules that prescribed visit length and frequency along with counselor behavior. Compliance was assessed through detailed reports for each visit (Chapter Four). But once again, the findings pointed to even narrower companionship parameters that were associated with boy improvement. Most findings from the unpartitioned* sample showed that most boys improved a little—with or without companionships.

A. DERIVED CHANGE MEASURES—FROM DIFFERENCES BETWEEN ASSESSMENT OCCASIONS

1. There were few differences between all companionship participants and controls at the time of application (I), program termination (II), and follow-up (III) as described by parents on the Adjective Check List (ACL) and the Problem List (PL).
2. Change patterns derived from differences between periods I, II, and III were quite similar for participants and controls, with a tendency for ACL ratings on controls to become more favorable and defensive and with an emphasis on increased manageability.

* Drawn from the gross samples containing mixed boy, counselor, and companionship characteristics. All findings significant at <.01 or <.05 unless indicated.

3. Both participants and controls showed a reduction in 20 per cent of their problems between the application (I) and termination (II) testings on the Problem List.
4. Participants and controls were again similar in showing an additional 5 per cent reduction in problems between termination (II) and follow-up (III) testings.

B. DIRECT CHANGE MEASURES—FROM RETROSPECTIVE DESCRIPTIONS

1. Participants showed more improvement on their specific presenting problems than controls (91 per cent versus 61 per cent) over the entire research span (I to III) according to retrospective change ratings by parents on the smaller follow-up samples.
2. Presenting problems became worse over the entire research span (I–III) for 3 per cent of the participants according to parents' retrospective ratings, in contrast to 28 per cent of the controls over the same span.
3. Retrospective change ratings by parents at termination and follow-up described both participants and controls as typically becoming "a little" better in schoolwork, school activities, peer relations, and self-esteem.
4. Most participants' parents rated the counselors' contribution to boy improvement as "some" or "much." (No Controls.)
5. Control parents offered various causes for improvement—mostly new structured or task-oriented activities, professional psychotherapy, and more contact with significant males.
6. Participants improved more than controls (75 per cent to 47 per cent) on global retrospective ratings of "gets along with others" over the companionship period. Almost twice as many controls as participants were seen as not changing over the entire research period.
7. Almost all (97 per cent) of the participants' parents said that if they had a chance to do it over they would join the project again.
8. Seventy per cent of the counselors saw specific initial problems similar to those described by parents. Of those counselors, 81 per cent described some degree of problem improvement at termination: 42 per cent "very little" or "little," 20 per cent "some," 19 per cent "much" or "very much."

In addition, the larger sample generated findings that suggested the existence of a method factor in parent measures, but provided some indication of measurement validity for the entire battery of instruments as parents, teachers, classmates, and counselors produced similar patterns of boy change over the research period.

Outcome Findings. The unpartitioned samples of participants and controls improved a little according to teacher and classmate ratings.

A. DERIVED CHANGE MEASURES
   1. Change indices drawn from teacher and classmate sociometric ratings of hostility, likeability, attention-seeking, and atypicality taken before and after the companionships were similar for participants and controls: insignificant improvement on the majority of measures.

B. DIRECT CHANGE MEASURES
   1. Teachers' retrospective change ratings on school attitude, peer relations, schoolwork, and self-esteem indicated "a little" improvement in all areas for both participants and controls.
   2. At termination, almost all (95 per cent) of the participant boys said the companionships could change boys. Areas of change most frequently mentioned were categorized as gains in interpersonal relations, skill acquisition, social awareness, and self-concept.
   3. Over half the participant boys claimed improved social relations with adults at termination, and almost 70 per cent did the same for peer relations. Typical changes involved more contact and less hostile interaction.
   4. When asked about skills or knowledge acquired, 30 per cent of the participant boys mentioned social communication, 21 per cent described athletic skills, and 20 per cent specified some academic knowledge.

Parents' "derived" change measures (drawn from discrepancies between successive sets of contemporary ratings on the same dimension) also indicated that both participants and controls improved a little. The picture changed for parents' "direct" measures of change, drawn from retrospective estimates of movement occurring over the past year. While both groups showed a little improvement on school attitude, schoolwork, peer relations, and self-esteem items, the participants gained significantly more than controls on two major scales. One scale asked parents to recall the particular presenting problem and rate change for that problem following the follow-up period. Almost all (91 per cent) of the participant parents saw some degree of improvement, in contrast to 61 per cent of the controls. The presenting problem became worse for one of every four control boys (28 per cent) while hardly any (3 per cent) of the participant parents rated the presenting problem as worsening.

Another direct change measure that favored participants was obtained in a follow-up interview. Parents were given a full-page flow chart that gathered impressions of global change in the boys' social relations over the entire research span. Improvement was indicated for three fourths of the participants and less than half of the controls over the companionship period. Participants also gained a bit more than controls over the follow-up span. About twice as many controls were seen as unchanging over the two periods as compared with participants (roughly 37 per cent versus 19 per cent).

These two indices drawn from the smaller follow-up sample are the only controlled sources of support for assuming that companionships *in general* are effective. Some of the noncontrolled findings fall in the same direction. Counselors complement the participant parents' strong improvement ratings on presenting problem (91 per cent) by posting an 81 per cent improvement rate on a similar set of specific boy problems. A large segment of the boys in the unpartitioned sample indicated that companionships could help boys to improve peer and adult social relations and to gain skills in communication, athletics, and academics.

Taken as a whole, the findings on unspecified companionships do not offer convincing evidence for their success or failure. The tendency for control groups to generate automatic gains and the canceling effect of subgroups with differing change patterns probably confounded measurement. Nevertheless, some findings from parents' direct change measures do show the companionships effective in reducing presenting problems and enhancing the participants' ability to "get along with others." These findings were complemented by a set of unsystematic parent observations that enthusiastically described improvement for a wide range of special problems. The mixed findings on unspecified dyads slightly favor companionships as a useful device, but a more appropriate picture of companionship effectiveness comes from findings on specific subgroups.

As a start, here is a condensed review of subgroup findings.*

* From data covering the companionship span—application to termination.

Subgroups were formed around boy, counselor, and companionship characteristics. Findings on these subgroups are summarized below.

Subgroups Based on Boy Characteristics

Fatherless Participants $(N = 27)$ Compared with Fatherless Controls $(N = 21)$:

1. Gained less on dimensions of manageability, docility, orderliness, timidity, and solitary play as rated by mothers.
2. Became more assertive, headstrong, unusual, and easily upset as rated by mothers.
3. Improved less in their attitudes toward school on teachers' retrospective measures.

Fatherless Participants Compared with Intact-Home Participants $(N = 61)$:

1. Showed few significant differences in change measures, but patterns suggested they became slightly more autonomous, self-asserting, with less self-control.
2. Were described by mothers as engaging in less solitary play.
3. Were in companionships where counselors reported more fun.

Quiet Participants $(N = 43)$ Compared with Quiet Controls $(N = 39)$:

1. Became more competitive, gained more self-esteem, fought more frequently—but gained less on independence and social confidence according to parent ratings.
2. Improved more on 70 per cent of the remaining nonsignificant comparisons of means.

Outgoing Participants $(N = 45)$ Compared with Outgoing Controls $(N = 36)$:

1. Became less mannerly, meek, rude, and headstrong according to parents' derived change measures.

Quiet Participants Compared with Outgoing Participants:

1. Showed more improvement on their presenting problem, and less improvement with their problems of dependence, sadness, playing alone, and self-esteem according to parents.
2. Improved more in the quality of their schoolwork and showed more reduction in classroom isolation according to teachers.
3. Gained more on 85 per cent of the remaining nonsignificant comparisons.

High Pathology Participants ($N = 19$) Compared with High Pathology Controls ($N = 15$):

1. Became more independent, bossy; gained more self-esteem, while reducing problems with appetite, speech, and physical modesty according to parents' derived change measures.
2. Gained more in likeability on the sociometric ratings by classmates.
3. Had more favorable mean change scores on almost two thirds of the remaining nonsignificant comparisons.

Low Pathology Participants ($N = 21$) Compared with Low Pathology Controls ($N = 19$):

1. Were essentially similar on most measures of change.

Black Participants ($N = 25$) Compared with Black Controls ($N = 20$):

1. Showed a greater reduction in phobias; became less timid, mannerly, manageable; more rude and attention-seeking; increased their self-esteem more—all according to parent measures.
2. Gained more on 70 per cent of the remaining nonsignificant comparisons of mean scores.

Black Participants ($N = 25$) Compared with White Participants ($N = 62$):

1. Improved more in problem areas of playing alone and phobias. Their self-esteem also showed stronger gains on parent ratings.
2. Became more likeable and hostile (aggressive boasting) over the school year according to classmates.
3. Improved more on about three fourths of the remaining nonsignificant comparisons.
4. Frequently (two thirds) had parents who saw the counselors' influence as a very important factor in their improvement.
5. Described their companionships in more favorable terms—more fun, understanding, and disclosure.

Subgroups Based on Counselor Characteristics

Moderately Trained Counselors ($N = 45$) Compared with Slightly Trained Counselors ($N = 42$):

1. Were described as more self-disclosed, more understood, and more controlling by their boys.
2. Had boys who described their own feelings as more understood during the companionships.
3. Had boys described as becoming more assertive and less mannerly

according to parents; improved more on 58 per cent of the remaining nonsignificant comparisons.

Counselors' Age and Quiet-Outgoing Self-Concept:

1. Counselors who were atypically old for an undergraduate population (25–35) had boys who improved less on a wide range of parent-rated problems—stealing, temper tantrums, bed wetting, irritability.
2. Boys with counselors who initially described themselves as outgoing showed a greater reduction in total problems according to parents and were rated as becoming more likeable by classmates.

Boys with Counselors Rated High on GAIT Open ($N = 26$) Compared with Boys Assigned to Medium Open Counselors ($N = 27$):

1. Gained more on a parents' composite adjustment measure and showed greater reduction in problems involving speech, irritability, sadness, and mood swings.
2. Were described as less angry at termination by their counselors.
3. At marginal significance (.10) tended to improve more on presenting problem and be seen as less hostile by teachers and classmates.
4. Gained more on 70 per cent of the remaining nonsignificant comparisons.

Boys with High Understanding Counselors ($N = 28$) Compared with Boys Assigned to Medium Understanding Counselors ($N = 28$):

1. Showed a tendency to reduce problems much more frequently according to parent ratings—particularly fighting, teasing others, shyness, and speech problems.
2. Improved more on 65 per cent of the nonsignificant comparisons of teacher and classmate ratings.

Boys with Low Quiet Counselors ($N = 28$) Compared with Boys Assigned to High Quiet Counselors ($N = 29$):

1. Became more likeable and less atypical according to classmates.
2. Became less hostile according to both teachers and classmates.
3. Became more thoughtful, neat, and serious according to parents.
4. Received nonsignificantly higher improvement scores on most (75 per cent) remaining indices.

Boys with Low Blue (not sad) Counselors ($N = 28$) Compared with Boys Assigned to High Blue (sad) Counselors ($N = 29$):

1. Improved more on presenting problem according to parents.

2. Got along better with peers and improved school attitude according to teachers.
3. Improved schoolwork according to counselors.
4. Gained more on two thirds of the remaining nonsignificant comparisons.

Boys with Low Rigid $(N = 23)$ Counselors Compared with Boys Assigned to High Rigid Counselors $(N = 26)$:

1. Became more likeable according to classmates.
2. Grew less sad and reduced eating problems according to parents.
3. Improved more on 63 per cent of the remaining nonsignificant comparisons—and 80 per cent of the Problem List items.
4. Rated themselves less angry at their counselors.

Subgroups Based on Companionship Characteristics

Double Quiet Dyads: Quiet Boys with Quiet Counselors $(N = 21)$:

1. Showed the least improvement—especially with sleep problems, self-esteem, temper tantrums, irritability, school attitudes, classmates' likeability ratings, and playing alone frequently.
2. Were the least improved on almost three fourths of the comparisons made among the four dyad types.

Quiet Counselors with Outgoing Boys $(N = 22)$:

1. Gained more than boys in double quiet dyads, but less than boys in the other two dyad types.
2. Gained least in schoolwork as rated by both parents and teachers.

Double Outgoing Dyads: Outgoing Counselors with Outgoing Boys $(N = 23)$:

1. Showed much more improvement than boys in double quiet or quiet (counselor)-outgoing dyads.
2. Made outstanding improvement in total problem reduction as seen by parents and by classmates' likeability ratings.

Outgoing Counselors with Quiet Boys $(N = 21)$:

1. Showed about the same level of improvement as boys in double-outgoing dyads.
2. Still involved in much solitary play according to parents but showed outstanding gains in classmates' likeability ratings.
3. Showed much improvement in schoolwork, sleep problems, manageability, and attention seeking according to parents.

Boys in Companionships with a Low Frequency (x = 40) of Visits (N = 28) Compared with Boys in High (x = 58) Visit Companionships (N = 28):
1. Showed more reduction on parent-rated problems.
2. Became more likeable according to classmates and less hostile according to teachers.
3. Made a better showing on 87 per cent of the remaining nonsignificant comparisons.

Boys in Long-Visit (3.4 hours) Companionships (N = 32) Compared with Boys in Short-Visit (2.7 hours) Companionships:
1. Gained more on parent-rated adjustment measures and improved more on a range of problems.
2. Improved more on schoolwork as seen by teachers; parents saw counselors as influencing schoolwork gains.
3. Became less isolated according to classmates and teachers.
4. Had more favorable means of 91 per cent of the remaining nonsignificant comparisons.

Boys in More Favorable Companionships as Rated by Counselors (N = 29) Compared with Boys in Less Favorable Companionships (N = 30):
1. Showed a greater reduction of problems according to parents.
2. Became less hostile and isolated according to both teachers and classmates.
3. Improved more on 80 per cent of the remaining nonsignificant comparisons of mean scores.

Boys in Attrition Companionships (x = 19 visits, N = 15) Compared with Boys in Full-Term Companionships (x = 99 visits, N = 88):
1. Became more hostile, isolated, atypical, and less likeable on both teacher and classmate ratings.
2. Could not be systematically assessed on parent ratings due to missing data, but appeared to gain less than full-term boys on informal inspection.

Among the subgroups formed on boy characteristics, black participants gained the most. Boys with quiet problems (isolation, withdrawal) and high pathology boys also showed gains. Fewer gains occurred for subgroups based on fatherless, intact-home, outgoing, low pathology, and white participants.

Boys with outgoing counselors did better on the outcome

measures than boys with quiet counselors. Counselors who scored high on GAIT open and understanding and low on GAIT rigid and blue also appeared more therapeutic. Training did not seem to make much difference, but older counselors were measured as less effective.

There are many useful ways to form types of dyads. We chose the quiet-outgoing dimension because it is very visible, is commonly found in factor studies, and can embrace a variety of boys' characteristic problems and counselors' interpersonal styles (Chapter Four). Boys in the double quiet companionships improved least. More improvement was measured for the quiet (counselor)—outgoing pairs. The best combinations we found were double outgoing and outgoing (counselor)–quiet.

Companionships with a lower frequency of visits produced better results along with companionships characterized by longer visits. Companionships rated more favorable by counselors produced more improved outcome measures for their boys. Boys in attrition companionships (x = nineteen visits) gained less than boys in full-term companionships. The findings point to characteristics associated with more effective companionships: black participants; quiet problems; more severe problems; outgoing, open, understanding, blue, and flexible counselors; double outgoing and outgoing counselor–quiet boy dyads.

Interpreting the findings. Our control group has been a measurement villain, frustrating efforts to make uniform sense of findings from the unpartitioned sample. Partitioning the control sample eventually helped us locate therapeutic variables, as can be seen in the subgroup findings. But even when cleaner results were obtained, the control group appeared to attenuate the strength of positive findings. That is, some enduring properties of control groups in therapy studies may stack the deck against measuring strong gains. The major problem may be a general tendency for "no-treatment" control groups of troubled children to register improvement in repeated measurement designs using parent ratings. Besides our own improved control sample we noted three large studies showing systematic gains in troubled children without treatment (Shepherd, Oppenheim, and Mitchell, 1969; Glidewell, 1968; Levitt, 1971). One factor contributing to improvement tendency in these control groups is the motivation to seek alternative therapeutic types of intervention. The parents of our control group discovered a variety of new situations for alleviating their boys' problems and, in most cases, regarded the substitute activity as therapeutic (Chapter Seven). Obviously, they could not be asked to postpone these alternative approaches in order to enhance our research. However, there is a possible and expensive solution to this design problem through a detailed study of all therapeutic activities attempted by the control group. A very large sample would be needed for partitioning along a continuum of therapeutic-intervention classes.

We also speculated on another factor that might have contributed to the measured improvement of the control sample. They were similar to participants in having initially applied to the project, which allowed us a control group matched on motivation for seeking help. By necessity, they were subsequently denied the opportunity to participate. The effects of that rejection could have been reflected in their responses to our questionnaires administered one and two years later. We do know that many of the rejected parents refused to serve as controls. Occasional resentment was expressed by parents despite our emphatic early announcements of small acceptance quota. Some residual resentment may have existed in those who did volunteer for the control group and, with other dynamics, might have influenced their ratings of change. It is easy to imagine these parents wanting to show us that they were not helpless without companionships and did manage to alleviate their boys' problems through other resources. However, our hypothesis is somewhat weakened by the less sensitive but more bias-free findings from teachers and classmates, who also registered improvement for control boys. The most reasonable causes for the mixed findings on the unpartitioned sample are (1) alternative therapeutic activities sought by controls had some measurable effect, (2) specific types of change for particular subgroups were masked by opposing changes in other subgroups or attenuated by no change for the larger majority, (3) idiosyncratic gains (like those described informally by parents) slipped past our nomothetic measures and appeared only on individualistic indices such as the presenting-problem item, (4) control parents tended to report gains automatically or because of defensive dynamics—perhaps linked to their initial rejection, (5) the impact of companionships were minimal or negative for some classes of boys and could not be measured, and (6)' companionships instituted some general change processes that become evident only after the two-year follow-up assessment. Our guess is that all of these factors affected our large sample findings but were rendered less effective against the more powerful actual gains occurring for some successful subgroups. Future investigators can expect to find some idiosyncratic gains from gross samples after discarding nomothetic measures; but accurate detection of companionship effects will require a multifactorial approach to dyadic composition, companionship process, and outcome measurement. Support for this view comes from the more conclusive findings on specific subgroups which can now be discussed in greater detail.

Black participants do appear to gain much from companionships—but boys' race alone cannot be isolated as a predictor of success (see Chapter Eight)'. We must also consider the cross-race aspect of dyads as a predictor, because all black participants were paired with white counselors. One of the more dramatic changes for boys in black participant–white counselor companionships appeared as parent-rated improvement "in the way he feels about himself—in terms of self-contentment, self-esteem, happiness." Three fourths of the boys in black-white companionships were seen to gain sharply on this self-esteem item. This frequency is almost double that observed for black controls and white participants. Black participants also posted sharp gains in their attitudes toward school; almost two thirds were rated as "much" or "very much" improved, compared to roughly one third of black controls and white participants. The trend of results are very promising for the prediction of therapeutic gains from black-white companionships: a marked reduction in boys' phobias, less timidity, more independence and rebelliousness, heightened self-esteem, less solitary play, and improved attitudes toward school, when compared to black children without companionships.

What are the elements of these cross-race companionships that make them effective? Perhaps the demand for relating to an unaccustomed partner and public curiosity about the atypical pairing generated a special set of experiences for counselor and boy. Visit Report data described an awareness of being regarded as special or unusual by strangers as the pairs made frequent excursions to public places. They sensed themselves being seen as a strange unit and attracting attention. According to Visit Reports, this special attention stimulated some important conversations early in the relationships. At first, the conversations seemed flavored with humor and some serious views of race relations, which appeared to shift into discussions of personal values and their attitudes toward each other. In this manner, the cross-race factor was responsible for some extended efforts toward understanding each other's experiences. Their shared adventures apparently served as a catalyst for more sensitive levels of listening and self-disclosure, which opened the way for a closer bond. We assume that the companionships were unique for most participants and became their most intimate cross-race relationship. Systematic findings are consistent with this speculation, since black participants rated themselves as receiving much more understanding and as disclosing more feelings and having and giving more fun in the companionships when compared with white participants. Clearly, the black-white companionship structure was one of the most enjoyable, empathic, open devices observed in our project. We assume that the special demands made upon both members in cross-race, cross-age dyads are converted into growth-producing relationships. Of course, we are led to speculation about the other combination, Black Counselor–White Boy; our guess is that a similar set of demands and interpersonal solutions makes them a strong bet for success. Expanding this notion a bit further brings a vision of research on the differential effectiveness of various pairings along cross-sex, cross-age, and cross-race dimensions. This level of pairing specificity has traditionally been outside the grasp of research projects on professional therapy, but such programs can be established and studied with comparative ease by investigators in the nonprofessional therapy field.

Another promising predictor of boy improvement involved a complex set of counselor characteristics labeled "outgoing." Three sets of findings involving these counselor characteristics indicate that they are important elements in successful companionship. In one study counselors were partitioned into upper and lower thirds from their scores on a GAIT item: "mild, reserved, quiet person" (see Chapter Eight). Those in the upper third were designated "high quiets" and the lower third were called "low quiets." Boys with low quiets improved more on various dimensions according to teachers, classmates, and parents. Another study separated companionships into four dyad types according to the quiet-outgoing characteristics of boy and counselor. Boys were classified according to problem type. Counselor types were somewhat similar to the low and high Quiet groups mentioned above; but, in addition to GAIT quiet scores, a direct self-description and scores from an introversion-extroversion scale were used to form a composite score. Composite scores were ranked, split in the middle, and the resulting two groups were designated quiet or outgoing Counselors. Of the four dyad types formed by this procedure, two were clearly most successful: quiet boys with outgoing counselors, outgoing boys with outgoing counselors. That is, outgoing counselors were more effective than quiet counselors with both types of boys. Additional evidence for the outgoing counselors' superiority comes from our separate study of attrition dyads. An extremely low proportion of these unsuccessful dyads had outgoing counselors: three of fifteen instead of the expected 7.5 (Chapter Eight). Separating counselors solely by their initial direct self-descriptions of either outgoing or quiet-reserved generated boy outcome findings similar to those above, but somewhat weaker.

These two counselor types, outgoing and low quiet, were formed for different phases of our investigation, but they are obviously quite similar and quite effective. To consider them simply as more outgoing or extroverted or more surgent is an error. Other measures used in our study help to form an expanded profile of this counselor type. The more outgoing counselors are less "sad, blue, and discontented"; choose more person-oriented academic majors; are more self-disclosed and assertive with peers; view human nature as quite complex and changeable; tend to see themselves low on abasement, deference, and succorance; and were not strong academic achievers in high school. They tend to have had previous experience working with children, participate in many extracurricular school activities, have strong faith in the efficacy of therapy, are self-confident, use more adjectives to describe themselves, and are less orderly than their quiet peers (Chapter Eight). In the companionship program, they had longer visits with their boys, spent more money, pursued more activities per visit, rarely worked on hobbies, and saw more similarities between themselves and their boys.

We did not expect such positive findings for boys with out-going counselors. Initially, our staff was biased toward the more gentle, reserved applicants who were less verbal during GAIT screening sessions. The more quiet applicants seemed to be better listeners because they gave less advice, did less interrupting, and appeared less aggressive—just like the stereotype of the old-fashioned nondirective therapist. But the GAIT procedure combined both staff and peer ratings as selection criteria to dilute our bias. Assertive and emotionally expressive applicants did pass the screening test when they also displayed a capacity for empathy, acceptance, and warmth. Apparently, these qualities comprise a winning combination for helping troubled boys with both quiet and outgoing types of problems. The quiet, unassertive counselors had less positive effect on boys, especially the boys who were withdrawn, isolated, concealed, and depressed.

A third pair of variables strongly related to positive companionship effects was visit length and frequency (Chapter Eight). Boys in companionships with longer visits ($x = 3.4$ hrs.) improved more in various areas according to parent, teacher, and classmate ratings. The findings suggest that Short-Visit ($x = 2.7$ hrs.) boys had less success with problems involving self-esteem, phobias, stealing, temper tantrums, isolation, and schoolwork. Our rules called for visits no less than one or more than four hours, but casual inspection of Visit Reports suggest that long-visit dyads had a higher incidence of five-hour and sometimes six-hour visits. That is, they occasionally chose to spend much of the day together. In some companionships, longer visits could have been the product of expediency due to tight schedules. On the other hand, longer visits allowed a wider range of activities such as country hikes and football afternoons. Regardless of cause, long-visit companionships appeared to provide more fun and interest. Counselors also reported more talk about their boys' behavior, including expressed feelings about the counselor.

A similar pattern was obtained from the low visit ($x = 40$) group; the boys in this group (approximately two visits per week) gained more than those in high visit ($x = 58$) companionships (roughly three visits per week). Outcome differences were similar to those found between the long- and short-visit groups (details in Chapter Eight). Low visit counselors were assessed as more disclosing and more autonomous. There was a slight tendency for fewer visits to be associated with longer visits, as evidenced by a weak negative correlation between visit frequency and length ($-.13$).

Apparently, companionships with fewer and longer visits have more therapeutic potential. Longer visits produced gains of greater magnitude and are easier to explain as a therapeutic agent; but why should two versus three visits a week make a difference? A small clue comes from the higher proportion of group-trained counselors in the low visit group: two thirds versus less than half for the high visit group. These counselors were seen as more empathic and disclosed by their boys. We could also speculate that a heavy saturation of visits deprived boys of opportunities for generalizing any gains to relationships with neighborhood peers. But these speculations are strained, and we must leave the more successful low visit pattern as a minor mystery. What does appear clear is that a larger number of shorter visits will produce fewer therapeutic gains. Three-and-a-half-hour visits twice a week were the averages for the most beneficial companionships.

So far, the more powerful predictors of boy improvement have come from three diverse companionship dimensions: dyad type, counselor type, and visit pattern. Obviously, the total project sample ($N = 88$) was not large enough for studying the combined effects of all three dimensions. However, our curiosity motivated a casual search and inspection that located six black-white companionships with outgoing counselors that had fewer and longer visits. As expected, their improvement scores from all observer groups were exceptionally high. This clue lends some support to the speculation that these more successful predictors may be additive.

Companionships also appear more effective with boys whose problems are rather severe—roughly the upper 3 per cent of a random sample and the upper quartile of our participant sample. Our small group of more severely troubled boys ($N = 19$) gained more than their controls. A majority had quiet problems: passivity, withdrawal, depression. They became more popular in school, more assertive, more dominant, and less self-abasing and physically modest. Less severely troubled participants (lower quartile of our participant sample) had change scores very similar to their mildly troubled controls. Casual inspection of eight high pathology participants and controls with distinctly quiet problems showed greater improvement for participants in every pairing on all major outcome measures. We suspect that extremely withdrawn boys were able to practice assertive and even dominant behaviors in the safely egalitarian companionships that were structured to demand collaboration. Their heightened likeability among school peers could be viewed as a function of generalized assertion learned in the companionships. In any case, the findings recommend companionships as most useful for severely or moderately troubled boys as opposed to those with mild problems.

The remaining predictors we studied gave findings that fall into two classes: (1) some companionship effects positive but at lower levels than seen for black-white dyads, outgoing counselor type, low-frequency–long-visit patterns or high problem-severity subgroups; (2) no measurable companionship effects, or negative effects.

The lower-level positive predictors were the following: quiet initial problems, group training for counselors, high scores on GAIT open and understanding. Some of these predictors were contaminated by other variables or distorted by the project design. Obviously, some contamination crept into most of the predictor studies; for instance, long-visit companionships had a higher-than-expected proportion of black boys, and low visit dyads had more group-trained counselors. Typically, the contaminant created less than a 10 per cent bias in the successful subgroups (see Chapter Eight). More serious problems diluted the effects of group training on counselors and the measurement of differences between counselors high and low on open and understanding.

The best test of training effects would use a simple split of counselors into trained and untrained subgroups. We did partition a matched half into weekly in-service training groups, but ethical considerations urged us to administer a six-lesson automated course on interpersonal relations to all counselors (Chapter Four). In addition, all counselors had easy access to professional consultants, which introduced another form of training. Thus, our study of training effects was diluted to a comparison of more and less training. Despite the dilution, we did measure a greater increase in assertiveness for boys with group-trained counselors. These counselors were also rated higher (by their boys) on measures of empathy, openness, and control ("tries to get me to do what he wants"). The high control scores were probably caused by the counselors' attempts to introduce some of the therapeutic "gimmicks" occasionally touted by fellow group members. Overall gains associated with group training are minor, more valuable for quiet boys, and poorly tested.

Impaired study of high open and understanding as predictors was also caused by an ethical issue. We publicly promised a suspicious community that special effort would be expended to select the best counselor applicants. The promise was converted into the rejection of any applicant scoring low on GAIT open, understanding, or accepting-warm (Chapter Three). Obviously, equating high scores on these variables with therapeutic aptitude requires some moderate assumptions, and we were tempted to use all applicants in a study of high versus low GAIT scores as outcome predictors. Temptation was resisted, and low-scoring applicants were rejected. The result was a truncated sample of counselors that could be dichotomized only into medium and high subgroups on open, understanding, and accepting-warm. Even with this severe limitation, the high open and understanding scores predicted some improvement in boys. High and medium levels of accepting-warm failed to predict differential boy outcome—although the trend of nonsignificant differences favored the high group.

GAIT open was the better predictor. Boys with medium open counselors did gain on most improvement indices, but the boys with high open counselors did much better with problem reduction and somewhat better (marginally significant: $p < .10$) in reducing hostility and attention-seeking in school. Boys with high understanding counselors also showed more problem reduction—especially, reduction of the presenting problem.

Both groups of high counselors differed from their medium counterparts by scoring lower on GAIT rigid, being chosen more frequently as a learning partner by peers, and describing human nature as more complex. Actually, high and medium counselors did not differ greatly on GAIT open and understanding scores: highs typically were seen as open or understanding by almost all of the raters, compared to roughly 70 per cent for mediums. Finding measurable differences in their impact on boys was most encouraging. We must seriously consider these interpersonal traits as capable of establishing a therapeutic environment within companionships. Evidence from other studies supports this view, and one other investiga-tion corroborates the differential predictive capacity of high and medium scores (Chapter Three)'. There is a good chance that indi-viduals scoring low on GAIT open and understanding will prove to effect less improvement. Our findings from other measures repeatedly show some association between empathy, self-disclosure, and thera-peutic gains. Of course, the findings presented here on GAIT open and understanding do not settle the matter of selecting nonprofes-sional therapists, but they may make it difficult for program directors to maintain good conscience while pairing low-scoring individuals with troubled children.

Two subgroups of participants showed gain patterns similar to those of their matched controls; that is, slight improvement. Twenty-one of the least troubled participants (low pathology)', and those outgoing participants with quiet counselors ($N = 22$) were assessed as gaining little or nothing from companionships. We could assume that low pathology boys had less room for improvement or were difficult to measure because their scores were suppressed by a ceiling effect. Another guess is that the "automatic gains" described by control parents are more likely to cover any small improvement resulting from the companionships. In any case, therapeutic gains for mildly troubled individuals are usually difficult to measure—except for enthusiastic self-reports. We are reluctant to conclude that companionships are ineffective for low pathology boys because measurement issues dominate the picture. What does seem clear is that high pathology boys improve much more than controls and should be given priority until research indicates otherwise.

Better speculations can be made for the weak showing by outgoing boys with quiet counselors. We know that the quiet coun-selors were assessed to be much less effective and that the outgoing group of participant boys gained a little less than their quiet counter-parts. But the cross-age factor interferes because even our quiet counselors were unlikely to be "taken over" twice or three times a week by their juniors. That is, quiet counselors tended to be unasser-tive, but they were not pathologically passive. Visit Reports from quiet counselor–outgoing boy dyads reveal that boys frequently attempted to control activities and frequently succeeded—up to a point. When the counselor finally resisted, conflict occurred. These were stormy dyads with contrasting stretches of affection and conflict. In a few cases, counselors received some physical abuse. One counselor complained to us when his books and papers were thrown into a lake by his angry boy. With all its problems, this dyad type does not seem entirely unproductive. True, the boys improve less in school and show little improvement with problems of irritability and temper tantrums, but their feelings get hurt less easily and they become less dependent on parents and gain much in self-esteem (Table 15). When there is no choice, the quiet counselor–outgoing boy dyad is a possibility—and clearly better than the double quiet type. However, it seems easier to use counselors that fit the more successful outgoing profile.

Double quiets are the worst combination, according to our data. We have labeled them "resentment factories" because their Visit Reports and complaints usually described the pair as unwilling to take initiatives, failing to "reach out," and concealing their disappointment from one another. Boys in these dyads were measured as markedly less improved (Table 15). We recommend that such pairings be avoided.

The double quiet variable was our best negative predictor. Not too far behind were counselor traits of rigidity and sadness measured by GAIT. Counselor age also appeared related to less improvement for boys. A small number of high rigid counselors were frequently described as more "set in his ways" during the GAIT sessions. This group tended to see human nature as simpler and more stable, felt more confident and dominant, claimed more religious commitment, were closer to parents, and (with marginal significance) described themselves as more concealed with friends. Their boys gained somewhat less than boys with low rigid counselors. A casual inspection of their Visit Reports suggested that they maintained "tight" companionships with more formality, some sermonizing, and a narrower range of activities. These counselors were not extremely rigid, and their therapeutic talent ratings were high enough for acceptance to the project. Some clinicians would expect them to be more effective—especially with acting-out boys, who are assumed to need formal relationship boundaries. We found no support for this contention, since outgoing and quiet boys produced similar outcome patterns.

High blue Counselors were rated "sad, blue, discontented" by a majority of peer and professional observers. Their boys did not do as well as boys with low blue counselors—especially with presenting problems and peer relations. As expected, high blue counselors received high quiet scores. They were seldom chosen as learning partners by peers and, with mild significance ($<.10$), tended to want object-oriented careers such as chemistry and engineering. In companionships, they were clearly more controlling and felt less understanding and understood when compared with the low blues. Once again, quiet, withdrawn, controlling traits are associated with less effectiveness. Combined with discontent or sadness and lower levels of empathy, the prospects look grim. But, remember, these counselors were also rated adequate on therapeutic potential, and it appears that they were open. Without these latter qualities we would expect high blue counselors to be retarding. As it is, they were merely less effective than counselors who were not as depressed and controlling.

A set of significantly negative correlations between counselor age and improvement on boys' problems gives warning about using atypically older undergraduates (23 to 35 in our sample). It is not a powerful finding, but if we were expending great effort to ensure successful companionships, the atypically older undergraduate would be excluded. Perhaps the age disparity between these counselors and their boys was just too much—roughly averaging at fifteen years, compared to about nine years in most companionships. Older undergraduates may also be atypical on other dimensions affecting companionships. We thought that they were more severe or serious and condescending. They also appeared to be more isolated from their school peers.

Summary. Here is a summary of boys measured as gaining most from companionships: (1) black boys who were paired with white counselors, (2) boys with outgoing Counselors, (3) boys in companionships with *relatively* long ($x = 3.4$ hours) and less frequent (two per week) visits, (4) boys with more severe problems— primarily passivity, withdrawal, depression. The following groups also showed some positive gains, but at lower levels than those listed above: (1) boys with quiet problems, (2) boys with counselors who received in-service group training, (3) boys with counselors who received high scores on GAIT open or understanding. Improvement

levels similar to those of noncompanionship controls (slight gain)'
were measured for (1) mildly troubled boys, (2) boys with outgoing
problems paired with quiet counselors. The groups of boys that
gained the least were (1) boys in double quiet companionships, (2)
boys with blue counselors, (3) boys with more rigid counselors, (4)
boys with counselors atypically old as undergraduates (23 to 35
years)'.

Effects on Counselors

The companionships and group training had significant impact on counselors. All our findings indicate that the impact was
positive, with some parallels to other projects using students as therapeutic agents. We compared changes in our counselors with those for
a control group matched on motivation, vocational goals, quiet-outgoing styles, age, and socioeconomic status. Details of counselor
change are described and summarized in Chapter Nine. Here is a
capsule of the highlights:

(1) In the area of interests, counselors, compared with controls, reported sharp increases for (a) children's behavior, (b) working with troubled people, (c) their own interpersonal behavior. They
cited project activities as having much effect on their enhanced interests.

(2) Counselors saw themselves as becoming more aggressive
and as needing more autonomy, more change, and less control when
compared with their matched control group.

(3) The self-descriptions of counselors became more critical
and less defensive than those of the control group.

(4) Quiet counselors gained more in the areas of assertion
and openness than their outgoing counterparts.

(5) Outgoing counselors became more interested in person-
oriented careers and came to view people as more trustworthy when
compared with quiet Counselors.

(6) Group training appeared to increase counselors' general
self-disclosure and further enhanced interests in their own interpersonal behavior and in their fields of study (mostly social science),
but decreased the quality of their schoolwork. These counselors also
gained somewhat more in ability to conceptualize social relations.

(7) Counselors with more severely troubled boys seemed to become more assertive.

(8) Counselors with black boys increased interest in cross-race relations and black culture.

Our earlier study of the applicants' motives (Chapter Three) allows us to compare what the counselors wanted and what they eventually received from the program. Most of all, they wanted to develop better interpersonal skills, to take action in giving to someone as opposed to their more passive and taking student roles, to clarify career goals. Some joined the project in search of academic relief, autonomy, or a new adventure. One theme threaded its way through most of their expressed motives: the need for converting pent-up ideals into some humanitarian action. Apparently, many counselors got what they wanted—and more. It is becoming clear from our findings and those reported by others (Chapter Nine) that companionship programs sharply heighten interest in human interaction and psychopathology and direct some into mental health careers. Some students get their wish for a greater sense of independence, and many take on a less idealistic self-concept in their push for self-improvement. At least some of the counselors wanting academic relief got it with a side effect—their academic performance dropped a notch. But, in general the changes were positive and appeared to further the developmental tasks critical to young adulthood: learning about intimacy and sharpening career goals. Comparing the students' initial motives and our findings on change makes us feel that their expectations were quite appropriate.

The implications for undergraduate education are clear: students working in structured companionships acquire competencies and knowledge that cannot be taught in the classroom. Mixing such mental health work with academic studies in the social sciences could enhance the generalizability of classroom learning. The instant relevancy gained from commerce with immediate and real human problems can provide the firsthand experiences needed to make conceptual learning easier and more pertinent. This blending of experiential and conceptual learning is not necessarily expensive or cumbersome. Programs like ours can be largely administered by graduate students in psychology, social work, psychiatry, pastoral counseling, and the like. Rappaport and his associates (1971) used graduate student administrators with much success and described such secondary gains as learning how to supervise and obtaining dissertation data. We also believe that students headed toward careers that are not in mental health but demand one-to-one interaction skills (dentistry, medicine, law, religion, business) need much early practice in helping–relation situations.

Finally, our findings, along with those from other investigators, show that change in nonprofessional therapeutic agents is a fruitful area for study.

Recommendations Based on Boy Outcome

Most companionship programs are rapidly conceived action projects without research. Project descriptions can be found in newspapers or magazines rather than professional journals. The programs vary in structure, but it seems that most use college students in one-to-one relationships. Thus far, only a small fraction of the six million United States college students have participated; but it is obvious that many are motivated for such idealistic and double-edged therapy activities. Current predictions call for a dramatic increase in the number of programs during the 1970s. We estimate the number of nonprofessional projects to exceed one thousand by 1975. This national movement should foster many outcome studies. Meanwhile, our findings, along with those from the few systematic investigations of companionship therapy (Chapter One), will have to serve as guidelines for program and research development.

A major lesson learned from our work involves the issue of specificity level. It is becoming clear that the successful design and study of companionship programs will demand sharper specification of outcome predictor variables. Unclassified, heterogeneous counselor and client populations, diffuse relationship processes, and gross tests of effects will yield inconclusive knowledge. Findings from our unpartitioned sample underline this point. What appeared to be a fairly homogeneous sample of boys, counselors, and companionships became a hiding place for several therapeutically promising variables. The promising variables began to emerge only after a partitioning of the larger sample into small bipolar subsamples. Thus, our search for grand effects imitated the historical pattern of classical therapy research. If research into nonprofessional therapy follows the same developmental route as traditional therapy research, it will produce a literature filled with conflicting evidence. Classical designs for testing global effects of an ostensibly uniform therapy with actually diverse populations and processes are now seen as doomed to failure. In a compilation of therapy research over the past thirty years, Bergin (1971) concludes that "gross tests on the effects of therapy are obsolete. . . . It is small wonder that such efforts have provided only the slimmest positive evidence of any effects, that results have usually been ambiguous, and that failures to replicate have been abundant" (p. 253). Workers in the nonprofessional therapy field should have an easier time avoiding the old pitfalls. Greater freedom in selecting particular nonprofessional therapists and clients, along with many opportunities to modify therapeutic procedures, can produce stronger research. In addition, nonprofessional projects usually allow more access to observations from counselor, client, and significant people in their lives. In sum, our findings recommend the need for a very specific classification of participant companionship characteristics; and we believe investigators of nonprofessional therapy can achieve such classifications with *relative* ease.

Our experience recommends the need for classifying companionship phenomena into four categories that appear to hold important outcome predictors: counselor type, dyad type, client type, and companionship process. We found important predictors in all four dimensions and cannot see any one dimension as expendable in a serious investigation. Counselor and dyad type seem especially promising and are probably most available to experimental maneuvers. The companionship process dimension is by far the most difficult to control and assess, but it contains the therapeutic events that are targets of the static predictors. Obviously, the great number of potential variables in each dimension can make the choice of what to study overwhelming. However, findings from psychotherapy research, along with findings and implications from our investigation, do offer a useful list of starters for research and program design.

Successful Counselor Variables. The outgoing profile was the best counselor predictor found in our study. As mentioned earlier, the profile involves more than gregariousness or social surgency. All outgoing counselors had to meet our screening criteria of relatively

high scores on GAIT understanding, accepting-warm, and open—
but so did the less successful quiet counselors. Here is a list of variables describing the outgoing profile which might be better labeled
as emotionally expressive (details are in Chapters Three and Eight):
(1) Low score on GAIT quiet (below 40 per cent); (2) Self-
description generally outgoing rather than quiet; (3) Low score on
GAIT blue (below 20 per cent); (4) academic majors more "person oriented" on Rosenberg scale; (5) described as more assertive
and disclosed by peers after many group sessions; (6) higher labile
and exhibit scores on ACL; (7) lower abasement, deference, and
succorance scores on ACL; (8) Lower GPA in high school (near
$3.0 = B$).

A few other variables were marginally associated ($p < .10$)
with the profile and round out the outgoing-expressive picture:
previous experience working with children, many extracurricular
activities in high school and college, high scores on number of adjectives checked and self-confidence and lower scores on order (on
ACL). The person-oriented variable (number 4 above) does seem
an obvious predictor at first glance, but some have argued that there
is a long speculative leap between career preference and therapeutic
talent. It has been asserted that strong motivation toward people can
frequently mask a sublimated need for self-correction that is denied
through social extroversion. We feel that this dynamic may operate
quite frequently, but does not commonly counterindicate therapeutic
effectiveness. Our findings are not alone in associating person-
oriented career preference to therapeutic talent. In their classic
clinical performance study, Kelly and Fiske (1951) found a set of
negative correlations between ratings of therapeutic competence and
more object-oriented vocational interest scores: engineer, chemist,
and production Manager. Apparently, a strong orientation toward
people is a valuable, easy-to-use predictor. It characterizes much of
our outgoing profile and should be used in investigations of nonprofessional therapists.

Here are some other variables for studying counselor type
that appear associated with better outcome. They are listed in order
of judged importance: (1) high scores on GAIT understanding
(>75) and open (>80); (2) Low scores on GAIT rigid (<20)
and relaxed (<50); (3) high complexity and changeability scores

on the Human Nature scale; (4) below 25 years of age (only for undergraduates); (5) low score on Jourard's lie scale; (6) above-average faith in psychotherapy.

The low relaxed score is not an error. We cannot be sure, but applicants that appear relaxed in the somewhat stressful GAIT sessions may frequently be faking. Some informal observation suggested that they were good actors with glib interpersonal styles. Specific criteria for all recommended counselor variables are detailed in Chapter Three, which also discusses Chapin's Social Insight Test —a somewhat dated instrument that may tap elements of interpersonal intelligence but not necessarily interpersonal competence in a performance situation.

Our recommended list contains variables drawn from paper-and-pencil tests, background information, and sociometric performance ratings. During its early stages, research into the characteristics of professional therapists used background information and paper-and-pencil tests. Therapist persuasion (theoretic orientation), length of experience, and level of expertise (sometimes judged by reputation) were used without much success. A paper-and-pencil test that designated therapists as type A or type B attracted some investigation (Betz, 1962; Heller, 1971). The scale was taken from items on the Strong Vocational Interest Blank, and differentiated therapists of type A as more successful with schizophrenic patients. The implication was that personal characteristics of therapists, rather than training, determined therapeutic skill (or, better phrased, therapeutic talent). An unpublished study by Carson, described by Heller (1971), found that type-A therapists were not interested in mechanics and manual activities, which appears to fit with some of our more successful counselors' lack of interest in object-oriented careers. The A-B therapist typology is another possibility for studying non-professional therapists; however, it has generated ambiguous findings and would be best used among a host of other predictors. That is, little is known about the characteristics of A and B therapists. This form of therapist typology involves locating enduring characteristics that are assumed associated with some unknown set of therapeutic interpersonal variables. Similar assumptions are involved when using therapist personality, background, and attitude variables to predict outcome; they are secondary predictors aimed at unknown interpersonal characteristics. It seems more efficient to study the interpersonal because the bulk of therapeusis or the therapeutic event is contained within interpersonal phenomena. This reasoning appears to be swinging investigation toward therapists' interpersonal talent, and we believe that research into nonprofessional therapy should follow the same direction. Truax and Mitchell (1971) have done an important review of this area and describe a group of recent studies on empathy, warmth, and genuineness as predictors of therapeutic effectiveness. These variables were found to be generally associated with positive outcome for a wide range of clients in many settings as described by fourteen separate studies. The variables were usually obtained through use of trained observers who reliably rate brief (typically three-minute) segments of audio- or videotape. This procedure is somewhat similar to our GAIT, but is geared more toward measuring the process of ongoing therapy rather than preselecting therapists. Nevertheless, the various interpersonal-measurement procedures pioneered by Truax could be modified into selection devices. Investigators planning to study counselor variables as predictors should be familiar with the work of Truax and colleagues before starting.

Boy Characteristics. Black boys did best, but they were only with white counselors. We strongly suspect that cross-race dyad type is the real predictor, and assume that white boys with black counselors would have done as well. At any rate, our design limitations make it appropriate to place this predictor under "dyad type."

In his review of research on client variables as outcome predictors, Garfield (1971) suggests that the best results have been obtained with the least disturbed clients. His review focused on individual professional therapy with adults, and the notion may not necessarily apply to children. At least, our findings support the opposing hypothesis: more severely troubled boys gain more than mildly troubled boys from companionships. Besides severity of problem, we also recommend that problem type be studied. Withdrawn, isolated, passive boys (quiets) gained somewhat more than hostile, acting-out boys (outgoings). Because many of the more severely troubled boys had quiet problems, we informally inspected a small group of high pathology–quiet boys. All of them improved more than their controls. Companionship may be a useful therapeutic device for quiet-problemed, more severely troubled boys.

Observers of our project expected fatherless boys to gain much from companionships. Unfortunately, our findings indicate that companionships make fatherless boys more aggressive, touchy, and isolated from peers. Perhaps the unstructured security of the companionships provided fatherless boys a place aggressively to explore the possibilities of relating to a man. If so, it is likely that such behavior would spill over into other relationships. Perhaps more than a year is generally required for the aggression to level off. In any case, it does seem best to continue study of fatherless versus intact-home boys because there are many programs now operating on the assumption that an adult male friend is the best therapy for troubled fatherless boys.

Our findings do not recommend any other boy variables as outcome predictors. Social class was not found independently associated to outcome, and our design did not allow study of other frequently studied client variables: intelligence, sex, age, and motivation. Actually, there is not much to be learned from the collection of past studies relating client attributes to outcome (Garfield, 1971). Client type seems to be a poorer predictor of outcome than therapist type.

Dyad Types. Race and the quiet-outgoing dimension were very useful in forming dyad types. We suspect that cross-race dyads have a therapeutic advantage. Double quiet dyads may generate more resentment than improvement. Boys in double quiet dyads clearly improved least, and the separately studied group of attrition dyads ($n = 15$) contained twice the expected proportion of double quiets (8 instead of 3.7—see Chapter Eight). Better results come when the reserved counselor is paired with an outgoing boy. Both quiet and outgoing boys do well with counselors fitting our outgoing profile. The use of gross constructs like similarity and complementarity does not help explain our data. At this early stage of nonprofessional therapy research, it seems best to build dyad types on dichotomies of several variables. Forming dyads on the basis of similarity-dissimilarity requires far too many variables that are typically inconsistent across age (child-adult), race, and sex. We need to locate promising dyad types that can be established and studied in the demanding atmosphere of applied settings. Constraints imposed by recruitment and sample sizes will limit most projects to four or five variables in forming dyad types; for example, black boys with quiet problems that are more severe and outgoing counselors scoring high on GAIT understanding. Traditional therapy research has moved slowly in this area because administrative constraints and sample deficiencies prohibited the formation of contrasting dyad types. With greater opportunity for manipulating sample composition, the investigators of nonprofessional programs could generate a body of evidence pointing to the most therapeutic dyad types.

Process Variables. Interpersonal-process variables are the most difficult to pin down and are probably the most potent predictors of behavior change. Our process variables included visit length and frequency, topics discussed, and activities pursued, along with a range of feelings and behaviors described by the participants. Because of the obvious measurement problems, most of our findings can serve only to suggest promising outcome predictors. The strongest results came from gross process measures and do not fit the trend of findings from traditional therapy research. That is, we found the longer and less frequent visit pattern associated with better outcome, while studies of professional therapy with children generally show no relation between outcome and length of session (Hartmann et al., 1968) and frequency of visits (Lessing and Schilling, 1966; Phillips, 1960). The findings are similar for studies on adult therapy. Comparing professional office therapy with companionship therapy on these dimensions is probably inappropriate. For professional child therapy, the mean visit length is probably the well-known fifty minutes with a standard deviation of, perhaps, fifteen minutes. Our mean visit length was almost three hours with a standard deviation of thirty minutes. The same is true for visit frequency: usually once a week in professional child therapy to two or three times a week in our project. We hope that those studying companionship therapy will not be diverted from the visit length and frequency variables by the lack of prediction observed for traditional therapy.

The remaining process variables associated with positive outcome represent phenomena that are frequently difficult to institute when companionships begin. Some variables can be used as indicators of satisfactory progress during early visits. Details on the following recommended variables can be found in Chapters Five, Six, and Eight: (1) sharing meals during visits; (2) low frequency of movie attendance; (3) frequent automobile or bike rides; (4) spending little money during visits; (5) conversing about counselor's skills; (6) conversing about the boy's mother; (7) discussions of project rules limited to early visits; (8) conversing about the boy's role in the family; (9) infrequent talk about boy's father; (10) infrequent talk about counselor's mother; (11) counselor describing independent visits as quite nondemanding, comfortable, warm, and, relaxed; (12) counselor infrequently describing interaction as quiet.

Some of these more successful process predictors do not make easy sense as elements of therapeutic interaction. With some strained reasoning, vigorous speculation, and a bit of corroborating data, we attempt explanations in Chapters Five and Six. Several of the variables listed above were supported by an independent study of fifteen attrition companionships (Chapter Eight). Attrition pairs rarely shared meals and attended movies more frequently than pairs in continuing companionships over equivalent time spans. Attrition counselors described the visit interaction as much less warm, comfortable, and more quiet. The attrition findings also provided a few more process variables that could be predictors of negative outcome: very low Visit Report scores on emotionally open, and a strong tendency for counselors to describe dissimilarity between themselves and their boys on the feelings and behavior items—especially on warm and closed (Chapter Six). In addition, findings from attritions indicate that their visits were extremely short, which strengthens the notion that shorter visits are associated with negative outcome.

Conclusions on Boy Outcome

After the customary search for a global therapy outcome picture, and the customary inconclusive answer, we moved to the appropriate question: Which boy and counselor in what companionship are more successful? The answers were varied: some specific arrangements were therapeutic, others appeared neutral, and a few may have been of disservice to boys. When we failed to classify companionships according to counselor, boy, dyad, and process variables, the resulting unpartitioned sample gave inconclusive results quite similar to typical findings from traditional child therapy studies: a majority of participants and controls improve. This contention is supported by Levitt's review of forty-seven studies on over nine thousand children spanning a thirty-five-year period (1971). His summary of all reported findings revealed that (1) a majority of cases were seen as improved, (2) a similar majority of no-therapy controls were seen as improved, (3) improvement rates were roughly similar for studies of neurotic and psychotic children, (4) acting-out children have somewhat lower improvement rates. Thus, the customary findings from typically unpartitioned studies of orthodox child therapy are equivalent to findings from our unpartitioned companionship sample: modest gains for both clients and no-therapy controls.

In addition, we found fewer gains for acting-out (outgoing) boys. These parallels, along with our studies showing greater gains for *particular* subgroups of participants over controls, serve to point out the masking effect of unpartitioned samples. Most of the investigations reviewed by Levitt did not attend to therapist type, dyad type, or process variables. Taken together, these issues should warn the investigator of nonprofessional therapy (and orthodox therapy) against using unpartitioned samples as the only vehicle for outcome research. It is time to abandon the search for global outcome effects from heterogeneous therapy conditions, and set our sights on the detailed situational variables. We expect a new direction in research to come out of the nonprofessional movement, where unheard-of freedom in design choice will foster the discovery of very specific therapeutic predictors.

We are not concluding that the refined study of predictors will solve most measurement problems. Fastidious selection of narrow samples should aid in establishing appropriate control groups, but careful sampling is not enough. If motivation is matched (as in our study), then alternate "treatment" must be provided because the motivation will ensure other forms of help-seeking activity. A matched no-therapy control group seems to exist only in the researcher's dreams. In our case, denying control parents their first choice of therapeutic activity seems to have biased their ratings: "I'll solve my boy's problems without you." That is, we matched for motivation

but not for rejection. There can be little doubt that control groups
of troubled children will register automatic gains and that alternatives
to treatment cannot be true placebos. We have suggested a partial
solution, involving the surveillance of idiosyncratic help-seeking
activities by no-treatment control subjects. The procedure will require considerable ingenuity but should allow experimental conditions
to stand out with greater clarity.

In lieu of anything better, we have recommended that cross-
age companionship programs integrate our best predictors of improvement—especially when programs are without a research
component. We have also recommended a set of secondary variables
under four rubrics—counselor, boy, dyad type, and companionship
process—intended for those planning studies of companionship
therapy. Counselor type and dyad type seem especially promising
dimensions for study. We assume that the most powerful predictors
will come from the dimension most difficult to study—companionship
process.

Most of our work has been geared to the serious investigator
or program director who has resources for implementing our research
products. However, some readers may be responsible for low-budget,
non-research programs that cannot afford the structuring suggested
by our work. Such programs are frequently initiated by administrative expediency and must justify their existence on some expedient
faith in the efficacy of nonprofessional therapeutic agents. Glowing
program reports are often based on hope and good intentions rather
than systematic study and further the impetus to proliferate untested formats. Reasoning that assumes anything should be tried
because nothing is known is no longer appropriate for designing
companionship programs. Findings from our project and other
studies described in this book provide guidelines for enhancing positive outcome and avoiding nonproductive or even damaging procedures. For example, we hope that companionship programs without research components will consider avoiding double quiet dyads
until further studies strengthen or weaken the generalizability of our
findings. We also recommend that such programs explore cross-race
dyads and attempt to select therapeutic agents that approximate our
outgoing profile: emotionally expressive, empathic, open, person
oriented, less rigid. That is, we suggest that quickly built programs

consider our best predictors as possibilities for their particular needs and capacities. The predictors are far from sure things, but they do offer better-than-chance probabilities for providing some therapeutic gains.

Appendices

Appendix A

Problem List for Elementary School Boys

These sentences describe problems that are found in elementary school boys. Please check the number (0 to 8) that comes closest to describing your boy. Describe your boy as he really is—please be frank. Do no skip any items.

	0 Never	1	2 Seldom	3	4	5	6 Often	7	8 Always
Example: He loses things									
1. His appetite is poor.									
2. He has problems with speech (stutters, baby talks, etc.)									
3. He asks for help with schoolwork.									
4. He gets into fights with children.									
5. He is quiet and shy.									
6. He must win at all costs.									
7. He plays alone.									
8. He bites his nails.									
9. He takes things not his own—steals.									

10. He is restless in sleep *or* has disturbing dreams.

11. He ruins toys or destroys belongings.

12. His feelings are easily hurt.

13. He does not like to share things.

14. He depends on parents too much.

15. He tries to get attention from others.

16. He is modest—doesn't like to be seen undressed.

17. He has mood swings—strong changes in feeling.

18. He wets his bed *or* soils during the day.

19. He has "temper tantrums"—anger outbursts.

20. He gets "on edge," annoyed, irritable at small things.

21. He wants to do the opposite of what is expected of him.

22. He has sad moods.

23. He is afraid or upset by certain things (dogs, fire, dark, high places, thunder, etc.) ⋮ ⋮ ⋮ ⋮ ⋮ ⋮ ⋮

24. He becomes very jealous. ⋮ ⋮ ⋮ ⋮ ⋮ ⋮ ⋮

25. He teases others. ⋮ ⋮ ⋮ ⋮ ⋮ ⋮ ⋮

26. He acts unusual—not like other children. ⋮ ⋮ ⋮ ⋮ ⋮ ⋮ ⋮

27. He keeps his feelings to himself. ⋮ ⋮ ⋮ ⋮ ⋮ ⋮ ⋮

28. He swears or curses. ⋮ ⋮ ⋮ ⋮ ⋮ ⋮ ⋮

29. He thinks poorly of himself. ⋮ ⋮ ⋮ ⋮ ⋮ ⋮ ⋮

30. He tells fibs or lies. ⋮ ⋮ ⋮ ⋮ ⋮ ⋮ ⋮

31. He feels everyone picks on him. ⋮ ⋮ ⋮ ⋮ ⋮ ⋮ ⋮

32. New situations and activities upset him. ⋮ ⋮ ⋮ ⋮ ⋮ ⋮ ⋮

33. He is not satisfied with his schoolwork. ⋮ ⋮ ⋮ ⋮ ⋮ ⋮ ⋮

34. He becomes very upset when scolded. ⋮ ⋮ ⋮ ⋮ ⋮ ⋮ ⋮

35. He is not sure of himself with people. ⋮ ⋮ ⋮ ⋮ ⋮ ⋮ ⋮

Appendix B

Classmate Descriptions

Print Boy's or Girl's Name Here➔

Boy............. Girl.............. School ....

Grade .... Teacher 1   2   3

1. He's a fast runner.
2. He plays all by himself a lot.
3. He makes fun of people.
4. He is one of my friends.
5. He's always clowning around.
6. He is very quiet and shy.
7. When he doesn't get his way, he gets real mad.
8. He's a nice guy.
9. He wants to show off in front of the kids.
10. He does not like to tell about himself.
11. If someone gets in his way, he shoves them away.
12. Many of the kids like him.
13. He tries to get attention.
14. Hardly any boys like to play with him.
15. He's just plain mean.
16. Some kids like him very much.
17. He does crazy things.
18. On the playground he just stands around.
19. He says he can beat everybody up.
20. He has a lot of friends.
21. He does not act like the rest of the kids.
22. He doesn't have very many friends.
23. He likes to pick on little kids.
24. He's the kind of kid I like.
25. Sometimes he acts very strange.
26. He cries easily.

Appendix C

Group Description Scale

Instructions. We want your impressions of every group member (except yourself). Please give us your best guesses and speculations on the first eight items. Indicate how each person appears to you from his behavior in today's group. Many items have three descriptive words. If one word doesn't seem to fit the pattern of the other two, then just use the other two words. It's the meaning of the item that we want you to use. We cannot elaborate on these items. Answer *every* item for *every* person.

Start with the first item, "I feel he understands what others really mean," and rate group member A. Continue using this same item and rate all the members in the group. When you have finished rating each group member on the first item, then move on to the second item, "He seems sad, blue, discontented," and rate each person on this one item. Then proceed to the third item and then on down the page using the same procedure. It is important that you rate all persons on one item before moving on to the next.

Place one or more plus (+) or minus (−) marks in each square to represent the following answers:

+++ I feel this is very much like him.

++ I feel this is like him.

+ I feel this is probably like him, or more like him than not.

− I feel this is probably *not* like him, or more unlike than like him.

−− I feel this is *not* like him.

−−− I feel this is very much *not* like him.

After completing items 1–8, tell us which four applicants you feel might make the best counselors, which might be most successful with an emotionally troubled person. Indicate your choices in order by numbering them 1 through 4. Since we cannot be certain of what makes a good counselor, we can't expect you to be sure of your guesses either. Use your intuition so we can compare it with ours.

GROUP MEMBERS

ITEMS	A	B	C	D	E	F	G	H	I
1. I feel he understands what others really mean.	....	....	....	....	....	....	....	....	....
2. He seems sad, blue, discontented.	....	....	....	....	....	....	....	....	....
3. He appears honest, frank, emotionally open.	....	....	....	....	....	....	....	....	....
4. I see him as a mild, reserved, quiet person.	....	....	....	....	....	....	....	....	....
5. He seems warm, patient, and accepting.	....	....	....	....	....	....	....	....	....
6. He appears set in his ways.	....	....	....	....	....	....	....	....	....
7. I see him as a relaxed, easygoing person.	....	....	....	....	....	....	....	....	....
8. Indicate in order of preference (1, 2, 3, 4) the four students you feel would make the best counselors.	....	....	....	....	....	....	....	....	....

Appendix D

Counselor-Boy Relationship Index

The questions below are necessarily direct and the instructions simple, as the same form is being given to the boys in the program. While the questions are worded as if you are still seeing your boy, we recognize that many of you have stopped by now. These are questions on how *you* are with your boy. Try to remember how things were. Indicate one of the following for each item: (0) never, (1) almost never, (2) not very often, (3) about half the time, (4) most of the time, (5) almost always, (6) always.

1. I tell him all about myself. ....

2. I get angry at him. ....

3. I have fun when we are together. ....

4. I understand how he feels. ....

5. I try to get him to do what I want. ....

Here are some questions about your *boy:*

1. He tells me all about himself. ....

2. He gets angry at me. ....

3. He has fun when we are together. ....

4. He understands how I feel. ....

5. He tries to get me to do what he wants. ....

274

Appendix E

Retrospective Questionnaire

A. We will use your impressions to get some idea of how boys changed over the past school year.

B. Indicate for each question: (1) much less, (2) somewhat less, (3) a little less, (4) no change, (5) a little more, (6) somewhat more, (7) much more. If you are not sure about how to answer, just give your best guess and put a question mark next to your response.

C. Please give this task your careful thought. Our work depends upon the sincerity of your descriptions.

1. Have you noticed any change in the boy's ATTITUDE TOWARD SCHOOL? He seems to like school: ....

2. Have you noticed any change in the way he GETS ALONG WITH OTHER CHILDREN? It appears that he enjoys being with other children: ....

3. Has the general quality of his SCHOOLWORK changed? Generally, his schoolwork seems: ....

4. Any change in the way he FEELS ABOUT HIMSELF (in terms of self-contentment, self-esteem, happiness)? He seems to like himself: ....

5. On a previous form you told us why you wanted your boy to join the project. That is, you described a problem. We would like to know if you have observed any change in your boy's behavior or feelings concerning that problem over the past school year. Please indicate the amount of change, if any. ....

275

Problem: ....

....

During the past school year the problem became: (1) much worse, (2) somewhat worse, (3) a little worse, (4) no change, (5) a little better, (6) somewhat better, (7) much better.

6. It is possible for a boy to change for better or for worse *during* the project but the change may not *last*. Was this true of your boy, or did the changes last? (Please do not hesitate to tell us if you have noticed that certain improvements did not last.)

7. It is also possible for the project to have effects on a boy which do not show up until *after* the project is over. Have you noticed any changes in your son—that you believe may be due to the project—which showed up *after* the project was over? Please give us details.

8. Did your son and his activities counselor have any contact with each other after the project was over in June of last year (visit, letter, phone call, etc.)? Yes............ No............ If yes, please describe:..

9. At any time since June of last year has your son received individual help from any professional person such as a school guidance counselor, social worker, minister, psychiatrist, psychologist? Yes............ No............ If yes, please describe: ....

10. No matter why you applied, we need to know if your son has changed in the way he gets along with people in general. The chart below can help you tell us how your boy changed in his personal relationships during the

project year *and* during this past year after the project was over (even if your boy never had a project counselor). We know the chart will not allow a perfect description—just check the description which will best tell what really happened.

a. *My son got along with others:*
   much better, a little better, about the same, a little worse, much worse, during the project year.

b. *My son got along with others:*
   much better, a little better, about the same, a little worse, much worse, during the year after the project ended.

If the above categories do not let you tell us what you think we should know, please use the space below.

Appendix F

Follow-Up Interview with Parents

1. Could you tell us whether .... was affected in any way by being in a companionship with ....? (In what ways was he affected? What makes you think the companionship was responsible? Did these changes seem important to you? How do you feel about these changes?)

2. Was the companionship pretty much what you expected it to be, or were you disappointed or surprised?

3. We are interested in two time periods: (a) the first is when your boy has a counselor; that would be when he was in the 5th-6th grade(s); (b) the second time period covers the past year, after the project was over.

    (a) During the time that your boy had a counselor, what changes did you notice?

    (b) Have you noticed any changes in your boy during this past year, since the project was over?

4. Here is a chart which will give us a better picture of the past two time periods, when added to what you have already told us. (Hand chart to parent and describe as necessary.) Could you tell us what *you* mean by "improvement"?

5. When you applied for the program you filled out a Problem Check List. Problems you checked as happening quite often were: (Show original PCL.) How are things now with these problems?

6. Does your boy have a problem now that concerns you?

7. At the beginning of the project did you hope your boy would become more *quiet* or more *outgoing?* Did your hopes come true in any way?

8. Please describe the companionship between .... and his counselor in terms of how close they were and how much fun they had. (Show Card A.)

9. Boys are different in the way they adjust to being separated from someone they like. Losing classmates or neighborhood friends because of moving or going home from summer camps may be a terrible experience for some boys, but only a sad fact of life for others. How does your boy generally adjust to separation from friends?

(b) Was .... surprised by the end of the companionship? How did he feel about the official ending? (Interviewer's rating—extremely, quite, or slightly: relieved, sad, angry, hurt, other.)

(c) How long did this feeling last?

10. In general, would you say (or guess) that *professional* psychotherapy or counseling offers benefit or produces positive personality change in grade school children? (Show Card B.) ....

(b) How about in adults? ....

11. At any time since June of last year has your son received individual help from any professional person such as a school guidance counselor, social worker, minister, psychiatrist, or psychologist? Yes................. No.................. (If so, please describe.)

279

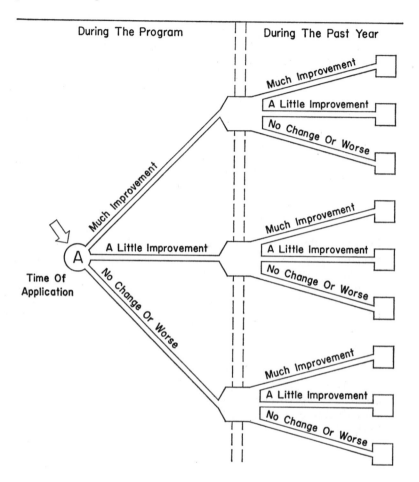

Appendix G

Boys' Story of Companionship

All the boys in the project have been telling us what happened when they had a counselor. We want to know what they liked and didn't like about the project. We also want to know if it made them any happier. We will not tell anyone what you say, including your counselor, but we need to know so we can help build better projects for boys.

Now, we need to know the story of you and your counselor. I'll start each part of the story and you tell me about the things I leave out. Let's try one.

_____ was a boy who joined the project. Some of the things he likes to do when he has free time are _____
_____.

That's the idea. Just say whatever comes to your mind first.

How We Got Started. A group of men decided to start a project so boys and college students could be friends until school was out in June. When _____ mother told him about the project he _____
_____. _____ joined the project because he _____
_____. _____ thought his mother wanted him to join because _____
_____.

Now in the next part of the story you meet each other.

The Beginning of Friendship. Soon, _____ and _____ met each other. _____ was a college student. He was taller than _____ and he looked _____
_____. _____ wasn't sure what a counselor like _____ was supposed to do, but he imagined that _____
_____. was not exactly like _____ expected. _____ thought _____ would be _____
_____. Instead, _____ was
_____.

After their first meeting _____ wondered what _____

281

thought about him. He guessed that _____ thought he was a boy who _____

_____.

In the beginning, _____ and _____ did different things at home and away from home. Most of the time the decision about what to do was made by _____. Now we go on to when you knew each other better.

We Come to Know Each Other Better. After a while they got to know each other better, and then when _____ came over _____ was _____. Sometimes they had fun together. One of the best times _____ had was _____ because _____ seemed to have less fun when _____ would _____. At times it was easier to talk to _____ than to other people. _____ could tell _____ about things like _____ _____. Sometimes it was not so easy to talk to _____ about things like _____ _____. _____ wished they could have talked more about _____

_____.

Sometimes _____ got the feeling that _____ wanted him to be _____. This made _____ feel _____. Let's move on to when you had known each other several months.

After Many Months Have Passed. What _____ liked most about their whole friendship was _____. Things had changed since they first met. Now that they knew each other better, _____ was _____ and _____ was _____. During those visits when _____ and _____ were not getting along so well, _____ usually _____. During these visits _____ usually _____

_____.

How We Felt About Each Other. Most of the time _____ made _____ feel _____ _____ because _____

282

_____. _____ thought
the best thing about _____ was _____
_____. Another thing he
liked about _____ was _____
_____. _____ was not sure how much _____
liked him but he guessed _____
_____. It seemed that one of the things _____ liked
about _____ was _____
_____. The best way to describe how much _____
liked _____ is _____
_____, _____ liked _____ a little less
when _____ was _____
_____.

_____ was a friend to _____ in a different way
than other people. Some of the ways he was different were _____
_____, _____ thought
about whether he wanted to be like _____ and decided that
_____
_____ [P]

Our Companionship Comes to a Close. At the beginning of the
project _____ had not been sure about what a counselor
was supposed to do. But by the end of the project _____
guessed that a counselor was supposed to _____
_____. After
the project was officially over, _____ _____
_____. This made _____
feel _____.

As I Look Back. When it was all over, _____ thought
about whether he learned new things when he was with _____.
_____ thought _____
_____. _____ also wondered
if he had learned anything new about the way he acted or got along
with others, and guessed that _____
_____.
Once in a while it was a help to talk with _____. One of the
best talks _____ and _____ ever had was about
_____.
That's the end of the story. Now you can help us out by answering
just a few questions.

283

Were you two very much alike in the way you acted or in things you wanted to do? ....
....

So you would say that you two were really not alike, just a little alike, more than a little alike, much alike, very much alike.

Do you think a project like this one can change boys in some ways?
....
....

Since you joined the project has there been any difference in the way you are with other boys? ....
....

Do you think that your friendship with .... had something to do with this change? ....
....

Since you joined the project has there been any difference in the way you are with adults? ....
....

Do you think your friendship with .... had something to do with the change? ....
....

Do you think the project helped you in any other way? ....
....
....

If you could have changed the project what would you have done?
....
....

Thank you for doing the story and answering the questions. Now, can you think a while to see if we missed anything? ....
....

References

ADELSON, D. D. and KALIS, B. (Eds.) *Community Psychology and Mental Health.* Scranton, Penn.: Chandler Publishing, 1970.

ALBEE, G. W. "Conceptual Models and Manpower Requirements in Psychology." *American Psychologist,* 1968, *23,* 317–320.

ARNHOFF, F. N., RUBINSTEIN, E. A., and SPEISMAN, J. C. (Eds.) *Manpower for Mental Health.* Chicago: Aldine, 1969.

BARNETT, O. J. "The Use of Nonprofessionals in the Rehabilitation of Mentally Disordered Sex Offenders." Unpublished doctoral dissertation, University of California, Los Angeles, 1972.

BARRETT-LENNARD, G. T. "Dimensions of Therapist Response as Causal Factors in Therapeutic Change." *Psychological Monographs,* 1962, *76,* (Whole No. 562).

BERGIN, A. E. "The Evaluation of Therapeutic Outcomes." In A. Bergin and S. L. Garfield (Eds.), *Handbook of Psychotherapy and Behavior Change.* New York: Wiley, 1971.

BERLIN, J. I., and WYCKOFF, B. L. "Human Relations Training through Dyadic Programmed Instruction." Paper presented at American Personnel and Guidance Association Convention, 1964.

BETZ, B. J. "Experiences in Research in Psychotherapy with Schizophrenic Patients." In H. Strupp and L. Luborsky (Eds.), *Re-*

search in Psychotherapy. Vol. II. Washington, D.C.: American Psychology Association, 1962. Pp. 41–60.

CAMPBELL, D. T., and FISKE, D. W. "Convergent and Discriminant Validation by the Multitrait-Multimethod Matrix." *Psychological Bulletin,* 1959, *56,* 81–105.

CARKHUFF, R. R., and TRUAX, C. B. "Training in Counseling and Psychotherapy: An Evaluation of an Integrated Didactic and Experiential Approach." *Journal of Consulting Psychology,* 1965, *29*(4), 333–336.

CHAPIN, F. S. "Preliminary Standardization of a Social Insight Scale." *American Sociological Review,* 1942, *7,* 214–225.

CHINSKY, J. M. "Nonprofessionals in a Mental Hospital." Unpublished doctoral dissertation, University of Rochester, 1968.

CHINSKY, J. M., and RAPPAPORT, J. "Attitude Change in College Students and Chronic Patients." *Journal of Consulting and Clinical Psychology,* 1970, *35*(3), 388–394.

CHINSKY, J. M., and RAPPAPORT, J. "Evaluation of a Technique for the Behavioral Assessment of Nonprofessional Mental Health Workers." *Journal of Clinical Psychology,* 1971, *27,* 400–402.

COOK, P. E. (Ed.) *Community Psychology and Community Mental Health.* San Francisco: Holden-Day, 1970.

COWEN, E. L. "Emergent Directions in School Mental Health: The Development and Evaluation of a Program for Early Detection and Prevention of Ineffective School Behavior." *American Scientist,* 1971, *59,* 723–733.

COWEN, E. L., DORR, D., and POKRACKI, F. "Selection of Nonprofessional Child-Aides for a School Mental Health Project." *Community Mental Health Journal,* 1972, *8,* in press.

COWEN, E. L., DORR, D., TROST, M. A., and IZZO, L. D. "A Follow-Up Study of Maladapting School Children Seen by Nonprofessionals." *Journal of Consulting and Clinical Psychology,* 1972, *36,* in press.

COWEN, E. L., GARDNER, E. A., and ZAX, M. (Eds.) *Emergent Approaches to Mental Health Problems.* New York: Appleton-Century-Croft, 1967.

COWEN, E. L., IZZO, L., MILES, H., TELSCHOW, E., TROST, M., and ZAX, M. "A Mental Health Program in the School Setting: Description and Evaluation." *Journal of Psychology,* 1963, *56*(2), 307–356.

COWEN, E. L., ZAX, M., and LAIRD, J. D. "A College Student Volunteer Program in the Elementary School Setting." *Community Mental Health Journal,* 1966, *2,* 319–328.

CRAIG, M., and FURST, P. W. "What Happens after Treatment." Report from New York City Youth Board, Research Department, 1965.

D'AUGELLI, A. R., CHINSKY, J. M., and GETTER, H. "The Effect of Group Composition and Time on Sensitivity Training." Unpublished manuscript, Department of Psychology, University of Connecticut, 1971.

DAVIS, W. J. "The Berkeley Big Brother Project." In A. de Grazia (Ed.), *Grass Roots Private Welfare*. New York: New York University Press, 1957. Pp. 41–44.

DAVISON, G. C., "The Training of Undergraduates as Social Reinforcers for Autistic Children." In L. Ullman and L. Krasner (Eds.), *Case Studies in Behavior Modification*. New York: Holt, Rinehart & Winston, 1966.

DOOLEY, C. D. "A Reliability and Validity Study of a Self-Administered Version of the Group Assessment of Interpersonal Traits." Unpublished manuscript, Department of Psychology, University of California, Los Angeles, 1972.

ERICKSON, E. H. *Childhood and Society*. New York: Norton, 1950.

EWALT, P. L. (Ed.) *Mental Health Volunteers*. Springfield, Ill.: Charles C Thomas, 1967.

GARFIELD, S. L. "Research on Client Variables in Psychotherapy." In A. Bergin and S. Garfield (Eds.), *Handbook of Psychotherapy and Behavior Change*. New York: Wiley & Sons, 1971.

GETTER, H., KORN, P. R., and ANCHOR, K. "Group Interaction Profile." Unpublished manuscript, Department of Psychology, University of Connecticut, 1970.

GLIDEWELL, J. C. "Studies of Mothers' Reports of Behavior Symptoms in Their Children." In S. B. Sells (Ed.), *The Definition and Measurement of Mental Health*. Washington, D.C.: National Center for Health Statistics, 1968. Pp. 181–217.

GOODMAN, G. *The Interpersonal Relations Project: Second Year Progress Report*. Berkeley: Institute of Human Development, University of California, 1966.

GOUGH, H. "The Adjective Check List as a Personality Assessment Research Technique." *Psychological Reports*, 1960, supplement 2.

GOUGH, H., and HEILBRUN, A. B., JR. *Manual for the Adjective Check List*. Palo Alto: Consulting Psychologist Press, 1963.

GOUGH, H., and HEILBRUN, A. B., JR. *The Adjective Check List Manual*. Palo Alto: Consulting Psychologist Press, 1965.

GREENBLATT, M., LEVINSON, D. J., and WILLIAMS, R. H. (Eds.) *The Patient and the Mental Hospital*. Glencoe, Ill.: Free Press, 1957.

GROSSER, C., HENRY, W. E., and KELLEY, J. G. (Eds.) *Nonprofessionals in the Human Services.* San Francisco: Jossey-Bass, 1971.

GRUVER, G. G. "College Students as Therapeutic Agents." *Psychological Bulletin,* 1971, *76*(2), 111–127.

GUERNEY, B. G. (Ed.) *Psychotherapeutic Agents.* New York: Holt, Rinehart & Winston, 1969.

HART, J., and TOMLINSON, T .M. (Eds.) *New Directions in Client-Centered Therapy.* Boston: Houghton Mifflin, 1970.

HARTMANN, E., GLASSER, B. A., GREENBLATT, M., SOLOMON, M. H., and LEVINSON, D. J. *Adolescents in a Mental Hospital.* New York: Grune & Stratton, 1968.

HELLER, K. "Laboratory Interview Research as Analogue to Treatment." In A. Bergin and S. Garfield (Eds.), *Handbook of Psychotherapy and Behavior Change.* New York: Wiley & Sons, 1971.

HOBBS, N. "Helping Disturbed Children: Psychological and Ecological Strategies." *American Psychologist,* 1966, *21,* 1105–1115.

HOLLINGSHEAD, A. B. *The Two-Factor Index of Social Position.* New Haven, Conn.: Yale Station, 1957.

HOLZBERG, J. D., GEWIRTZ, H., and EBNER, E. "Changes in Moral Judgment and Self Acceptance as a Function of Companionship with Hospitalized Mental Patients." *Journal of Consulting Psychology,* 1964, *28,* 299–303.

HOLZBERG, J. D., KNAPP, R. H., and TURNER, J. L. "College Students as Companions to the Mentally Ill." In E. L. Cowen, E. A. Gardner, and M. Zax (Eds.), *Emergent Approaches to Mental Health.* New York: Appleton-Century-Crofts, 1967.

HOLZBERG, J. D., WHITING, H. S., and LOWY, D. G. "Chronic Patients and a College Companion Program." *Mental Hospitals,* 1964, *15*(3), 152–158.

ISCOE, I., and SPIELBERGER, C. D. (Eds.) *Community Psychology Perspectives in Training and Research.* New York: Appleton-Century-Crofts, 1970.

JAHN, J. A. "An Experimental Study of Services for Fatherless Boys." Research Center, University of Pennsylvania School of Social Work, 1962.

KANTOR, D. "Impact of College Students on Chronic Mental Patients and on the Organization of the Mental Hospital." Proceedings of the College Student Companion Program Conference, Stratford, Conn., November 1962. Reprinted in C. C. Umbarger et al., (Eds.), *College Students in a Mental Hospital.* New York: Grune & Stratton, 1962.

KELLY, E. L., and FISKE, D. W. *The Prediction of Performance in Clinical Psychology.* Ann Arbor: University of Michigan Press, 1951.

LESSING, E., and SCHILLING, F. "Relationship between Treatment and Selection Variables and Treatment Outcome in a Child Guidance Clinic: An Application of Data Processing Methods." *Journal of American Academic Child Psychiatry,* 1966, *5,* 313–348.

LEVITT, E. L. "Research on Psychotherapy with Children." In A. Bergin and S. L. Garfield (Eds.), *Handbook of Psychotherapy and Behavior Change.* New York: Wiley & Sons, 1971.

LINDEN, J., and STOLLACK, G. "Training of Undergraduates in Play Techniques." *Journal of Clinical Psychology,* 1969, *25,* 213–218.

LINTON, E. F. "The Nonprofessional Scene." *American Child,* 1967, *49*(1), 9–13.

MAGOON, T. M., GOLANN, S. E., and FREEMAN, R. W. *Mental Health Counselors at Work.* New York: Pergamon, 1969.

MANNING, W. H., and DUBOIS, P. H. "Correlational Methods in Research on Human Learning." *Perceptual and Motor Skills,* 1962, *15* (Monogr. Suppl. 3), 287–321.

MATARAZZO, J. D. "Some National Developments in the Utilization of Nontraditional Mental Health Manpower." *American Psychologist,* 1971, *26*(4), 363–371.

MCCORD, J., and MCCORD, W. "A Follow-Up Report on the Cambridge-Somerville Youth Study." *Annals of the Academy of Political and Social Science,* 1959, *322,* 89–96.

MCWILLIAMS, S. A. "A Process Analysis of a School-Based Mental Health Program." Unpublished doctoral dissertation, University of Rochester, 1971.

MITCHELL, W. E. "Student Volunteers with Troubled Children." Summary progress report to National Institute of Mental Health, the Hope Foundation, Cuttingsville, Vermont, 1963.

MITCHELL, W. E. "Amicatherapy: Theoretical Perspectives and an Example of Practice." *Community Mental Health Journal,* 1966a, *2*(4), 307–314.

MITCHELL, W. E. "The Use of College Student Volunteers in the Out-Patient Treatment of Troubled Children." In H. R. Huessy (Ed.), *Mental Health with Limited Resources.* New York: Grune & Stratton, 1966b. Pp. 28–37.

PALMER, T. "Types of Treaters and Types of Juvenile Offenders." *California Youth Authority Quarterly,* 1965, *18*(3), 14–23.

PARKER, G. V., and MEGARGEE, E. I. "Factor Analytic Studies of the Adjective Check List." Proceedings of the 75th Annual Convention of the American Psychological Association, 1967, pp. 211–212.

PATTERSON, N. B., and PATTERSON, T. W. "A Companion Therapy Program." *Community Mental Health Journal,* 1967, *3*, 133–136.

PHILLIPS, E. "Parent-Child Psychotherapy: A Follow-Up Study Comparing Two Techniques." *Journal of Psychology,* 1960, *49*, 195–202.

POSER, E. G. "The Effects of Therapists' Training on Group Therapeutic Outcome." *Journal of Consulting Psychology,* 1966, *30*(4), 283–289.

POWERS, E., and WITMER, H. *An Experiment in the Prevention of Delinquency: The Cambridge-Somerville Youth Study.* New York: Columbia University Press, 1951.

RAPPAPORT, J., CHINSKY, J. M., and COWEN, E. L. *Innovations in Helping Chronic Patients: College Students in a Mental Institution.* New York: Academic Press, 1971.

REINHERZ, H. "The Therapeutic Use of Student Volunteers." In B. Guerney (Ed.), *Psychotherapeutic Agents.* New York: Holt, Rinehart & Winston, 1969.

RIOCH, M. J., ELKES, C., and FLINT, A. A. "Pilot Project in Training Mental Health Counselors." Public Health Service Publication No. 1254. Washington, D.C.: U.S. Government Printing Office, 1965.

ROGERS, C. R. "The Necessary and Sufficient Conditions of Therapeutic Personality Change." *Journal of Consulting Psychology,* 1957, *21*, 95–103.

ROSENBERG, M. *Occupations and Values.* New York: Free Press, 1957.

SCARR, S. "The Adjective Check List as a Personality Assessment Technique with Children: Validity of the Scales." *Journal of Consulting Psychology,* 1966, *30*(2), 122–128.

SCHEIBE, K. E. "College Students Spend Eight Weeks in Mental Hospital: A Case Report." *Psychotherapy: Theory, Research, and Practice,* 1965, *2*(3), 117–120.

SHEPHERD, M., OPPENHEIM, A. N., and MITCHELL, S. "Changes in Parents' Views of Their Children's Problems." *Transaction: Social Science & Modern Society.* April 1966, 5.

SIMON, R. *Experiments in Mental Health Training.* Public Health Service Publication No. 2157. Washington, D.C.: U.S. Government Printing Office, 1971.

SOBEY, F. *The Nonprofessional Revolution in Mental Health.* New York: Columbia University Press, 1970.

TAIT, C. D., and HODGES, E. F. *Delinquents: Their Families and the Community.* Springfield, Ill.: Charles C Thomas, 1962.

TRUAX, C., and MITCHELL, K. M. "Research on Certain Therapist Interpersonal Skills in Relation to Process and Outcome." In A. Bergin and S. Garfield (Eds.), *Handbook of Psychotherapy and Behavior Change.* New York: Wiley & Sons, 1971.

TURNER, J., HOLTZBERG, J. D., and KNAPP, R. H. "Effects of Companionship with Mental Patients on Students' Stereotype of the Typical Mental Patient." Paper presented at Eastern Psychological Association meeting, Boston, April 1967.

UMBARGER, C. C., DALSIMER, J. S., MORRISON, A. P., and BREGGIN, P. R. *College Students in a Mental Hospital.* New York: Grune & Stratton, 1962.

VAN COUVERING, N. "One-to-One Project." Stiles Hall, 2400 Bancroft, Berkeley, Calif., 1966. (Mimeographed Report)

WEIGEL, R. G., and CHADWICK, P. C. "Reported and Projected Self Disclosure." Paper presented at the joint meeting of the Oregon and Washington Psychological Associations, Department of Psychology, Oregon State University, 1966.

WIGGINS, J. S., and WINDER, C. L. "The Peer Nominations Inventory: An Empirically Derived Sociometric Measure of Adjustment in Preadolescent Boys." *Psychological Reports,* 1961, *9* (Monogr. Suppl. 5), 643–677.

WRIGHTSMAN, L. S. "Measurement of Philosophies of Human Nature." *Psychological Reports,* 1964, *14,* 743–751.

WRIGHTSMAN, L. L. "Annotated Bibliography of Research on the Philosophies of Human Nature Scale." Nashville, Tenn.: George Peabody College for Teachers, 1968.

ZAX, M., and COWEN, E. *Abnormal Psychology: Changing Conceptions.* New York: Holt, Rinehart & Winston, 1972.

ZUNKER, V. G., and BROWN, W. "Comparative Effectiveness of Student and Professional Counselors." *Personnel and Guidance Journal,* 1966, *44,* 738–743.

Index

A

A-B therapist typology, 259
Activity choices, 80–94
ADELSON, D. D., 5
Adjective Check List: applied to children, 20, 129–137; compared with Problem List for Elementary School Boys, 144–148; and self-descriptions by counselors, 209–211. *See also* Boys, therapeutic change in; Counselors, change in
ALBEE, G. W., 5
ALLPORT, G., 9–10
ANCHOR, K., 46
ARNHOFF, F. N., 5
Attrition of companionships, 80, 196–199, 230, 241, 263

B

BARNETT, O. J., 44
BARRETT-LENNARD, G. T., 28
BERGIN, A. E., 257

Berkeley Project: announcement of to parents, 16; first pilot year of, 1–2; instruments used in, 267–284; overview of, 1–5, 16; second pilot year of, 3–5, 227
BERLIN, J. I., 57
BETZ, B. J., 259
Boys, therapeutic change in: associated with conversation and activity patterns, 194, 263; associated with visit length and frequency, 192–194, 241, 247–248; and attrition, 196–199, 241–263; best predictors of, 244–249, 253, 257–263; and black versus white, 151, 178–179, 238, 244–245; and boy characteristics, 174–179, 237–238, 260–261; for control group, 152–153, 242–244; and companionship character-istics, 188–198, 240–241, 247–

248, 261–262; and counselor age, 253; and counselor characteristics, 180–188, 238–240, 245–247, 250–251; counselor contribution to, 152; and counselor view of dyadic feeling, 194–196, 241; and cross-race dyads, 244–245, 260; direct versus derived measures of, 233–236; and double-outgoing dyads, 189–190, 240; and double-quiet dyads, 191–192, 240, 252, 261; and fatherless homes, 151, 174–175, 237, 261; global retrospective impressions of, 153–154; implications of, 256–266; interpretation of, 242–254; low level positive predictors of, 249–251, 254; measurement problems for, 125–126, 128, 263–265; negative predictors of, 252–254; observed from boy self-reports, 166–168; parent and counselor views of compared, 157–158; and presenting problems, 151–152; and process variables, 262–263; and severity of initial problem, 176–178, 238, 248–249, 251, 260; and quiet counselors, 185, 239, 251; and quiet-outgoing dyads, 189–191, 240–241, 251–252, 261; and quiet-outgoing problems, 151, 175–176, 237; related studies of, 127–128; as seen by classmates and teachers, 159–172; as seen by counselors, 156–159; as seen by parents, 129–156; and severity of initial problem, 176–178, 238, 248–249, 251, 260; study samples of 126; summarized, 232–242, 263–266; teacher retrospective ratings of, 163–166

Boys, therapeutic change in and counselor characteristics: age, 253; background, 181–182; depression, 186, 239, 252–253; empathic understanding, 184–185, 239; interpersonal traits, 182–188; outgoing-quiet, 191, 239, 245–247; openness, 183–184, 239, 250–251; relaxed, 186–259; rigidity, 187, 240, 252; self-concept, 181–182; training level, 180–181, 238, 249–250

Boys, troubled: general and family characteristics, 19; and matched controls, 17–19, 20, 226–227, 242–244, 264–265; parents' initial description of, 20–23; problem severity in, 17, 21–24; quiet versus outgoing problems in, 17; recruitment of, 16–17; sample composition of, 24–25; selection criteria for, 15, 17, 226; teacher and classmate initial descriptions of, 23–24

BREGGIN, P. R., 11
BROWN, W., 9

C

Cambridge-Somerville Youth Study, 9–10
CAMPBELL, D. T., 38
CARKHUFF, R. R., 28
CHADWICK, P. C., 213
CHAPIN, F. S., 39, 181, 204, 208, 259
CHINSKY, J. M., 9, 12, 35, 36, 44, 46, 201, 229, 255
College students. See Counselors
Companionship: activity choice and change in, 80–94; attrition in, 80, 196–199; characteristics predicting boy change in, 188–189; collaboration in, 80–81, 230–231, 251–252; conversation topics in, 97–107, 231; early and later verbal descriptions by counselors about, 66–68; feeling and behavior patterns in, 107–118, 231; initial meetings in, 79–80; length and frequency of visit in, 192–194;

and mechanics of visiting, 69–71, 93–94; methods for studying, 74–79, 257–265; outcome and child therapy studies about, 264; and psychotherapy, 96–97, 262; rationale for, 71–72; structuring, 51, 70–73, 229–232; termination of, 118–123, 231–232

Companionship programs: in colleges, 11, 256; and innovation, 14; prospects for, 256; and research design, 256–260

COOK, P. E., 7

Counselors: characteristics of affecting boy change, 183–189, 257–258; depressed, 186; emotionally open, 183–184; empathically understanding, 184–185; matched controls for, 203–204; motives of for joining project, 47–49, 255; orientation methods for, 54–59; quiet, 185; relaxed, 186; rigid, 187; therapeutic profile of, 188, 257–258; training and supervision of, 61–69; views of about change in boys, 156–159. *See also* Group Assessment of Interpersonal Traits

Counselors, change in: and black versus white boys, 221; and career choice, 207, 256; and intactness of boy's home, 221; in interests, 204–206, 254; measured at termination, 204–208; observed in previous studies, 200–203; pre-post measurement of, 208, 214; and quiet versus outgoing, 214–218, 254; related to boy companion type, 220–221, 255; related to training, 218–220, 254; in religious commitment, 206; in seeking personal therapy, 207; in self-concept, 209–211, 254; in self-disclosure, 211; and severity of boy's problem, 220; in social insight,

214; in social interaction styles, 206, 208; summarized, 221–223, 254–256; and undergraduate education, 255

COWEN, E. L., 5, 7, 9, 12, 13, 14, 44, 201, 202, 210, 255

CRAIG, M., 127

D

DALSIMER, J. S., 11
D'AUGELLI, A. R., 35, 44, 46, 229
DAVIS, W., 2, 3, 10
DAVISON, G. C., 14
Derived versus direct change measures, 233–236
DOOLEY, C. D., 36
DORR, D., 13
Dyad types: quiet-outgoing effects of on boys, 51–55, 189–192, 240, 261–262; structuring of, 51–55

E

EBNER, E., 9, 129, 210
ELKES, C., 8
ERIKSON, E. H., 103

F

Feeling and behavior patterns, 107–118, 231
FISKE, D. W., 38, 258
FLINT, A. A., 8
FREEMAN, R. W., 9
FURST, P. W., 127

G

GARDNER, E. A., 5, 7
GARFIELD, S. L., 260, 261
GETTER, H., 35, 44, 46, 229
GEWIRTZ, H., 9, 129, 210
GLASSER, B. A., 262
GLIDEWELL, J. C., 128, 242
GOLANN, S. E., 9
GOODMAN, G., 20
GOUGH, H., 38, 44, 130, 204, 208, 215, 216
GRASSER, C., 5, 7
GREENBLATT, M., 262
Group Assessment of Interpersonal

Traits (GAIT): accepting-warm characteristics in, 39; internal coherence of, 36–37; item means for, 32–37; items in, 31; measurement issues in, 29, 34; and prediction of field performance, 44, 239–240, 250; procedure for, 29–30; professional versus student ratings on, 42–43; quiet characteristics in, 39; relation of to change in boys, 44–46, 182–188, 239–240, 250; relation of to other instruments, 37–40, 44–47; reliabilities of, 34–36; scoring methods for, 32; rigid characteristics in, 39; selection criteria for, 40–41; suggested uses of, 228–229; understanding characteristics in, 39

Group training, 61–69; effectiveness of and group size, 66; effectiveness of rated by counselors, 68–69; measured effects of on counselors, 218–220, 254; process patterns in, 65

GRUVER, G. G., 7, 14, 202
GUERNEY, B. G., 5, 7, 11, 14

H

HART, J., 7
HARTMANN, E., 262
HEILBRUN, A. B., JR., 38, 44, 130, 204, 208, 215, 216
HELLER, K., 259
HENRY, W. E., 5, 7
HOBBS, N., 14
HODGES, E. F., 127
HOLLINGSHEAD, A. B., 19, 126
HOLZBERG, J. D., 9, 11, 41, 52, 129, 200, 201, 210

I

Initial meeting, 79–80
Intervention in the community: by Berkeley Project, 1; and disclosure, 4; as error, 3–4; principles of, 2
Intimacy: as emotional openness, 111, 114; and interpersonal

closeness, 107, 117–118, 123; as warmth, 116. *See also* Companionship

ISCOE, I., 7
IZZO, L., 12, 13

J

JAHN, J. A., 11
JOURARD, S., 39, 181, 182, 192, 208, 213, 259

K

KALIS, B., 5
KANTOR, D., 47
KELLY, E. L., 258
KELLY, J. G., 5, 7
KNAPP, R. H., 11, 201
KORN, P. R., 47

L

LAIRD, J. D., 12, 201, 210
LESSING, E., 262
LEVINSON, D. J., 262
LEVITT, E. L., 125, 128, 242, 264
LICHTENBERG, B., 11
LINDEN, J., 14
LOWY, D. C., 41, 52, 200
LINTON, E. F., 40

M

MC CORD, J., 10
MC CORD, W., 10
MC WILLIAMS, S. A., 13
MAGOON, T. M., 9
MATARAZZO, J. D., 7
Matching boys and counselors, 51–55. *See also* Dyad types
MEGARGEE, E. I., 210, 216
MILES, H., 12
MITCHELL, K. M., 8, 260
MITCHELL, S., 128, 242
MITCHELL, W. E., 12, 53
MORRISON, A. P., 11
Motives of counselors, 47–49, 255

N

Nonprofessional therapists: client populations of, 8; types of, 7–8

Nonprofessional therapy: causes for, 6; literature on, 8; and mental health economics, 5–6; and professional therapy, 6–7; rationale for, 5; scope of, 5

O

OPPENHEIM, A. N., 128, 242
Orientation: of counselors, 54–59; of parents, 59–61

P

Pairing procedure, 51–55
PALMER, T., 53
Paraprofessionals, prospects for, 8
Parents: and family composition, 19; and initial descriptions of boys, 20–23; interest of in companionship therapy, 3, 17, 226; orientation of, 59–61
PARKER, G. V., 210, 216
PATTERSON, N. B., 14
PATTERSON, T. W., 14
Peer Nominations Inventory: boys' change scores on, 159–163; classmate-teacher correlations of, 23; format and administration of, 23–24, 225. *See also* Boys, troubled
PHILLIPS, E., 262
Philosophies of Human Nature Questionnaire, 217–218
POKRACKI, F., 13
POSER, E. G., 9
POWERS, E., 9
Problem List for Elementary School Boys: compared with ACL, 144–148; consistency of parents' reports with, 23; findings generated by, 137–144; format of, 20. *See also* Boys, troubled
Psychopathology. *See* Boys, troubled

R

RAPPAPORT, J., 9, 12, 35, 36, 44, 201, 255
Recommendations: for applying GAIT procedure, 228–229; on initial visits, 230; for pairing boys and counselors, 252, 261; for selecting troubled children, 226; for studying outcome, 244, 256–266; for undergraduate education, 255–256
Recruitment of college students, 26
Recruitment of troubled boys, pilot phase of, 2–3
REINHERZ, H., 14
RIOCH, M. J., 8
ROGERS, C. R., 28
ROSENBERG, M., 39
RUBINSTEIN, E. A., 285

S

SCARR, S., 20, 211, 215, 216
SCHEIBE, K. E., 201, 210
SCHILLING, F., 262
SCHNEIDERMAN, D., 11
Selection criteria: for boys, 15, 17, 226; for counselors, 40–41, 187–188
Self-disclosure: change of in counselors, 211; and counselor group training, 254; questionnaire on, 211–213, 217
SHEPHERD, M., 128, 242
SIMON, R., 7, 8
SOBEY, F., 7, 14
Social insight test, 214, 254, 259
SOLOMON, M. H., 262
SPEISMAN, J. C., 5
SPIELBERGER, C. D., 7
STOLLACK, G., 14
Students. *See* Counselors
Supervision of counselors, 61–69

T

TAIT, C. D., 127
Teachers descriptions of boys: initial, 23–24; retrospective, 163–166
TELSCHOW, E., 12
Termination of companionships, 118–123, 231–232
Therapeutic talent: assessment procedures for, 29; in client-centered theory, 28; criteria for, 27–29; and professional education 28; versus training,

27. *See also* Group Assessment of Interpersonal Traits

TOMLINSON, T. M., 7

Training: effects of on counselors, 218–220; program of for counselors, 61–69. *See also* Orientation, Group training

TROST, M., 12, 13

TRUAX, C. B., 8, 28, 260

TURNER, J. L., 11, 201

U

UMBARGER, C. C., 11

V

VAN COUVERING, N., 202, 210

Volunteers: reliability of, 3; versus paid workers, 12

W

WEIGEL, R. G., 213

WHILING, H. S., 41, 52, 200

WIGGINS, J. S., 23, 44, 225

WINDER, C. L., 23, 44, 225

WITMER, H., 9

WRIGHTSMAN, L. S., 39, 43

WYCKOFF, B. L., 57

Z

ZAX, M., 5, 7, 9, 12, 201, 210

ZUNKER, V. G., 9,